THE CONSULTANT'S TOOLKIT

High-Impact Questionnaires, Activities, and How-to Guides for Diagnosing and Solving Problems

Mel Silberman

McGraw-Hill

New York   San Francisco   Washington, D.C.   Auckland   Bogotá
Caracas   Lisbon   London   Madrid   Mexico City   Milan
Montreal   New Delhi   San Juan   Singapore
Sydney   Tokyo   Toronto

McGraw-Hill

A Division of The McGraw·Hill Companies

13 14 15 16 DOC/DOC 0

ISBN 0-07-136261-4

Printed and bound by R. R. Donnelley & Sons Company.

How to Contact the Publisher

To order multiple copies of this book at a discount, call the McGraw-Hill Special Sales Department at 800-842-3075, or 212-904-5427.

To ask a question about the book, contact the author, or report a mistake in the text, please write to Richard Narramore, Senior Editor, at:

richard_narramore@mcgraw-hill.com.

Important Guidelines for Photocopying or Downloading Pages from This Publication

Guidelines for requesting permission are available at:

www.mhhe.com/info/permission.mhtml

CONTENTS

PART II: HOW-TO GUIDES FOR SOLVING YOUR CLIENT'S PROBLEMS   93

PART III: INTERVENTION ACTIVITIES TO INCREASE YOUR CLIENT'S EFFECTIVENESS   *219*

TOPICAL INDEX
Find a Tool for Your Specific Topic

In the place of a traditional index, here is a classification by topic of the 45 tools found in *The Consultant's Toolkit*.

Organizational Effectiveness

Group
Exercises

PREFACE

For over 30 years, I have been a consultant to individuals, teams, and total organizations, helping them to improve their current effectiveness and to facilitate desired changes. I can't tell you how many times I wished that I could have at my fingertips a variety of consulting tools, designed by expert consultants, that I could use freely to meet the needs of my clients. Having such a toolkit would have been unthinkable at a time when consulting resources were limited to proprietary use or could cost the user a small fortune.

Times have changed. Many consultants view other consultants as their partners, not their competitors. Fortunately, I know a lot of them. And so, I have invited a talented and willing group of consultants to offer their tools to guide your efforts and, if you wish, to give directly to your clients. Best of all, the entire collection is freely reproducible or downloadable to your computer, so that you can customize whatever tools you choose.

The Consultant's Toolkit contains 45 resources: 13 assessment questionnaires to study your clients' needs, 15 how-to guides to solve your clients' problems, and 17 intervention activities to expand your clients' effectiveness.

Pick and choose those tools that best support your consultation efforts. To make it easier to make your selections, all the tools begin with a brief overview so that you can quickly establish their relevance to your consulting situations. In addition, a Topical Index is included to help you locate tools in the following categories:

✓ consulting basics
✓ leadership and management development
✓ organizational effectiveness
✓ performance improvement
✓ problem solving and teamwork
✓ strategic planning and organizational change

I hope you will find *The Consultant's Toolkit* to be a one-stop resource you can draw upon again and again in your efforts to be a top-notch consultant.

Mel Silberman
Princeton, New Jersey

ASSESSMENT QUESTIONNAIRES TO STUDY YOUR CLIENT'S NEEDS

INTRODUCTION

Your effectiveness as a consultant depends on the quality of the data you obtain to study your client's needs. While there are many ways to collect data ... from interviewing to observing ... the easiest way to obtain information from the greatest number of individuals is to utilize assessment instruments such as surveys, questionnaires, and other tools.

In Part I of *The Consultant's Toolkit,* you will find 13 questionnaires ready to use with your clients. They deal with a wide range of assessment issues, including the study of individual clients, teams, and entire organizations.

In selecting questionnaires for *The Consultant's Toolkit,* a premium was placed on survey forms that are easy to understand and quick to complete. Preceding each questionnaire is an overview that contains the key questions to be assessed. The questionnaire itself is on a separate page(s) to make reproduction more convenient. All the questionnaires are scorable and may contain guidelines for scoring interpretation. Some include questions for follow-up discussion.

Many of these questionnaires are ideal to utilize as activities *during* consultation sessions. After completion, ask clients to score and interpret their own results. Then, have them compare outcomes with other participants, either in pairs or in larger groupings. Be careful, however, to stress that the data from these questionnaires are not "hard." They *suggest* rather than *demonstrate* facts about people or situations. Ask clients to compare scores to their own perceptions. If they do not match, urge them to consider why. In some cases, the discrepancy may be due to the crudeness of the measurement device. In others, the discrepancy may result from distorted self-perceptions. Urge your clients to open themselves to new feedback and awareness.

You may decide to collect data *prior* to a consultation session. If you choose this option, be sure to explain the process clearly to respondents. You might want to use the following text:

We are planning to get together soon to identify issues that need to be worked through in order to maximize your future effectiveness. An excellent way to begin doing some of this work is to collect information through a questionnaire and to feed back that information for group discussion. I would like you to join with your colleagues in filling out the attached questionnaire. Your honest responses will enable us to have a clear, objective view of the situation. Your participation will be totally anonymous. My job will be to summarize the results and report them to the group for reaction.

1

DOES YOUR CLIENT'S BUSINESS STRATEGY MAKE SENSE?

Gina Vega

Overview   A situational analysis (SWOT) focuses on four areas of your client's business: Strengths (S), Weaknesses (W), Opportunities (O), and Threats (T). *Strengths* and *Weaknesses* cover internal issues, and *Opportunities* and *Threats* are external or environmental issues. Effective strategic planning requires a careful analysis of all four areas.

The following SWOT analysis form provides you with straightforward guidelines and questions to help your client through this process, as well as the means to quantify your client's current strategic position. Once you have established a strategic baseline score for the business or division, you can use this score at the next planning session (six months or one year from now). This will facilitate measurement of your client's improvement and of changes in the external environment. Each of the questions in the following form will have a different meaning depending upon the industry your client is in, but all the questions need to be answered when you perform a complete SWOT analysis. The planning process will become simpler in the future, once you have determined a baseline and can actually measure and quantify change.

Contact Information: Merrimack College, School of Business and International Commerce, 315 Turnpike Street, No. Andover, MA 01845, 978-837-5000 x 4338, gvega@merrimack.edu.

SITUATIONAL ANALYSIS (SWOT) ASSESSMENT OF YOUR ORGANIZATION

I. Strengths

For each statement below, put a ✓ in the appropriate column.			
	Disagree	*Neither agree nor disagree*	*Agree*
1. We have a high level of competence.			
2. We have competitive skill.			
3. We are ahead on the experience curve.			
4. We have adequate financial resources.			
5. We have a good reputation with buyers.			
6. We are an acknowledged market leader.			
7. We have well-conceived functional area strategies.			
8. We have access to economies of scale.			
9. We are somewhat insulated from strong competitive pressures.			
10. We have proprietary technology.			
11. We have better advertising campaigns than the competition.			
12. We are good at creating new products.			
13. We have strong management.			
14. We have superior technological/ technical skills.			
15. We have cost/pricing advantages.			
Total number of ✓'s			

SITUATIONAL ANALYSIS (SWOT) ASSESSMENT OF YOUR ORGANIZATION

II. Weaknesses

For each statement below, put a ✓ in the appropriate column.	Disagree	Neither agree nor disagree	Agree
1. We have no clear strategic direction.			
2. Our facilities are obsolete.			
3. We are lacking managerial depth and talent.			
4. We are missing some key skills or competencies.			
5. We have a poor track record in implementing strategy.			
6. We are plagued with internal operating problems.			
7. We are falling behind on Research & Development.			
8. We have a narrow product line.			
9. We have a weak market image.			
10. We have below average marketing skills.			
11. We are unable to finance needed strategy changes.			
12. We have higher overall costs relative to our key competitors.			
13. We have subpar profitability.			
Total number of ✓'s			

SITUATIONAL ANALYSIS (SWOT) ASSESSMENT OF YOUR ORGANIZATION

III. Opportunities

For each statement below, put a ✓ in the appropriate column.			
	No	*Maybe*	*Yes*
1. There are additional customer groups that we could serve.			
2. There are new markets or market segments to enter.			
3. We can expand our product/service line to meet customer needs.			
4. We can diversify into related products.			
5. We can control sourcing or supply activities (vertical integration.)			
6. Falling trade barriers are opening foreign markets to us.			
7. Our rivals are becoming complacent.			
8. The market is growing faster than in the past.			
9. Fewer regulatory requirements will making doing business easier for us.			
Total number of ✓'s			

SITUATIONAL ANALYSIS (SWOT) ASSESSMENT OF YOUR ORGANIZATION

IV. Threats

For each statement below, put a ✓ in the appropriate column.			
	No	*Maybe*	*Yes*
1. Low-cost foreign competitors are entering the market.			
2. Sales of substitute products are rising.			
3. The market is growing more slowly than we expected.			
4. There are adverse shifts in foreign exchange rates and/or trade policies.			
5. Regulatory requirements are becoming onerous.			
6. We are vulnerable to changes in the business cycle or to recessions.			
7. Our customers and/or suppliers are enjoying growing bargaining power.			
8. Buyers' needs and tastes are changing in directions that point away from our current expertise.			
9. Demographic changes are having a negative impact on business.			
10. It's easy to enter this industry (very low barriers to entry).			
11. Technology could change this industry with little or no warning.			
Total number of ✓'s			

SITUATIONAL ANALYSIS (SWOT) ASSESSMENT OF YOUR ORGANIZATION

V. Interpreting the Situational Analysis Assessment of Your Organization

1. Strengths and Weaknesses:

   a) Give yourself 1 point for each ✓ under "Disagree"
   b) Give yourself 2 points for each ✓ under "Neither agree nor disagree"
   c) Give yourself 3 points for each ✓ under "Agree"

2. Threats and Opportunities

   a) Give yourself 1 point for each ✓ under "No"
   b) Give yourself 2 points for each ✓ under "Maybe"
   c) Give yourself 3 points for each ✓ under "Yes"

Total Strengths	_____	Total Threats	_____
+Total Opportunities	_____	+Total Weaknesses	_____
(S + O)	_____		
Minus **(T + W)**	_____		
Strategic Baseline	_____		

Use your Strategic Baseline at your next planning session to measure how much change your organization has experienced, how much improvement you have achieved in your strengths and weaknesses, and how the external environment has affected your progress.

2

HOW MOTIVATING IS YOUR CLIENT'S ORGANIZATION?

Dean Spitzer

Overview   Did you ever wonder how to measure *organizational* motivation (in contrast to *personal* motivation)? The Motivated Organization Survey is an easily administered self-reporting instrument that provides a valid and reliable method for assessing motivation in any organization, department, or work unit. It consists of 60 items drawn from the characteristics of high-motivation organizations (Spitzer, *SuperMotivation,* AMACOM, 1995). When taken together, the items that comprise the survey provide a kind of vision, or operational definition, of the highly motivated organization.

Contact Information: Dean R. Spitzer & Associates, Inc., 5150 S. Florida Avenue, Suite 316, Lakeland, FL 33813, 941-648-2754

THE MOTIVATED ORGANIZATION SURVEY

In the space to the right of each statement, place a number (from 1 to 5) indicating *how true* the statement is *about your organization,* using the following rating scale:

1 = not true at all

2 = true to a small extent

3 = true to some extent

4 = mostly true

5 = completely true

1. Employees in this organization are energetic and enthusiastic. _____

2. Employees are highly productive. _____

3. Employees have positive and optimistic attitudes. _____

4. There is little or no wasted effort. _____

5. This organization is highly customer-focused. _____

6. Unsafe conditions are identified and promptly corrected. _____

7. Employees are made to feel like true business partners. _____

8. Employees have a strong sense of organizational identity. _____

9. Employees are very careful in how they use the organization's resources. _____

10. Employees have a clear understanding of the organization's mission, vision, and values. _____

11. Employee input into organizational strategic planning is solicited and used. _____

12. Employees are encouraged to make significant choices and decisions about their work. _____

13. Employees are involved in making key production decisions. _____

14. Employees are empowered to improve work methods. _____

15. Employees are encouraged to work closely with their internal customers and suppliers. _____

16. There is a no-fault approach to problem solving in this organization. _____

---

17. A concerted effort is made to identify and use the full range of abilities that employees bring to work. _____

18. Employees are challenged to strive for ambitious goals. _____

19. Obstacles to effective employee performance are promptly identified and eliminated. _____

20. Personnel decisions are perceived to be fair and consistent. _____

21. There are few, if any, unnecessary policies and rules. _____

22. Effective communication is a high organizational priority. _____

23. Employees throughout this organization are well informed. _____

24. Management explains to employees the rationale behind all important decisions. _____

25. There is frequent communication between employees and management. _____

26. Senior managers regularly visit employees' work areas. _____

27. No secrets are kept from employees. _____

28. Meetings are well led and highly productive. _____

29. Company publications are informative and helpful. _____

30. Management is highly responsive to employees' needs and concerns. _____

31. Employees feel that management has their best interests at heart. _____

32. When labor–management conflicts arise, they are promptly and constructively resolved. _____

33. Management is quick to take personal responsibility for its mistakes. _____

34. Employees are encouraged to assume leadership responsibilities. _____

35. Employees receive a great deal of encouragement and recognition. _____

36. Outstanding performance is always recognized. _____

37. Both individual and team performance are appropriately rewarded. _____

38. Poor performance is never rewarded. _____

39. Creativity is encouraged and rewarded. _____

40. Employees consider their pay to be fair and equitable. _____

41. Employees are willing to pay part of the cost of their benefits. _____

42. Employees feel that their ideas and suggestions are genuinely welcomed by management. _____

43. Employees' suggestions receive prompt and constructive responses. _____

44. Everyone in the organization is committed to continuous improvement. _____

45. There are no barriers between departments or units. _____

46. There is a high level of trust between workers and management. _____

47. There is excellent teamwork throughout the organization. _____

48. There is a high level of interdepartmental communication and cooperation throughout the organization. _____

49. Management views problems as opportunities for improvement, rather than as obstacles to success. _____

50. Learning is a high priority in this organization. _____

51. Employees are encouraged to learn from each other. _____

52. There is consistent follow-up after training. _____

53. Employees are involved in making training decisions. _____

54. Employees are involved in determining performance requirements, measures, and standards. _____

55. Employees view performance evaluation as a positive development process. _____

56. Self-evaluation and peer evaluation are integral components of performance appraisal. _____

57. Discipline is perceived to be fair. _____

58. Employees consistently give extra effort. _____

59. Tardiness, absenteeism, and turnover rates are extremely low. _____

60. Employees are excited about working in this organization. _____

Total score (add all item responses): _____

Percentage score (divide by 300): _____%

Add all your responses to determine your total score. (If surveys were completed by a group, compute a mean score for each item.) A perfect score would be 300 (based on a maximum response of 5 for each of the 60 items on the survey). When you divide your total score by 300, you will obtain an overall percentage score. The higher the percentage score, the higher the perceived level of organizational motivation.

INTERPRETING THE MOTIVATED ORGANIZATION SURVEY

Here are some guidelines for helping you interpret your organization's percentage score:

90%–100%	Congratulations! Your organization has already attained high-motivation status.
80%–89%	Your organization is well on its way to high motivation.
70%–79%	Your organization has some of the characteristics of a high-motivation organization.
60%–69%	Your organization has a slightly above average* motivational climate.
50%–59%	Your organization has an average* motivational climate.
Below 50%	Your organization has a below average* motivational climate.

*Based on national norms for this survey.

3
WHAT DOES A TEAM NEED TO IMPROVE?

Kevin Lohan

Overview Before teams undertake the challenging task of collaborating on a temporary or permanent project, they need to ascertain whether they are all reading from the same metaphoric sheet of music. This assessment instrument enables teams to determine whether they have reached the readiness point at which optimal performance takes place. The instrument affords insights into the specific aspects of their collective functioning that may require fine-tuning, by addressing four dimensions of team effectiveness: Goals, Roles, Interpersonal Relationships, and Procedures.

Contact Information: 2 Windsor Rd., Wamberal, NSW 2260, Australia, +64-2-4385-2049, endeavr@terrigal.net.au, www.endeavour.net.au

GETTING A GRIP ON YOUR TEAM'S EFFECTIVENESS

GOAL-SETTING CHECKLIST

Directions: The ten items that follow are associated with establishing and maintaining goals for your team. Consider the two statements in each item and then encircle a number between the two options to indicate how closely your team fits one or the other description.

I never discuss objectives with others on the team.	0 1 2 3 4 5	I always discuss objectives thoroughly with others on the team.
Our goal-setting sessions are a year or more apart.	0 1 2 3 4 5	Sessions to update our goals are held at least every 3 months.
We have fewer than 3 or more than 6 major goals this year.	0 1 2 3 4 5	We have a manageable 3 to 6 major goals this year.
We rarely clarify how we will measure our success.	0 1 2 3 4 5	We have tangible measures of our success or otherwise.
We rarely meet to discuss performance.	0 1 2 3 4 5	Performance is either part of our regular agenda or discussed often.
Once set, our goals rarely change as circumstances change.	0 1 2 3 4 5	When unexpected situations arise, our goals are open to renegotiation.
Only staff (and not the manager) have clear accountabilities.	0 1 2 3 4 5	Everyone has clear accountabilities (including the manager).
Unachievable goals are often set for the team.	0 1 2 3 4 5	When we set goals, they are almost always achievable.
We rarely check the organizational ensure relevance of our goals.	0 1 2 3 4 5	Individual goals are checked to they are relevant to the organization.
No steps are taken to ensure that people share information about their goals.	0 1 2 3 4 5	We ensure that people share information about their goals.

Total of 10 circled numbers: _____

GETTING A GRIP ON YOUR TEAM'S EFFECTIVENESS

ROLES CHECKLIST

Directions: The ten items that follow are associated with roles within the team. Consider the two statements in each item and then encircle a number between the two options to indicate how closely your team fits one or the other description.

There are no clear, written job descriptions for team members.	0 1 2 3 4 5	Written job descriptions exist for each role.
Lines of responsibility are unclear and people often question their parts of a task.	0 1 2 3 4 5	People know their responsibilities very well and rarely question them.
It is difficult to assign work without making waves.	0 1 2 3 4 5	Assigning work is easy. Team members know their roles and accept them.
When one person is absent, other people are uncertain about how to fill in.	0 1 2 3 4 5	When one person is absent, important things still get done.
No one is being groomed to learn a new role.	0 1 2 3 4 5	People are always being groomed for the next position.
There is no program for addressing staff weaknesses.	0 1 2 3 4 5	Staff development is addressed continuously.
We do not openly discuss our roles.	0 1 2 3 4 5	We openly discuss our roles.
There is very little respect for each other's part in the process.	0 1 2 3 4 5	Everyone respects the part played by every other team member.
Informal roles are often adopted that take over from formal roles.	0 1 2 3 4 5	The formal roles are followed by everyone and attempts to adopt informal roles are not made.
Leadership of the team is unclear.	0 1 2 3 4 5	Team leadership is clearly understood.

Total of 10 circled numbers: _____

GETTING A GRIP ON YOUR TEAM'S EFFECTIVENESS

INTERPERSONAL RELATIONSHIPS CHECKLIST

Directions: The ten items that follow are associated with interpersonal relationships among team members. Consider the two statements in each item and then encircle a number between the two options to indicate how closely your team fits one or the other description.

Some people on the team treat others as inferiors.	0	1	2	3	4	5	Everyone treats others as equals and there is clear evidence of empathy.
There is no evidence that people on the team trust each other.	0	1	2	3	4	5	There is plenty of evidence that people on the team trust one another.
If people have problems, they keep them to themselves.	0	1	2	3	4	5	If people have problems, they discuss them with each other.
There is no feedback among the team about each other's work.	0	1	2	3	4	5	Everyone accepts feedback happily and gives it appropriately.
I do not find out about problems I have created until it is too late.	0	1	2	3	4	5	Problems I create are promptly brought to my attention so that corrective action can be taken.
Anger and frustration are displayed as violent outbursts.	0	1	2	3	4	5	Anger and frustration are resolved rationally.
I do not treat others on the team as friends but as coworkers.	0	1	2	3	4	5	Friendships among the team are common and do not cause problems.
During conflicts, one person usually wins at the expense of others.	0	1	2	3	4	5	Conflicts are resolved to the satisfaction of everyone concerned.
Participation in decision making and at meetings is unequal and some people dominate.	0	1	2	3	4	5	Participation in decision making and at meetings is equally shared.
Perceptions held by team members about our relationships are not the same as those of people outside the team.	0	1	2	3	4	5	Our perceptions about the way we get along are the same as the perceptions of those outside the team.

Total of 10 circled numbers: _____

GETTING A GRIP ON YOUR TEAM'S EFFECTIVENESS

PROCEDURES CHECKLIST

Directions: The ten items that follow are associated with the procedures the team follows. Consider the two statements in each item and then encircle a number between the two options to indicate how closely your team fits one or the other description.

There are few, if any, clearly communicated policies and procedures.	0 1 2 3 4 5	Clearly written policies and procedures are readily available for our use.
We have trouble agreeing on tough team decisions.	0 1 2 3 4 5	We have agreed-on procedures for reaching tough team decisions.
We have no procedure for resolving conflict.	0 1 2 3 4 5	We have an agreed-on procedure for resolving conflict when it arises.
Communication is confused and comes and goes in many directions.	0 1 2 3 4 5	Communication is appropriate and we know how and from whom we get information.
Formal rules are rarely followed.	0 1 2 3 4 5	Formal rules are almost always complied with.
Our organization does not welcome ideas for change.	0 1 2 3 4 5	Our organization encourages innovation.
Our operating procedures are out of date.	0 1 2 3 4 5	Our operating procedures are regularly updated to reflect current methods and technology.
Our meetings are usually a waste of time.	0 1 2 3 4 5	Our meetings are productive and well run.
Policies favor labor-intensive, time-consuming procedures that cover all the bases.	0 1 2 3 4 5	Policies favor getting things done rather than guarding against error.
Policies appear inconsistent for different parts of the organization.	0 1 2 3 4 5	Policies are the same for everyone, with a few necessary exceptions.

Total of 10 circled numbers: _____

GETTING A GRIP ON YOUR TEAM'S EFFECTIVENESS

SCORING AND INTERPRETATION

There is no best or worst total score. Your own interpretation of what each of the statements means, together with the variables that exist in a numerical rating system, would make such a diagnosis worthless. The instrument is intended to help you diagnose what you perceive as the strengths and weaknesses of the team as related to a range of team activities and behaviors. Thus, the diagnosis is achieved by comparing your responses within the team, rather than making an assessment against the scores of other teams.

Each response is rated from zero to five points, as shown in the rating scale. The total maximum score for each of the four team dimensions is 50 points. By comparing the score for each dimension against the other three, you can determine which area has the greater need for development. Similarly, within each of the dimensions, you can determine the issues that need the most urgent attention by comparing the scores for each of the ten items with others in that dimension.

4

IS IT A LEARNING ORGANIZATION?

Michael Marquardt

Overview   Becoming a learning organization is critical for succeeding in the twen-
ty-first century. Organizations that can increase the quality and speed
of knowledge management will possess a significant advantage over
their slow-learning competitors.

Many organizations, however, are neither aware of their existing
learning capacities nor cognizant of how they can increase their potential as learning organizations. If they are familiar with the concepts
and practices of the learning organization, it is often only one or two of
the diverse elements of a learning organization.

The Learning Organization Profile is the first comprehensive
instrument that examines each of the five key components of a learning organization: 1) learning dynamics, 2) organizational transformation, 3) people empowerment, 4) knowledge management, and 5) technology application. The instrument has been used by hundreds of
organizations around the world, both in determining their present status as learning organizations and in providing specific guidelines for
developing themselves as learning organizations.

The Profile should be completed by as many and as representative
a number of employees as possible. It is useful for senior management to
be familiar with the basic concepts of a learning organization, so as to
demonstrate commitment to transforming the company into a learning
organization. The Learning Organization Profile may be administered in
a group meeting or by having individuals complete the instruments on
their own and then return them.

Contact Information: Global Learning Associates, 1688 Moorings Drive, Reston,
VA 20190, 703-437-0260, mjmq@aol.com

LEARNING ORGANIZATION PROFILE

Below is a list of various statements about your organization. Read each statement carefully and decide the *extent* to which it actually applies to your organization. Use the following scale:

4 = **applies totally**
3 = **applies to a great extent**
2 = **applies to a moderate extent**
1 = **applies to little or no extent**

I. Learning Dynamics: Individual, Group/Team, and Organization

In this organization ...

_____ 1. We are encouraged and expected to manage our own learning and development.

_____ 2. People avoid distortion of information and blocking of communication channels through skills such as active listening and effective feedback.

_____ 3. Individuals are trained and coached in learning how to learn.

_____ 4. Teams and individuals use the action learning process (that is, learning from careful reflection on the problem or situation, and applying it to future actions).

_____ 5. People are able to think and act with a comprehensive systems approach.

_____ **Learning Dynamics Score**

II. Organization Transformation: Vision, Culture, Strategy, and Structure

In this organization ...

_____ 1. Top-level management supports the vision of a learning organization.

_____ 2. The climate supports and recognizes the importance of learning.

_____ 3. We learn from failures as well as successes.

_____ 4. Learning opportunities are incorporated into operations and programs.

_____ 5. The organization is streamlined, with few levels of management, to maximize communication and learning across levels.

_____ **Organization Transformation Score**

III. People Empowerment: Employee, Manager, Customer, Alliances, Partners, and Community

In this organization ...

_____ 1. We strive to develop an empowered workforce that is able to learn and perform.

_____ 2. Authority is decentralized and delegated so as to equal one's responsibility and learning capability.

21

_____ 3. Managers take on the roles of coaching, mentoring, and facilitating learning.

_____ 4. We actively share information with our customers, to obtain their ideas and input in order to learn and improve services and products.

_____ 5. We participate in joint learning events with suppliers, community groups, professional associations, and academic institutions.

_____ **People Empowerment Score**

IV. Knowledge Management: Acquisition, Creation, Storage/Retrieval, and Transfer/Utilization

In this organization ...

_____ 1. People monitor trends outside our organization by looking at what others do (e.g., benchmarking best practices, attending conferences, and examining published research).

_____ 2. People are trained in the skills of creative thinking and experimentation.

_____ 3. We often create demonstration projects whereby new ways of developing a product and/or delivering a service are tested.

_____ 4. Systems and structures exist to ensure that important knowledge is coded, stored, and made available to those who need and can use it.

_____ 5. We continue to develop new strategies and mechanisms for sharing learning throughout the organization.

_____ **Knowledge Management Score**

V. Technology Application: Information Systems, Technology-Based Learning, and Electronic Performance Support Systems

In this organization ...

_____ 1. Learning is facilitated by effective and efficient computer-based information systems.

_____ 2. People have ready access to the information highway (local area networks, Internet, on-line, etc.)

_____ 3. Learning facilities (e.g., training and conference rooms) incorporate electronic multimedia support and a learning environment based on the powerful integration of art, color, music, and visuals.

_____ 4. We support just-in-time learning, a system that integrates high-technology learning systems, coaching, and actual work on the job into a single, seamless process.

_____ 5. Our electronic support performance systems enable us to learn and to do our work better.

_____ **Technology Application Score**

GRAND TOTAL TO 5 SUBSYSTEMS _____
(Maximum score: 100)

22

SCORING AND INTERPRETING THE LEARNING ORGANIZATION PROFILE

Score the Learning Organization Profile by adding the individual scores and developing average scores for each subsystem as well as for each department. The interpretation of compiled data can be significantly enhanced by asking and discussing some of the following questions:

✓ Which subsystems have the highest scores and which have the lowest? What are the causes for these high and low scores?

✓ Are there significant differences among the scores within each of the subsystems? What can be done to increase the scores in each subsystem?

✓ What differences emerge among the various departments? Between management and nonmanagement? What may be the reasons for these different perspectives?

✓ Which statements are seen as being the most important and providing the greatest leverage for changing the organization?

✓ How can the results of the Profile be used to establish an action plan to begin building a learning organization?

5

DOES YOUR CLIENT'S STRATEGIC PLAN GIVE THEM THE COMPETITIVE EDGE?

Tom Devane

Overview The nature of strategic planning has changed dramatically in the past few years. These changes have been in response to the increasingly difficult environment in which companies must operate: global markets; unexpected new competitors; dizzying technology changes. All these factors create an environment in which it is difficult to develop any sort of continually relevant, long-term plans that have lasting significance. Companies that attempt to forecast the future even for four years forward are often treated to unwelcome surprises.

The Strategic Plan Assessment Tool is a self-administered questionnaire that can provide insights into how well an organization's strategic plan is posturing the organization for success in today's turbulent business environment.

These assessment criteria are widely applicable and have been used in a variety of industries including electronics assembly manufacturing, health care, pharmaceuticals, paper products, telecommunications, and software development. The assessment criteria have also been used in government agencies.

The assessment tool can be used in a variety of ways:

- ✓ Preplanning checklist
- ✓ Evaluating the existing strategic plan
- ✓ Interim reviews of business direction
- ✓ Mergers, acquisitions, and partnership arrangements
- ✓ Evaluating departmental fit with the organization's larger strategic objectives
- ✓ Roll-out of the existing strategy to the entire organization

Contact Information: Premier Integration, 317 Lookout View Court, Golden, CO 80401, 303-279-1099, tdevane@iex.net

STRATEGIC PLAN ASSESSMENT TOOL

Directions: The Strategic Plan Assessment Tool consists of ten categories, each representing an important aspect of maximizing the usefulness of a strategic plan. These categories are:

✓ Strategic Focus

✓ Organizational Identity

✓ Environmental Scans and Plans

✓ Internal Scans and Plans

✓ Products and Services

✓ Reinvention and Renewal

✓ Performance Measurement

✓ Leadership

✓ Strategy Process Effectiveness

Under each of these categories are subcategories that are the criteria by which the strategic plan is assessed.

When using this tool, simply evaluate your strategic plan based on the criteria included in the tool. Rate each criterion using a scale of 1 to 7 (1 = poor example of the criterion, 7 = excellent example of the criterion). Record your rating in the space provided. We strongly recommend that you make comments in addition to the numerical rating, particularly if the rating is low. This qualitative information will help support the quantitative ratings and provide you with ideas on actions to take to improve the current rating. (Examples are provided for clarification where needed.)

STRATEGIC FOCUS

The following categories help assess the organization's articulation of specific areas upon which to focus attention, mobilize resources, and set it apart from competitors.

Criteria	Rating	Comments
Value Proposition The organization has a clearly defined strategy for adding unique value in its selected markets.		
Trade-Off Articulation The organization recognizes that a single organization can't do everything well, and that it shouldn't try to be everything to everybody. In keeping with this concept, the organization has selected one, or possibly two of the following as areas for excellence: innovation, customer intimacy, operational excellence (Treacy and Wiersewa, 1995).		
Key Goals for the Year The organization has established 2 to 5 goals for the year. The organization recognizes that it is unlikely that more than 5 goals will be understood, embraced, and acted upon by the general workforce within a one-year time frame.		
Key Strategic Initiatives The organization has identified and staffed 2 to 3 key efforts to move the organization forward in its articulated strategic direction.		
Alignment Mechanism In order to provide organizationwide, consistent focus, communications, standard tools, and methods exist to ensure that local departmental efforts are aligned with the organization's overall focus and goals for the year.		
"Nonfocus" Articulation To discourage activities outside its strategic boundaries, the organization has clearly stated the businesses that it is not in so that employees do not spend time and resources in these areas.		
Value Chain Emphasis Within the organization's value chain the organization has clearly articulated its key leverage points (areas where a small amount of resources yields a disproportionate return). *(Term explanation: A value chain is the sequence of activities that add value to a product or service as it moves through the chain. Value chains differ by industry and individual companies, but tend to have a similar high level chain of events: product conception, product development, manufacturing, and distribution.)*		

ORGANIZATIONAL IDENTITY

The following categories help assess the organization's articulation of what the organization stands for and what it is trying to accomplish.

Criteria	Rating	Comments
Vision The organization has a clearly articulated view of what the business will be like and its external impact (the world, its niche markets, its industry) in the next 3 to 20 years. *(Example: "A personal computer on every desktop.")*		
Mission The organization has documented the central reason why it is in business. *(Example: McDonald's mission is "To satisfy the world's appetite for good food, well-served, at a price people can afford.")*		
Values The organization has articulated a set of deeply ingrained operating rules or guidelines for behaviors and actions of members of the organization. Once articulated, these values act as a set of choice principles for individuals to help them decide among behavior alternatives. *(Examples: "None of us is as smart as all of us"; "Customers are the focus of everything we do.")*		
Culture The organization has identified key factors that impact how the organizational culture can be instrumental in achieving the business strategy. Once identified, the organization uses established conditions for those factors to activate, then reinforces them when they appear. *(Examples: "We encourage risk taking because it leads to innovation breakthroughs"; "We use teams to reduce cycle times and slash costs"; "We use straight talk and in-your-face communications to get at the truth quickly and make a decision.")*		
Broadcast of the Identity Where appropriate, the organization has sent the message of its identity to key outside parties through marketing, advertising, or other mechanisms.		

ENVIRONMENTAL SCANS AND PLANS

The following categories help assess the organization's effectiveness in gathering relevant information from the outside world and in developing plans to react to and in some cases influence the outside world.

Criteria	Rating	Comments
Competitor Assessment The organization has examined and evaluated the strengths, weaknesses, opportunities, and threats of known competitors.		
Noncompetitor Assessment The organization has examined and evaluated the strengths, weaknesses, opportunities, and threats of unlikely but potential competitors.		
Customer Assessment The organization has examined and evaluated the strengths, weaknesses, opportunities, and threats of its primary targeted customers.		
Noncustomer Assessment The organization has examined and evaluated the strengths, weaknesses, opportunities, and threats of organizations or individuals that have declined to purchase products or services from the organization. The organization has examined and evaluated the strengths, weaknesses, opportunities, and threats of organizations or individuals that were not previously considered to be potential customers.		
Uncontrollable but Important Forces The organization has examined and evaluated key external forces over which the organization has no direct control, but that could impact the viability of the organization. Examples include the economy sociodemographics, international unrest, technology and government regulations.		
Partnership Building and Maintenance The organization has identified strategic partnerships with customers and suppliers that result in high-leverage, win-win situations for all parties. After developing these, we take painstaking care in monitoring them and maintaining good relations.		

The following categories help assess the organization's effectiveness in gathering relevant information from its internal operations, integrating that information from external scans, and developing plans to shape internal variables and situations as needed.

Criteria	Rating	Comments
Core Competencies Identified The organization has identified its unique combination of capabilities that provide exceptional customer value, distinguish it from competitors, and provide a platform for building similar capabilities in the future.		
Core Competencies Managed With respect to the identified core competencies, the organization: ✓ actively manages competencies as an asset. ✓ provides special rewards for the desired competencies ✓ provides adequate training to ensure the competencies remain current.		
Leadership Regarding leadership, the organization: ✓ has defined a style of leadership consistent with meeting the company's business strategy; ✓ attempts to develop leaders at all levels of the organization; ✓ removes leaders who do not demonstrate the desired leadership style and behaviors.		
Organizational Structure ✓ The organization's structure is designed to carry out the articulated business strategy. ✓ The organization makes use of teams where appropriate to support business strategy. ✓ Decisions about work are made by the people doing the work where the work is done. ✓ Information and communication are used where possible to obviate the need for multiple levels in the organization chart. ✓ When it supports business needs, workers at any level of the organization may reorganize themselves to address problems and capitalize on opportunities.		

Criteria	Rating	Comments
Strategic Compensation and Rewards The organization currently compensates employees based on the value they provide to the organization. If it is in keeping with the organization's philosophy, employees holding identified core competencies are reimbursed appropriately. When people are expected to exhibit team behavior, there are team rewards. Pay for skills and pay for competencies has been implemented where those are the basis for contributing to the organization's objectives. When the organization does well, all share in some of the proceeds as dictated by corporate philosophy. Nimble reward systems provide one-time bonuses for exceptional performance and special skills, instead of providing increases to the salary base. Rewards are made for both results and behaviors.		
Cost Model The organization knows its true costs for dealing with customers and classes of customers. The organization knows its true costs of producing its products and providing services. The organization has strategically considered what to sell and what to give to customers for free. The organization has decided the appropriate mix of fixed and variable costs for its overall cost structure. The organization has outsourced all activities that are not strategic and that the organization does not perform at the lowest cost compared to alternative sites.		
Information Technology The information technology infrastructure supports the business strategy. The organization has evaluated which information systems activities should be outsourced. If so decided in the company strategy, the information technology provides a competitive advantage.		

PRODUCTS AND SERVICES

The following categories help assess the organization's effectiveness in developing products and services that meet the strategic needs of the business.

Criteria	Rating	Comments
Product and Service Strategies The organization has developed strategies for specific products and services and groups of products and services. In developing these strategies the organization has considered: ✓ the growth of its selected market; ✓ its share of the selected market; ✓ cyclical trends in this market and related markets that impact the organization's product and service; ✓ competitor strengths, weaknesses, opportunities and threats relative to the organization's.		
Customer Retention There are active plans to retain existing customers and use that group as a base from which to expand.		
Customer Assessment Using customer input, the organization conducts systematic reviews of product and service features for existing and new offerings.		
Noncustomer Assessment The organization has examined and evaluated the strengths, weaknesses, opportunities, and threats of organizations or individuals that have declined to purchase products or services from the organization. The organization has examined and evaluated the strengths, weaknesses, opportunities, and threats of organizations or individuals that were not previously considered to be potential customers.		
Uncontrollable but Important Forces The organization has examined and evaluated key external forces over which the organization has no direct control, but that could impact the viability of the organization. Examples include the economy, sociodemographics, international unrest, technology, and government regulations.		

REINVENTION AND RENEWAL

The following categories help assess the organization's effectiveness in continually adapting to the organization's external environment.

Criteria	Rating	Comments
Assumptions and Beliefs The organization has identified and challenged the assumptions that were used in previous years' strategic plans. The organization has been especially critical of those assumptions and beliefs that have brought them success over the years. *(Example: assuming that the future of computing would always be mainframe-based.)*		
Observation and Analysis Filters The organization has considered whether or not its observations of the outside world are colored by its wishful thinking and previous assumptions and beliefs. *(Example: Auto companies' assessment that Japanese increase in auto sales 20 years ago was a temporary blip that would never repeat itself.)*		
Porous Organization: Inside to Outside Mechanisms or processes exist to ensure that information flows freely between members inside the organization and the external environment. Important trends are quickly detected and passed on to those who can act upon them.		
Porous Organization: Inside Level-to-Level Mechanisms or processes exist to ensure strategic planning information flows freely among members of the organization, irrespective of organizational level. *(Example: Department store clerks signal changes in customer buying patterns to senior management faster than the traditional forecasting system does.)*		
Discussions about Ways to Reinvent How the Industry Does Business At least once a year the organization conducts discussions about how the organization might change the way that its entire industry does business.		

PERFORMANCE MEASUREMENT

The following categories help assess the organization's ability to translate its strategy to measurable, easily communicated objectives.

Criteria	Rating	Comments
Balanced Measurement The organization emphasizes the balance of financial objectives, customer service objectives, process improvement objectives, and learning objectives.		
Process There is a process by which objectives at a higher level in the organization are disseminated to lower levels of the organization.		
Performance Measurement Is Part of a Management System The organization's focus on measurement isn't just a narrow one on "the numbers"; rather measurement is part of the overall management system of how the organization is run.		
Feedback for Adjustments to Behaviors and Assumptions Mechanisms exist for incorporating learning that may necessitate changing the existing measurements in the organization.		
Basis for Communication, Discussion and Negotiation Clearly articulated performance objectives form the foundation for information dissemination, discussion, and negotiation among organizational levels.		
Local Goal-Setting Based on Objectives and Goals at Higher Levels Groups of people set their own goals based on information they receive from higher levels in the organization.		

The following categories help assess how well leaders are helping the organization survive and thrive in its environment.

Criteria	Rating	Comments
Ensuring That a Vision Exists Leadership ensures that there is a vision of the impact that the organization wishes to have on the world. (Note: In some cases the leader at the top of the organization may not need to personally develop the vision; the leader only need ensure that one exists.)		
Clearly Articulate Reality Leaders paint a clear picture of the world external to the organization, and how the organization interacts with the world. The leader is not blinded by existing assumptions and beliefs, and helps people in the organization see opportunities and threats in a realistic light.		
Mobilize Resources The leadership is able to recognize high-priority, high-leverage activities for the development of the organization, and ensures that resources (money, people, time) flow to those activities.		
Develop Leaders at All Levels Plans exist to develop leaders at all levels of the organization, not just at the top of the organizational hierarchy.		
Upward and Downward Responsibility Leaders at all levels in the organization recognize that they are responsible to those above them and responsible to those below them.		
Distribution of Power and Responsibility Leaders actively seek out ways in which to distribute decision-making capability and authority throughout the organization.		

STRATEGY PROCESS EFFECTIVENESS

The following categories help assess the effectiveness and efficiency of the process that the organization uses to develop strategic plans.

Criteria	Rating	Comments
Customer and Market Input Considered A mechanism exists to ensure that preferences and trends in the marketplace are considered in the planning process.		
Strategic Planning and Action Planning Are Linked In addition to developing strategies, the organization develops action plans to implement those strategies.		
Participative Development The strategic plan and associated action plans are developed in a group setting with key members in attendance.		
Concentration of Time for the Plan The strategic plan is not developed in 1- or 2-hour sessions over a period of time. Instead, it is often developed in 2- or 3-day blocks of time in which participants can focus their energies and attention.		
History and Assumption Review Members of the strategic planning group take time to understand the factors that have shaped the organization into what it is today, and critically review key assumptions upon which its success has been based.		
Communication of the Plan Members of the strategic planning group have developed a process for communicating essential elements of the plan so that people at all levels of the organization know how best to structure their work to contribute to the organization's strategy.		
Monitoring of the Action Plans Mechanisms have been set up to ensure that day-to-day pressures of the business do not interfere with the action plans necessary to implement the strategy.		
Continual Environmental Scanning and Replanning The organization understands that the nature of the marketplace is so dynamic that it needs to scan the environment more that just once a year. Processes have been established to rapidly identify key trend and customer taste preference changes, and incorporate those into the plan.		

INTERPRETING THE RESULTS OF THE STRATEGIC PLAN ASSESSMENT TOOL

Many organizations use this tool as a type of "report card" that indicates how well they are developing and deploying their strategic plans. This is a valid use, but there is at least one other use that organizations have found to be particularly helpful.

Instead of using this assessment tool as a report card, many strategic planning groups use it to have an in-depth conversation about an item on the assessment list and how it relates to their business situation. For example, in the Reinvention and Renewal section there is an assessment item, "Discussions about Ways to Reinvent How the Industry Does Business." The vice president of engineering for a major electronics assembly firm remarked that he had never thought about how they might change the industry before, but believed that with the talent they had inside the company they could certainly do that. He and the marketing vice president formed a special task team and, within six months, they radically changed the configuration and pricing of their product, which in turn changed the way the entire industry conducted business in their niche segment.

One final note on the assessment: Organizations that have used this assessment have commented that it is best done with groups of people, instead of by one or two individuals. The quality of conversations, assumption sharing, and group commitment to action appear to have a synergistic effect when groups of people participate in the assessment.

REFERENCES

Emery, M., and Purser, R. *The Search Conference.* San Francisco: Jossey-Bass, 1996.

Fogg, C. D. *Team-Based Strategic Planning.* New York: AMACOM, 1994.

Halal, William E. *The New Management.* San Francisco: Berrett-Koehler, 1996

Hamel, Gary. "Strategy Innovation and the Quest for Value." *Sloan Management Review,* 39, 2, Boston, 1998.

Harrington, H. J., and Harrington, J. S. *Total Improvement Management.* New York: McGraw-Hill, 1995.

Mintzberg, Henry. *The Rise and Fall of Strategic Planning.* New York: The Free Press, 1994.

Quinn, James Brian. *The Intelligent Enterprise.* New York: Free Press, 1992.

Reading, J. C., and Catalanello, R. F. *Strategic Readiness.* San Francisco: Jossey-Bass, 1994.

Thompson, A., and Strickland, A. J. *Strategy Formulation and Implementation.* Burr Ridge: Irwin, 1992.

Treacy, M., and Wiersema, F. *The Discipline of Market Leaders.* Reading: Addison-Wesley, 1995.

6

WHAT MAKES TEAMS EFFECTIVE?

George Truell

Overview   Many organizations today are restructuring themselves into groupings of self-managed work teams. Often consultants are assigned to help these teams get under way and to support a team's efforts by acting as a coach, facilitator, or resource person. Once the teams are up and running, it is helpful to periodically assess how effectively they are functioning from three dimensions:

1. how well members are working together as one cohesive group;

2. the overall effectiveness of the person assigned to support them; and

3. the amount of support and encouragement team members are receiving from members of top management.

The Assessing Team Effectiveness instrument identifies three key areas of behaviors and attitudes that affect a team's performance. In addition to arriving at one score for overall team effectiveness, you can evaluate specific persons or groups of people to determine what improvements in their own behaviors and attitudes would enable the team to improve its overall performance.

Contact Information: George Truell Associates, 495 North Forest Road, Williamsville, NY 14221-5036, 716-634-3491, gtabuffny@aol.com

ASSESSING TEAM EFFECTIVENESS

HOW I SEE THE OVERALL OPERATING EFFECTIVENESS OF OUR TEAM

Directions: Read each statement below. Using the ranking scale of 1 through 5, determine how true the statement is for your team. Place the numerical ranking in the space to the left of the statement.

5 - Definitely Agree
4 - Inclined to Agree
3 - Neither Agree Nor Disagree
2 - Inclined to Agree
1 - Definitely Disagree

AS TEAM MEMBERS:

___ **1.** We all fully understand and support our team's basic mission and its current objectives.

___ **2.** We all have a clear understanding of our assigned duties and responsibilities, the various roles we are expected to play, and our accountabilities to the total team, as well as to each other.

___ **3.** We all place a high level of importance on providing quality products and services to our internal or external customers (i.e., the people who receive the output from our team).

___ **4.** We are all willing to engage in cross-skills training so each of us can perform the duties and responsibilities of our fellow team members.

___ **5.** We have all established a high level of trust and mutual respect for one another and provide a lot of support and encouragement to our fellow team members.

___ **6.** We are all very open and candid in expressing our opinions and in sharing information with each other.

___ **7.** We all have a genuine concern for each other and willingly help our fellow team members in performing their tasks and in handling work problems they may encounter.

___ **8.** We all understand the value of differing viewpoints and we handle any conflicts we may have by facing the issues openly and by focusing on "what's right" rather than on "who's right."

___ **9.** We all place a heavy emphasis on being certain that the knowledge, skills, and abilities of every person are fully utilized and reflected in the decisions we make as a team.

___**10.** We all have a high sense of urgency and actively participate in the identification and solution of any problems we encounter on the job.

___**11.** We all enjoy the work we do and our working relationships with one another.

___**12.** We all continuously seek information from our internal or external customers so we can find and develop new and better ways to function as a team.

ASSESSING TEAM EFFECTIVENESS

HOW I SEE THE OVERALL EFFECTIVENESS OF THE PERSON ASSIGNED TO SUPPORT OUR TEAM (I.E., OUR COACH, FACILITATOR, OR RESOURCE PERSON)

Directions: Read each statement below. Using the ranking scale of 1 through 5, determine how true the statement is for your team's support person. Place the numerical ranking in the space to the left of the statement.

5 - Definitely Agree
4 - Inclined to Agree
3 - Neither Agree Nor Disagree
2 - Inclined to Agree
1 - Definitely Disagree

THE PERSON ASSIGNED TO SUPPORT OUR TEAM:

___13. Encourages us to expand our range of skills and degree of involvement by delegating some of his or her own duties and responsibilities to our team.

___14. Provides encouragement, recognition, and positive reinforcement of our team's accomplishments.

___15. Willingly obtains and communicates whatever corporate, marketing, customer, supplier, departmental, cost, or related information we seek in order to help us monitor and improve our team's performance.

___16. Obtains from various staff groups, professional specialists, and members of management the physical and personnel resources, tools, equipment, materials, and technical support we request in order to improve our team's operating effectiveness.

___17. Serves as a spokesperson for our team and defends us when he or she feels that we are being unfairly criticized or treated poorly by members of management, by other teams, or by other organizational groups.

___18. Is readily accessible to us, listens well to what we have to say, answers whatever questions we ask, and responds quickly to any concerns we express.

___19. Arranges meetings for us with members of other teams, company personnel, customers, suppliers, and other outside groups whenever we request them so that we can exchange information and experiences, establish cross-functional task forces, and participate in joint problem-solving activities.

___20. Helps us develop proposals, obtains any required approvals, and assists us in implementing changes in work layout, work flow, physical arrangement of work centers, operating policies, practices, and systems that will facilitate and reinforce the continuous improvement of our team's operating effectiveness.

___21. Keeps us well informed about the goals and objectives of the total organization as well as the goals of other organizational units, so that we can develop and integrate our own team's goals in support of every other group.

___22. Helps us identify problems, define the sources of those problems, develop proposed courses of action, and successfully solve our problems.

___23. Helps us identify our training needs and supports our learning efforts by willingly sharing his or her own knowledge and experience with us; by providing time, support, and encouragement for learning to occur; and by obtaining whatever personnel or physical resources may be required.

___24. Places major emphasis on the accomplishments of our team, rather than on his or her own personal accomplishments.

ASSESSING TEAM EFFECTIVENESS

HOW I SEE THE OVERALL SUPPORT AND ENCOURAGEMENT WE RECEIVE FROM MEMBERS OF TOP MANAGEMENT

Directions: Read each statement below. Using the ranking scale of 1 through 5, determine how true the statement is for members of top management. Place the numerical ranking in the space to the left of the statement.

5 - Definitely Agree
4 - Inclined to Agree
3 - Neither Agree Nor Disagree
2 - Inclined to Agree
1 - Definitely Disagree

MEMBERS OF TOP MANAGEMENT:

___25. Serve as role models of employee involvement by willingly delegating some of their own duties and responsibilities to members of their managerial and supervisory teams.

___26. Allocate time, money, and other essential resources to encourage greater employee involvement throughout all organizational areas for which they are responsible and accountable.

___27. Personally and publicly recognize, compliment, encourage, and reward individual team members, as well as our total team, for our input in decision making, problem solving, creative thinking, and our overall operating effectiveness.

___28. Conduct their own meetings in a participative manner by such means as: having different people lead the meeting, openly soliciting team member input, inviting differing opinions, and frequently using consensus building in their decision making.

___29. Willingly assume responsibility for protecting newly-formed teams from external organization pressures, practices, and policies that may hinder or actually destroy the development of those teams.

___30. Are highly visible and make themselves readily available to us (in both formal and informal settings), in order to answer our questions and to provide leadership and help when we request it.

___31. Provide an ongoing flow of information to us about the organization's vision, its operating philosophy, our customers' requirements, the organization's current goals and objectives, and the level of success the organization is attaining in meeting those goals and objectives.

___32. Invite our input on issues that were formerly decided only by them, and willingly explain their actions whenever changes are made or their final decisions are questioned by team members.

___33. Treat the errors we make as learning experiences for us, rather than as opportunities for them to place blame on our team.

___34. Initiate changes in operating policies and practices in order to reinforce our team's development and effectiveness.

___35. Provide time to personally teach, coach, and counsel the men and women who work directly with us in order to improve the operating effectiveness of those people.

___36. Are highly involved in promoting the continuous growth and development of individual team members and the continuous improvement of our team's operating effectiveness.

ANALYSIS SHEET FOR ASSESSING TEAM EFFECTIVENESS

Directions: Record the numerical rating you selected (5, 4, 3, 2, or 1) for each statement in the spaces below. Work down the sheet for each of the 36 statements.

OTHER TEAM MEMBERS	SUPPORT PERSON	TOP MANAGEMENT
1. ___	13. ___	25. ___
2. ___	14. ___	26. ___
3. ___	15. ___	27. ___
4. ___	16. ___	28. ___
5. ___	17. ___	29. ___
6. ___	18. ___	30. ___
7. ___	19. ___	31. ___
8. ___	20. ___	32. ___
9. ___	21. ___	33. ___
10. ___	22. ___	34. ___
11. ___	23. ___	35. ___
12. ___	24. ___	36. ___

Totals: _____ + _____ + _____ =

Grand Total: ☐

ASSESSING TEAM EFFECTIVENESS

SCORING

Add the point values in each of the three columns to obtain subtotals. Then add the subtotals for the three dimensions to obtain the grand total.

SCORING INTERPRETATION

The team's overall effectiveness can be determined from the scores in the Grand Total box as follows:

Score Range	Overall Rating
168–180	Highly effective. All dimensions of the team's working relationships are in great shape.
156–167	Generally effective. Most dimensions of the team's working relationships are functioning quite well.
144–155	Somewhat effective. Some dimensions of the team's working relationships need to be improved. Analyze the scores in each of the three areas of interaction to see where fine-tuning is needed.
36–143	Not very effective. Many areas need to be addressed.

Scores for Each Area

The three areas of behaviors and attitudes are clustered under the following headings:

Other Team Members

Support Person

Top Management

Specific areas for improvement can be determined by analyzing the scores for each of the three columns. If an area of behaviors and attitudes has a score in the range of 48 to 60, it is helping the team to be highly effective. On the other hand, if the score is 47 or less, all of the statements in that area should be examined to determine which ones are not supporting team effectiveness and need to be addressed.

To determine specific action steps that might be taken, review the 12 statements in the column to see which ones scored low (3, 2, or 1). Ask yourself:

"What could we do to change this situation so people would agree with the statement; in other words, would rate it a 4 or a 5?"

7

WHY ISN'T THE TEAM MAKING DECISIONS?

Janet Winchester-Silbaugh

Overview This tool helps a team you are consulting with to figure out why it isn't making decisions. Once it has figured out what is blocking the decision, there are strategies to move the decision forward.

It is frustrating to be part of a team that can't seem to make a decision or keeps revisiting a decision you thought was made. Think of decisions as water flowing down a stream. When teams don't make decisions, their thought process gets sidetracked around a rock, or goes through a hole in the bank, or runs up against a dam. Once a team understands why the thought process is not flowing, it can develop effective strategies to help it make good decisions...with your help.

There are at least six key elements in any decision process:

1. the team or people making the decision,
2. the other stakeholders who care about what decision is made but aren't directly part of the process,
3. the problem itself and how it is defined,
4. the information you have to feed into the decision-making process,
5. the decision-making tool you've chosen to use, and
6. the management of the process.

When these elements are aligned, decisions, even difficult ones, can be made effectively. But when one element is not compatible with the rest, decisions are easily derailed.

This assessment tool makes it easier to spot the conflicts between different elements in the decision-making process, and gives strategies for solving the problems.

Contact Information: 51 Pinon Heights, Sandia Park, NM 87047, 505-286-2210, silbaugh@ccvp.com

TEAM DECISION BARRIER MATRIX

STEP 1: WHERE ARE THE BLOCKS?

Instructions: The first step is to see what is blocking the decision. Fill each box with a *yes* if you think there is a disconnect between the vertical and horizontal elements. Take box 1, for example. Ask yourself if the team members seem to be influenced by stakeholders outside the team. Then go on to box 2 and ask if the decision is framed in a way that is comfortable for and solvable by the team. Continue across the row: Do all team members have the same information, is the team comfortable with the decision rules, and is the team managing the decision-making process? Each element is listed twice, so that you can answer the question with that element as the actor and again as the element acted upon.

After you have completed the matrix, go to Step 2 for strategies to deal with the more common barriers to team decision making.

	Team Members	Stakeholders Outside the Team	Definition of the Problem	Information Available To Make Decisions	Decision Rules	Decision Process
Team Members		1	2	3	4	5
Stakeholders Outside the Team	6		7	8	9	10
Definition of the Problem	11	12		13	14	15
Information Available to Make Decisions	16	17	18		19	20
Decision Rules	21	22	23	24		25
Decision Process	26	27	28	29	30	

STEP 2: STRATEGIES FOR MANAGING COMMON BARRIERS TO TEAM DECISION MAKING

Here are strategies that might work for some of the particular mismatches that you marked "yes" on the Team Decision Barrier Matrix. Each situation calls for a different strategy, so read through the ideas and then modify them in whatever way fits your own needs.

The team is confined or influenced by other stakeholders who are not on the team. (Boxes 1 and 6)

It is difficult to make team decisions when people are worried about the opinions of people who are not on the team. Outside stakeholders, such as senior management, can block decisions when 1) they are not in the discussions, so there is no way to understand their views clearly, and 2) their views become absolute requirements, because they don't change as the discussion evolves.

✓   Add the external stakeholders to the team, so the team discussion now includes all the important viewpoints.

✓   Ask the outside stakeholders if they really want to make the decision themselves. Sometimes they had no intention of influencing the decision. At other times, they want to make the decision instead of letting the team make it.

✓   Get input from the outside stakeholders to present to the team. Their input becomes part of the decision-making process without blocking it.

✓   Use the outside stakeholders' opinion as a boundary and see if you can make a creative decision within their framework.

✓   Change the team's job to making a recommendation or providing input.

The problem to be solved is not appropriate for the team, or is phrased so it can't be solved. (Boxes 2 and 11)

You have to have the right people to solve the right problem. This means that a team needs authority over and knowledge about the problem, and the problem has to be defined in a way that encourages a solution.

✓   Change the composition of the team. Make sure that all the people who are impacted by the decision are represented in some way: as team members, by having team members ask them about their issues, or by having a team member formally represent them.

✓   Redefine the problem so it is appropriate for the team. Often this means making it more concrete and limited ("What new products should we develop?" rather than "Develop a strategic product plan.").

✓   Redefine the problem so you know what constitutes success.

✓   Separate different issues into sub-problems so you can deal with them one at a time.

✓   Look for precedents in decisions you have already made. See if it's possible to view this problem as a variation on an established pattern.

Team members don't have the right information or the information is not in a useful form. (Boxes 3 and 16)

✓ Realize that few decisions are made based on information alone. If they were, there would be no reason for having a team. A good decision mixes solid information with a team's knowledge, experience, and judgment.

✓ Ask people what's missing. This allows you to see whether information is missing or is just not usable in its current form. It also lets you spot people who use lack of information as an excuse to block a decision. In this case, figure out what is bothering the person. Sometimes, a decision involves more risks than a person is willing to take or upsets a comfortable position. In other cases, a decision in one team may seem to one person to be disloyal to another team of people.

✓ Get the information the team wants and present it to them in such a way that all members know what is available. Encourage questions. When information is not available, ask the team to define different information that would serve the same purpose.

✓ Make sure the information fits the preference of different team members. Use different presentation styles (text, tables, bullet points, graphs) if that will make it easier to understand.

✓ Stick to essential information. Don't get sidetracked by information that is nice to know, but takes a lot of time. Know when enough is enough for an effective decision.

✓ Build in time for the team to process the information. Many people can't understand the implications of information until they have "played with the numbers."

✓ Build in the expectation that people will do their homework.

✓ If people miss meetings and information, ask them to catch up outside the meeting rather than stop the team.

The decision rules don't fit the team. (Boxes 4 and 21)

We often think of decision making using a democratic process such as a majority vote. Other common decision rules are: consensus (everyone must be able to live with the decision even though it may not have been their first choice); "the boss decides"; "just do it" (whereby one member takes action and the team ends up going along with it whether they agree or not); majority rule; team consensus with certain people having veto power; analysis by experts; and working groups that feed their input to a decision-making committee. Figure out which decision rule is most effective for the particular decision you are trying to make.

✓ Always make sure the team knows how a decision will be made. In some cases, it is dictated by someone else (such as the boss); sometimes the team can change the decision process.

✓ Talk openly about conflict of interest between what is best for one member and what is best for the organization.

✓ Listen to determine whether any member of the team is too uncomfortable with the decision rules to go along with them. This often happens when members are used to a hierarchical style and simply can't see that consensus is a "real" decision.

✓ Talk about different preferences among team members in how they approach problems. Some will take lots of risk; others like a sure thing. Some look at the future as bright, while others want a decision that is safe even if the worst happens. Some think a "good enough" decision is fine, while others will spend a long time getting to the best decision. Some people are strongly driven by time, while others are not. Some people are global thinkers, while others go sequentially through each step.

The decision process is not effective for the team members. (Boxes 5 and 26)

✓ Make sure someone is responsible for managing (facilitating) the process itself. The facilitator usually keeps the discussion focused on the topic, makes sure everyone has a chance to express ideas, makes sure that many options are discussed, and keeps the discussion leading toward a resolution.

✓ Use the facilitator who is effective for that particular team. Change the facilitator if necessary.

✓ When there is an impasse, check to see if the impasse is over facts, methods, goals, or values.

✓ Set realistic deadlines, or deadlines driven by business necessity. Keep the process moving and at a pace comfortable for the team.

The information available doesn't seem to fit the decision. (Boxes 13 and 18)

✓ See the strategies listed under "Team members don't have the right information." (Boxes 3 and 16)

✓ Look for proxy measures that might not answer the whole question, but help chip away at it.

The rules for making the decision don't seem to work for that particular decision. (Boxes 14 and 23)

This is a much more common problem than you'd expect. Examples of common decision rules include: "the boss decides"; "just do it" (whereby one member takes action and the team ends up going along with it whether they agree or not); majority rule; team consensus; team consensus with certain people having veto power; analysis by experts; and working committees feeding their input to a decision-making committee. For a technical decision, analysis by experts may be the best approach. For a decision that many people will have to support, team consensus may be critical. "The boss decides" may be the most effective method for a controversial decision that must be made quickly. Pick the decision rule that fits your needs and environment.

Many common analysis techniques assume that you've seen similar problems before and that there is a fair amount of information available. Watch out if your decision involves something your organization hasn't seen before or if there isn't much information available.

✓ Ask yourself whether this decision is like others you have made. If it is, did the process you used last work well?

✓ When you choose a decision rule, think about: the time the decision process takes, the resources it requires, the skills the decision makers must have, the support it might generate, how it fits with the "corporate culture," the fallout if it doesn't work well, the amount of risk you can afford to take, and the skills you want the organization to learn for the future.

The decision process you chose requires different information than you have. (Boxes 19 and 24)

✓ Change the process so it is less dependent on information you can't get. This usually involves substituting "what if" analysis for information. For instance, if you can't get a good estimate of buying trends, then figure out whether your decision changes if buying is either very high or very low.

✓ Use several proxy measures to replace a concrete measure that is unavailable. If you can't get a percentage increase in hospital admissions, then see if you can get estimates for things that influence hospital admissions, such as the age of the population and technological advances.

The process doesn't lead to the decision rule you are trying to use. (Boxes 25 and 30)

✓ Make sure your decision makers have enough time to make the decision. The boss may want to make the decision, but if the boss doesn't have the time, the decision won't be made. Build in time to let teams get established and for all members to work from the same information. Allow enough time for team process to occur.

✓ The larger the team involved, the more formal the management process needed. Large teams may have difficulty with controversial decisions, because there are more points of view to be unified.

✓ Keep the process moving. Make small decisions early. Start building a fact and agreement base before the big decisions are needed.

✓ Let the decision rule determine your style of management. A consensus decision rule often means a more informal-feeling process, whereas a majority voting process lends itself to a more obviously structured process.

Decision making, just like a river, keeps flowing. Once you've overcome one barrier, ideas flow into another barrier. Spend some time watching the process of decision making and you will find that you get much better at spotting the root causes of the barriers that come up. Enjoy the journey.

HOW DO YOUR CLIENTS VIEW THEIR ORGANIZATION'S PERFORMANCE?

Scott Parry

Overview   Organizations today are constantly looking to improve their products, processes, services, and relationships. In order to be successful at this improvement, the organization needs to know where it is now and where it wants to be at multiple levels: organizational, departmental, and team. This instrument will help a consultant assess such things as performance expectations, performance standards, the way standards are established, types of rewards, and reward systems. It also provides a format for creating an action plan that addresses the findings. (A sample filled-in action plan appears on page 53.)

Contact Information: Training House, Inc., 96 Bear Brook Road, Princeton, NJ 08540, 609-452-1517, jsparry@erols.com, www.traininghouse.com

MEASURING OUR PERFORMANCE

1. This organization has always had certain goals and standards to be met. What changes have you seen in recent years in the way goals and standards are being set? In the way performance toward them is being measured?

2. What are some of the reasons for the increased emphasis this organization is placing on quality and continuous improvement?

3. Some organizations set standards as "minimum expectations that must be met." Examples: "No more than six sick days per year" or "Telephone should be answered by the fourth ring." Other organizations see standards as maximum expectations that require stretching and great effort to attain. Example: "Each salesperson will increase next year's total sales volume ($) by at least 20% over this year's volume." How are standards seen within this organization? Give examples.

4. Performance standards occur at many levels of the organization. At the highest level of a profit-making organization, the board of directors may set certain minimum expectations of return on investment so as to satisfy stockholders. At the middle level, managers and supervisors set standards regarding the time required and the funding needed to accomplish different projects and procedures. What standards are being set or could be set by the members of a team or work group? Give examples.

5. When new practices, procedures, or equipment are installed in an organization, it's difficult to set standards regarding employee performance (e.g., on error rate, time required, measures of quality). How are standards set in this organization as changes in operations are made?

6. Sometimes innovation and experimentation are keys to finding better ways of doing things and thereby improving the performance standards. Are employees in this organization encouraged to experiment and try out new ideas, or are such actions discouraged or even punished by supervisors? Give examples.

51

7. What kinds of rewards and recognition are used within this organization to acknowledge superior performance in consistently meeting or exceeding standards?

8. What rewards and recognition are used within teams to celebrate unusual performance by the team or one of its members?

9. What are the sources of standards and best practices used to benchmark (measure and improve) performance? Are there any that should be added by any of the teams?

10. Four types of performance standards are described in the table below. Beside each, describe an example that applies to the work performed by the team. If you can't think of a team-based example, describe an organizational example.

Type of Standard	Example
Competency/Ability: These standards set the minimum levels of knowledge, skill, and attitude that a person or group must have to perform.	
Activity/Process: These standards specify the required activities (procedures, sequences, steps, phases) to be performed.	
Tolerance/Acceptance Standards: These standards describe the required characteristics (minimum levels of acceptability) of a person's or group's output.	
Results/Outcomes: These standards spell out the desired consequences of performance: the return on investment (financial and other).	

Evaluation of Responses: Reviewing the answers to the ten questions, determine where there are gaps between what is and what should be. Detail this information on the What-Why-How Report and develop an action plan for eliminating the gap.

MEASURING OUR PERFORMANCE

SAMPLE WHAT-WHY-HOW REPORT
(Performance Gaps and Recommended Actions)

Task Force: _Selection, New Hires_   **Subset Responsibility:** _Interviewing Job Candidates_

Should be (Desired Performance)	*Actual* (Existing Performance)	*Constraints* (Reasons for the Gap)	*Recommendations* (Actions to Close the Gap)
Supervisor should study application form and prepare questions and a plan before conducting the interview.	Many interviews (est. 30%) are conducted without prior preparation...more of a "chat" than a selection interview.	Supervisor doesn't get paperwork in advance of applicant showing up, or doesn't study it.	Policy to require that supervisor gets paperwork at least a day before the interview. Supervisor to discuss plans and questions with HR prior to interviewing applicant.
Supervisors should avoid potentially damaging questions and issues (EEO, ADA).	Supervisors failed to indicate correctly 42% of list of questions that can/can't be asked during interviews.	They do not understand implications of EEO issues, and are unaware of the guidelines of the ADA (Disabilities Act).	Conduct workshop and/or issue 4-page folder with guidelines. Do this just before each selection interview (as paperwork is sent to supervisor).
Supervisor should evaluate each applicant immediately after an interview, and assign weight to each criteria.	Supervisors don't list the criteria before doing interviews. Also, they wait until they've done all (2–4) interviews before evaluating the candidates.	They've never prepared a decision matrix. They may also fear leaving a paper trail that could later prove to be damaging.	Prepare an example of a decision matrix for three candidates for a typical entry level job. Distribute this during supervisory training.

MEASURING OUR PERFORMANCE

WHAT-WHY-HOW REPORT
(Performance Gaps and Recommended Actions)

Task Force: _____ **Subset Responsibility:** _____

Should be (Desired Performance)	*Actual* (Existing Performance)	*Constraints* (Reasons for the Gap)	*Recommendations* (Actions to Close the Gap)

9

WHAT NEEDS CHANGING IN YOUR CLIENT'S ORGANIZATION?

Ernest Schuttenberg

Overview   What processes and outcomes in your client organization are perceived more and less positively by employees? Which areas might need changing, and which are priority change targets? What change goals should be formulated? How should your client organization get started in making needed changes?

The Organization Perception Questionnaire (OPQ) will help you and members of your client organization answer these questions and develop the bases for change planning.

This instrument may be administered at a consultation session or completed in advance and brought to the session by the participants. Since the instrument assesses a person's perceptions of "the organization," it is important to assign (write in the space provided) a specific definition of "the organization" so that respondents are thinking about the same organizational entity as they complete the instrument. It is possible that people from various departments or work units can complete the instrument, but during the Scoring and Discussion phases, subgroups should be set up so that separate discussions can be carried out for each department or work unit.

Contact Information: 6083 Park Ridge Drive, North Olmsted, OH 44070, 440-734-8249

THE ORGANIZATION PERCEPTION QUESTIONNAIRE (OPQ)

This questionnaire asks you to indicate your perception of several aspects of "The Organization" (TO). Before you respond to the items or issues, you will need to define "The Organization" as a business unit, division, department, or work group, if this has not been done for you. Focus on this organizational unit while completing the OPQ.

As you respond to the items on the OPQ, define "The Organization" (TO) as:

_____

There are two response columns: A and B.

Column A: The way I perceive "The Organization" *is now.* (current)

Column B: The way I perceive "The Organization" *should be.* (desired)

Using the response scale below, record your perceptions to the 40 items or issues listed, both as they are now and the way they should be.

> RESPONSE SCALE
>
> 1 = Practically none; to a very small degree
>
> 2 = Not very; not very much
>
> 3 = Moderately (on the low side)
>
> 4 = Moderately (on the high side)
>
> 5 = Very; to a high degree
>
> 6 = Extremely; to a very high degree

There are no right or wrong answers! Your perceptions are what are important!

A (Current)	B (Desired)	Issues
		1. The degree to which TO produces a high-quality product or service.
		2. The degree to which TO is concerned with solving problems in society.
		3. The degree to which TO will give you the opportunity to do and to learn to do all the things you consider yourself capable of.
		4. The degree to which the most knowledgeable people are consulted in making decisions in TO.

A (Current)	B (Desired)	Issues
		5. The degree to which you feel free to risk making mistakes in doing your job.
		6. The degree to which TO changes its way of doing things as new conditions and needs arise.
		7. The degree to which the various departments and work groups that make up TO work together cooperatively to get the job done.
		8. The degree to which management keeps abreast of outside developments affecting TO.
		9. The degree to which those in positions of authority are concerned to hear how members feel TO is being run—both pro and con.
		10. The degree to which reactions of clients or others on the outside cause changes to be made in TO.
		11. The degree to which TO's product or service is useful to society.
		12. The degree to which management stresses the responsibility of TO to society at large.
		13. The degree to which you get personal satisfaction from the work you do in TO.
		14. The degree to which you are involved in the making of plans and decisions in TO.
		15. The degree to which you feel free to suggest new ways of doing things.
		16. The degree to which TO is quick to change when change is needed.
		17. The degree to which you are kept informed about the things you need to know to do your job.
		18. The degree to which management correctly interprets the impact of current events and trends on TO.
		19. The degree to which you feel free to discuss problems and dissatisfactions with those TO who can do something about them.
		20. The degree to which those in position of authority in TO are responsive to your suggestions and wishes.
		21. The degree to which your personal goals and aspirations are taken into account in management decisions.
		22. The degree to which TO is successful in accomplishing its goals.

A (Current)	B (Desired)	Issues
		23. The degree to which TO commits money, time, and knowledge to the solution of social and environmental problems.
		24. The degree to which people at various levels in TO participate in planning and decision-making activities.
		25. The degree to which it is advantageous to your future in TO to stick your neck out and take risks in doing your job.
		26. The degree to which TO is strong in long-range planning.
		27. The degree to which you understand the goals of TO.
		28. The degree to which the product or service of TO is up to date.
		29. The degree to which the management is concerned to know how those outside TO view its effectiveness.
		30. The degree to which the ideas and desires of members of TO influence changes that are made.
		31. The degree to which TO is aware of new discoveries and methods of doing things in its field.
		32. The degree to which the product or service of TO has earned it a good reputation.
		33. The degree to which TO is directly involved in alleviating problems in society in addition to producing its primary product of service.
		34. The degree to which management is concerned about how people in TO feel and what they think.
		35. The degree to which you have opportunity to use all your abilities in your job.
		36. The degree to which group decision making is practiced in TO.
		37. The degree to which management is tolerant of people in TO trying out new ideas and methods even though they may be unsuccessful.
		38. The degree to which TO is effective in foreseeing potential problems in the accomplishment of its objectives.
		39. The degree to which the upward communication flow in TO is free of obstruction.
		40. The degree to which leadership is provided by management in TO.

INTERPRETATION

Individual Scoring and Interpretation

Place a check mark (✓) in front of the OPQ items or issues for which the number you wrote for Column A (Current) is 4 or less. According to your perception, these are potential items or issues for change. Next, review the checked items and circle the check mark in front of those items for which the number you wrote in Column B (Desired) is 2 or more numbers higher or lower than the number in Column A (for example: A=3, B=5 or A=4, B=2). These items are your Change Targets, areas in which you think substantial change should be made in The Organization.

Group Score Interpretation and Action Plan

On a flip chart, overhead, or computer projector, record the numbers of the Change Targets for each person who completed the OPQ. Identify the five to ten OPQ items that most respondents have identified as Change Targets. Discuss each of these items, identifying examples of behaviors in The Organization that illustrate each item. Next, through voting or discussion, rank order these five to ten from most to least important. Finally, brainstorm change goals for the top three to five ranked items and develop a list of "next steps" and persons responsible for change planning for each item.

10

WHAT ARE YOUR CLIENT'S LEADERSHIP COMPETENCIES?

Joan Cassidy

Overview As organizations embrace the notions of empowerment and team building, they must also stress the need for better leadership. Some individuals need a structured, controlled environment with continuous feedback to feel secure and to be productive. Others need a flexible, open, creative environment with little or no supervision. Successful leaders recognize these differences in themselves and others and then learn to adjust to optimize the performance of all individuals.

This instrument identifies 20 characteristics or competencies attributed to successful leaders. It is important to recognize that not everyone will be exceptional or even very good in all 20. Based on their own innate qualities and preferences, most individuals feel more comfortable engaging in some activities, and prefer to avoid others. On the other hand, highly successful leaders understand their own strengths and weaknesses. They engage in developmental activities and also supplement and complement their weaknesses by drawing on others. This instrument helps individuals to determine their strengths and weaknesses as well as the relevance of those strengths and weaknesses to current and future leadership roles. It also helps them develop an action plan for improvement.

Contact Information: Integrated Leadership Concepts, Inc., P.O. Box 523080, Springfield, VA 22152, 703-866-1184, DrJoanC@aol.com, www.DrJoanCassidy.com

360° LEADERSHIP DEVELOPMENT ASSESSMENT INSTRUMENT

Name of person being rated: _____

Name of person doing the rating: _____   Date: _____

Following are 20 competencies that represent knowledge, skills, abilities, and attitudes of successful leaders. Please read the description of each competency and then rate the individual identified above, using the following key:

5 = Exceptional; 4 = Very Good; 3 = Good; 2 = Needs Improvement; 1 = Very Weak

____ 1. **Creating a Vision and Setting Goals.** Without clear goals, team members perceive their work to have less purpose and impact and are less inclined to participate. A good leader has a clear vision about what needs to be accomplished and is able to set realistic goals to achieve that vision.

____ 2. **Explaining and Communicating Expectations.** Team members want to know and understand expectations for individual and group performance. Without these expectations, feedback is not as meaningful as it could be, making it difficult for individuals or a group to achieve goals and successes. Good leaders are clear about reporting relationships, and they establish evaluation criteria that are fair and appropriate.

____ 3. **Written Communication.** The successful leader writes clearly and concisely at the level needed by the person(s) receiving the information. In other words, the leader writes to *express,* not *impress.*

____ 4. **Oral Communication.** Good leaders inform others about what is going on and why. The leader engages in frank discussion about issues and how those issues affect individuals, and structures meetings to provide for needed dialogue.

____ 5. **Personal Integrity.** Personal integrity is becoming more and more an issue in the workplace. Good leaders demonstrate and model integrity in day-to-day interactions by:
- establishing a relationship of trust;
- being honest (even if it means making a different decision than the one recommended);
- treating everyone fairly;
- delivering on promises and meeting commitments;
- placing personal needs (ego) in second place to needs of the overall group; and
- admitting mistakes and accepting constructive criticism.

___ 6. **Creativity and Experimentation.** Great leaders value and establish an organizational climate built on trust and openness in order to ensure that creativity and new ideas flourish. Leaders encourage others to experiment and learn from mistakes, without fear of retribution. They are known for their out-of-the-box thinking.

___ 7. **Nurturing.** Good leaders demonstrate that they care about and are interested in others' individual growth by:
- noticing the work and accomplishments of the individual as a person;
- exhibiting understanding and empathy for a variety of personality types;
- saying "thank you" for a job well done;
- caring about individuals' personal and professional growth; and
- seeking input on decisions that others will be affected by.

___ 8. **Decisiveness.** Leaders make decisions in a timely and effective manner and explain the basis for their decisions. Ideal leaders base decisions on facts and priorities, rather than trying to please everyone. They know when to seek consensus as part of the decision-making process.

___ 9. **Making Appropriate Interventions.** Leaders must trust subordinates. Good leaders know when to leave a subordinate or team member alone to get the job done and when to make an intervention to resolve issues that are beyond the subordinate's or team member's span of control.

___10. **Active Listening.** Good leaders are available, attentive, unbiased, and responsive. They recognize the need to allow input as well as to follow up on the input given. Good leaders are open-minded and encourage other points of view. They frequently paraphrase what is being said to ensure that they understand the speaker's point.

___11. **Assertiveness.** Most people will acknowledge that the leader's role is not an easy one, especially in dealing with conflict. Conflict is a daily occurrence in the workplace. Good leaders understand that personality and other work conflicts do not go away, that they typically get worse if not addressed. Thus, leaders deal with conflict in a timely, straightforward manner. They are assertive and honest with all parties in dealing with any type of conflict.

___12. **Delegating.** The ability to delegate effectively and focus on performance and results is a key element of leadership. Leaders demonstrate trust by delegating authority along with responsibility. However, the leader must know subordinates and their capabilities in order to delegate effectively. Good leaders understand that effective delegation enhances team members' and subordinates' skills and ultimately leads to a higher success rate.

___13. **Fostering Team Building.** The best leaders are known for promoting team efforts. They recognize and reward individuals for outstanding performance. However, they work to minimize and eliminate harmful competitiveness that may undermine the team. Leaders continuously discourage we–they attitudes.

___14. **Acting as an Advocate.** Leaders are expected to be the "point persons" and to be responsible to the needs of the team. They have a dual loyalty, to team members as well as to others, particularly upper management. Leaders are advocates not only for an individual, but also for the team, the department, and the organization as a whole.

___15. **Appraisal and Feedback.** Good leaders are knowledgeable about what is required to get the job done and who is doing it. They engage in "management by walking around" to learn about work status. They also solicit input from internal as well as external customers concerning satisfaction. They use this data to provide appropriate and timely feedback to everyone concerned. Good leaders also distinguish between good and poor work and take the appropriate action (e.g., reward or recognition for good performance; coaching or corrective action for poor performance).

___16. **Coaching.** An ideal leader spends considerable time in devising professional development guidance for staff. The leader engages in the following types of activities, as appropriate:

- Tell the purpose and importance of the activity.
- Explain the process to be used (or allow freedom to design one).
- Show how it is done, completely and accurately (if it must be done a specific way).
- Ask whether the person has any questions and clarify if necessary.
- Observe while the person engages in the process.
- Provide immediate and specific feedback (coach again or reinforce success).
- Express confidence in the person's ability to be successful.
- Agree on followup action(s) as necessary.

___17. **Learning.** The ideal leader is a lifelong learner who:

- is open to change;
- engages others in problem solving;
- views ideas from different perspectives;
- experiments and learns from mistakes; and
- continues to build his or her own skills as well as the skills of staff members.

___18. **Mediating.** Leaders must be able to mediate problems between people fairly. Ideal leaders are assertive in using mediation skills when warranted. However, the leader does not take sides, but keeps an open mind, gathers all the information in a thorough manner, and makes decisions based on facts.

___19. **Dealing with Critics.** Every leader gains some critics. Successful leaders, however, do not tear others down in public. They remain objective. They learn to distinguish between those who are attempting to provide constructive advice and those who have more selfish agendas. They then take the appropriate steps to deal with the situation.

___20. **Technical Competence.** Leaders are expected to have technical competence. This does not mean that they can do the actual work better than their team members. Rather, it means that they have a basic understanding of what is required and can make informed decisions.

360° LEADERSHIP DEVELOPMENT ASSESSMENT INSTRUMENT

SCORING INTERPRETATION

1. Use the attached Individual Feedback Analysis Worksheet. Collect the assessments, record the results, and compare the ratings (i.e., self versus others). Is there congruence? How varied are the results? Try to understand these differences. Congratulate yourself on any 4s or 5s! Make a note to continue engaging in these successful activities.

2. Next, concentrate on any 1s and 2s. For example, who rated you as a 1 or 2? Prioritize the 1s and 2s in terms of relevance to what you currently do or aspire to do.

3. Seek out the individual(s) who rated you as a 1 or 2 and discuss the rating. Ask for **specific** feedback (i.e., why they think you are a 1 or 2). Next ask for **specific** strategies or actions that you might take to improve. If you gave yourself a 1 or a 2, discuss with others how you might improve.

4. Focus on one to three of the relevant competencies that are in most need of improvement. Develop an action plan that includes the competency, an improvement goal, strategy or action for improvement, resources needed, time frame, and method of evaluation. (See the **Individual Action Plan Worksheet** for suggestions.)

5. Share your strategies and action plan with those who rated you and ask for their continuing support. Set up a tickler system to periodically elicit feedback (e.g., about once every six months). Reward yourself each time you reach an important milestone!

360° LEADERSHIP DEVELOPMENT ASSESSMENT INSTRUMENT

DOWNLOADABLE

INDIVIDUAL FEEDBACK ANALYSIS WORKSHEET

Name of Person Being Rated: ______________________ **Date:** __________

Insert numerical rating from each of the Raters*

Competency	Raters' Scores 1	2	3	4	Notes
1. Creating a Vision and Setting Goals					
2. Explaining and Communicating Expectations					
3. Written Communication					
4. Oral Communication					
5. Personal Integrity					
6. Creativity and Experimentation					
7. Nurturing					
8. Decisiveness					
9. Making Appropriate Interventions					
10. Active Listening					
11. Assertiveness					
12. Delegating					
13. Fostering Team Building					
14. Acting As an Advocate					
15. Appraisal and Feedback					
16. Coaching					
17. Learning					
18. Mediating					
19. Dealing with Critics					
20. Technical Competence					

* Raters:

1. ______________________ 3. ______________________

2. ______________________ 4. ______________________

360° LEADERSHIP DEVELOPMENT ASSESSMENT INSTRUMENT

INDIVIDUAL ACTION PLAN WORKSHEET

Name: _____   **Date:** _____

It is important that you use a systematic process to ensure that you reach your improvement goal(s). After you have completed your Individual Feedback Analysis Worksheet, select one, two, or three competencies to work on. Use one sheet for each competency. Share your plans with others and encourage them to help you reach your desired goals.

Competency: _____
(Identify the competency that you need to work on.)

Goal for Improvement: _____

_____
(Be as specific as possible about what you want to improve.)

Strategies or Actions to Take for Improvement:
(Identify several strategies or actions you will take. To the extent possible, answer: Who, What, When, Where, How, and Why. This will help you to focus on resources that might be needed. Note: It is perfectly acceptable to delegate certain competencies that a subordinate may perform better than you. However, you need to be clear about what you are doing and why.)

_____

_____

_____

_____

Resources Needed: _____

Begin By: _____ **Target Completion Date:** _____

Evaluation: _____
(What data will you collect? From whom? When? How? What are significant milestones?)

_____

_____

_____

11

WHAT ARE YOUR CLIENT'S COACHING STRENGTHS?

Scott Martin

Overview One of the principal functions of today's managers is the development and support of those who report to them. How well they fulfill the role of coach is crucial to their own success and that of their associates. Here are two instruments to help a manager to assess strengths and discover undeveloped or underdeveloped areas in coaching activities, behaviors, and philosophies. The first instrument is to be completed by the manager, the second by his or her direct reports. Comparing the results of the two will provide the means for developing an action plan that addresses the underdeveloped areas and reinforces the strengths.

Contact Information: Organizational Solutions: S. Martin & Associates, 14 Heather Rd., Turnersville, NJ 08012, 856-582-7666, SCOTT5522@aol.com

COACHING INVENTORY: SELF

The Coaching Inventory (Self) has been developed to help managers assess the extent to which they engage in coaching activities and behaviors, embody coaching philosophies, and create a climate conducive to coaching. It is intended as a method for managers to get a general idea of the extent of their coaching, but not necessarily as a scientifically precise measurement. Managers can use the results, along with other learning and experience (e.g., the Coaching Inventory (Employee), etc.), to begin to determine what areas of coaching may need more of their attention.

Directions: The Coaching Inventory (Self) consists of 35 statements related to coaching. In Part I, please circle the number of the response that best identifies the extent to which you engage in this activity or behavior, according to the following three-point scale.

- I rarely or seldom engage in or display this behavior or activity.
- I sometimes or occasionally engage in this behavior or activity.
- I frequently engage in this behavior or activity.

Part II is a self-scoring key with directions.

Please fill out this inventory and score yourself. The plotted profile will indicate areas that you may want to work on improving.

Part I: Coaching Inventory (Self)

Directions: Circle the number of the response that best identifies the extent to which you engage in this activity or behavior.

	Rarely or Seldom	Occasionally or Sometimes	Frequently
1. I spend time with my employees to help them develop professionally and in their careers.	1	2	3
2. I spend time with my employees discussing with them how to perform to their highest abilities.	1	2	3
3. I observe my employees and target any skills or behaviors for further development.	1	2	3
4. When giving feedback to an employee, I prefer to guard the feelings of the employee by softening the feedback.	3	2	1
5. When meeting with an employee, I ensure privacy and uninterrupted time.	1	2	3
6. In a developmental meeting, I encourage an employee to tell me as much as he or she can about the issue.	1	2	3
7. I revise development plans that have previously been agreed upon with the employee as needed, and provide further coaching.	1	2	3
8. I resist losing my best employees to other opportunities within the company.	3	2	1
9. During a formal performance appraisal or employee progress review, I devote time to discussing plans to further improve performance.	1	2	3

	Rarely or Seldom	Occasionally or Sometimes	Frequently
10. I identify and communicate the consequence of an employee not developing to his or her potential.	1	2	3
11. In a performance or development discussion, I describe to the employee specifically what the ideal performance or behavior is.	1	2	3
12. In a developmental or performance discussion, we concentrate on my perspective rather than the employee's.	3	2	1
13. I encourage a two-way discussion by asking employees for their perspective on areas for development or improvement.	1	2	3
14. I periodically review with employees their progress toward established development goals.	1	2	3
15. I set time aside throughout the year, outside of performance appraisal and other formal processes, to discuss each employee's professional development and advancement.	1	2	3
16. I create a work environment that allows employees to change and improve their performance over time.	1	2	3
17. When I identify a development need for an employee, I just discuss it with them without worrying about any formal advance planning for the meeting.	3	2	1
18. I provide specific feedback to the employee on performance and development and suggest changes for improvement.	1	2	3
19. In a development or performance discussion, I pay attention to and consider the employee's perspective.	1	2	3
20. In a meeting with an employee, I tend to concentrate so much on what I want to say that I don't always hear what the employee is saying.	3	2	1
21. I evaluate my employee's development and reinforce any increase in competence.	1	2	3
22. During a formal performance appraisal or employee progress review, I devote time to discussing development and career advancement goals.	1	2	3
23. I leave performance discussions to performance appraisal meetings only.	3	2	1
24. Before actually conducting a developmental meeting with an employee, I determine specifically what I want the employee to do differently and why.	1	2	3
25. In a developmental meeting, I help the employee to identify barriers to future development and ways to overcome them.	1	2	3
26. When meeting with an employee, I show that I am interested and attentive through my nonverbal behaviors, such as facing the employee directly, making eye contact, etc.	1	2	3
27. I make sure I have understood everything an employee has said through behaviors such as concentrating, paraphrasing, and checking for understanding.	1	2	3
28. It is not appropriate for me to assist employees in implementing development plans, so I leave them on their own for the most part.	3	2	1

	Rarely or Seldom	Occasionally or Sometimes	Frequently
29. I help my employees to better understand the expectations of our organizational culture and environment, and how they can impact their professional aspirations.	1	2	3
30. I actively identify performance improvement opportunities for individual employees.	1	2	3
31. If and when I note a development need or opportunity for an employee, I take time to analyze the situation and to determine the root causes and barriers to improvement.	1	2	3
32. I give honest feedback that helps employees to better understand how their behaviors and performance are perceived within the organization.	1	2	3
33. I convey a positive attitude throughout a coaching session that communicates my belief in the employee's ability to reach agreed-upon goals.	1	2	3
34. I probe for further information from an employee through behaviors such as concentrating and paraphrasing and checking for understanding.	1	2	3
35. I monitor the employee's use of a skill or behavior that was targeted for improvement on the job.	1	2	3

PART II: SCORING (<u>SELF</u>)

Directions: Transfer the numerical values (1, 2, 3) you have given to each item to the spaces in the columns below. (Please record each individual number carefully, as some of the numerical values change within each column or category). Add the numbers in each column for a total score for each category.

Commitment toward Professional Development	Commitment toward Performance Development	Assessment, Diagnosis, and Planning
1.	2.	3.
8.	9.	10.
15.	16.	17.
22.	23.	24.
29.	30.	31.
Total:	Total:	Total:

Meeting Face-to-Face and Giving Feedback	Attending	Listening and Responding	Implementation and Follow-Up
4.	5.	6.	7.
11.	12.	13.	14.
18.	19.	20.	21.
25.	26.	27.	28.
32.	33.	34.	35.
Total:	Total:	Total:	Totals:

INTERPRETATION

Look at your scores in each category as one indication of the degree to which you use or are committed to this coaching philosophy, behavior, or skill.

Scores in the 12- to 15-point range indicate use of or commitment to these coaching areas.

Scores in the 5- to 8-point range indicate areas of coaching on which you may want to focus more attention.

PLOTING YOUR PROFILE

To create a profile of your coaching strengths and highlight opportunities for improvement, plot the scores from each of the seven categories on the graph below. Create a plot line by connecting the circled numbers.

	Commitment toward Professional Development	Commitment toward Performance Development	Assessment, Diagnosis, Planning	Meeting Face-to-Face, Giving Feedback	Attending,	Listening, Responding	Implementation Follow-Up
MOST	15	15	15	15	15	15	15
	14	14	14	14	14	14	14
	13	13	13	13	13	13	13
	12	12	12	12	12	12	12
	11	11	11	11	11	11	11
	10	10	10	10	10	10	10
	9	9	9	9	9	9	9
LEAST	8	8	8	8	8	8	8
	7	7	7	7	7	7	7
	6	6	6	6	6	6	6
	5	5	5	5	5	5	5

You may also want to plot your employees' scores (from the "Employee" inventories) on the graph in a different color to compare to your own scores.

COACHING INVENTORY: <u>EMPLOYEE</u>

Name of Person Being Rated: _____ **Your Name (optional):** _____

The Coaching Inventory (<u>Employee</u>) has been developed to help your Coach or Manager to better assess, through your perceptions, the extent to which he or she engages in coaching activities and behaviors, embodies coaching philosophies, and creates a climate conducive to coaching. Coaches can use the results, along with other learning and experience (e.g., the Coaching Inventory, <u>Self</u>) to begin to determine what areas of coaching may need more of their attention. Please be candid in your responses to the following items to help ensure that your Coach or Manager obtains the maximum benefit from the inventory.

Directions: The Coaching Inventory (<u>Employee</u>) consists of 35 statements related to coaching. Please circle the number of the response that best identifies the extent to which the Coach or Manager engages in this activity or behavior, according to the following three-point scale:

- Rarely or seldom engages in or displays this behavior or activity.
- Sometimes or occasionally engages in this behavior or activity.
- Frequently engages in this behavior.

Part II is a self-scoring key with directions.

	Rarely or Seldom	Occasionally or Sometimes	Frequently
1. My manager spends time with me to help me develop professionally and in my career.	1	2	3
2. My manager spends time with me discussing how to perform to my highest abilities.	1	2	3
3. My manager observes me and targets any skills or behaviors for further development.	1	2	3
4. When giving feedback to me, my manager prefers to guard my feelings by softening the feedback.	3	2	1
5. When meeting with me, my manager ensures privacy and uninterrupted time.	1	2	3
6. In a developmental meeting, my manager encourages me to tell him or her as much as I can about the issue.	1	2	3
7. My manager revises development plans that have previously been agreed upon with me as needed, and provides further coaching.	1	2	3
8. My manager resists losing his or her best employees to other opportunities within the company.	3	2	1
9. During a formal performance appraisal or employee progress review, my manager devotes time to discussing plans to further improve my performance.	1	2	3
10. My manager identifies and communicates the consequence of my not developing to my potential.	1	2	3

	Rarely or Seldom	Occasionally or Sometimes	Frequently
11. In a performance or development discussion, my manager describes to me specifically what the ideal performance or behavior is.	1	2	3
12. In a developmental or performance discussion, my manager concentrates on his or her own perspective rather than on mine.	3	2	1
13. My manager encourages a two-way discussion by asking me for my perspective on areas for development or improvement.	1	2	3
14. My manager periodically reviews with me my progress toward established development goals.	1	2	3
15. My manager sets time aside throughout the year, outside of performance appraisal and other formal processes, to discuss my professional development and advancement.	1	2	3
16. My manager creates a work environment that allows me to change and improve my performance over time.	1	2	3
17. When my manager identifies a development need for me, he or she just discusses it with me without worrying about any formal advance planning for the meeting.	3	2	1
18. My manager provides specific feedback to me on performance and development and suggests changes for improvement.	1	2	3
19. In a development or performance discussion, my manager pays attention to and considers my perspective.	1	2	3
20. In a meeting with me, my manager tends to concentrate so much on what he or she wants to say that he or she doesn't always hear what I am saying.	3	2	1
21. My manager evaluates my development and reinforces any increase in competence.	1	2	3
22. During a formal performance appraisal or employee progress review, my manager devotes time to discussing development and career advancement aspirations.	1	2	3
23. My manager leaves performance discussions to performance appraisal meetings only.	3	2	1
24. Before actually conducting a developmental meeting with me, my manager determines specifically what he or she wants me to do differently and why.	1	2	3
25. In a developmental meeting, my manager helps me to identify barriers to future development and ways to overcome them.	1	2	3
26. When meeting with me, my manager shows that he or she is interested and attentive through nonverbal behaviors, such as facing me directly, making eye contact, etc.	1	2	3
27. My manager makes sure he or she has understood everything I have said through behaviors such as concentrating, paraphrasing, and checking for understanding.	1	2	3
28. In implementing development plans, my manager leaves employees on their own for the most part.	3	2	1

	Rarely or Seldom	Occasionally or Sometimes	Frequently
29. My manager helps me to better understand the expectations of our organizational culture and environment, and how they can impact my professional aspirations.	1	2	3
30. My manager actively identifies performance improvement opportunities for individual employees.	1	2	3
31. If and when my manager notes a development need or opportunity for me, he or she takes time to analyze the situation and to determine the root causes and barriers to improvement.	1	2	3
32. My manager gives honest feedback that helps me to better understand how my behaviors and performance are perceived within the organization.	1	2	3
33. My manager conveys a positive attitude throughout a coaching session that communicates his or her belief in my ability to reach agreed-upon goals.	1	2	3
34. My manager probes for further information from me through behaviors such as concentrating, paraphrasing, and checking for understanding.	1	2	3
35. My manager monitors my use of a skill or behavior that was targeted for improvement on the job.	1	2	3

PART II: SCORING (EMPLOYEE)

Directions: Transfer the numerical values (1, 2, 3) you have given to each item to the spaces in the columns below. (Please record each individual number carefully, as some of the numerical values change within each column or category). Add the numbers in each column for a total score for each category. Then return the inventory to your coach or manager.

Commitment toward Professional Development	Commitment toward Performance Development	Assessment, Diagnosis, and Planning
1.	2.	3.
8.	9.	10.
15.	16.	17.
22.	23.	24.
29.	30.	31.
Total:	Total:	Total:

Meeting Face-to-Face Giving Feedback	Attending	Listening and Responding	Implementation and Follow-Up
4.	5.	6.	7.
11.	12.	13.	14.
18.	19.	20.	21.
25.	26.	27.	28.
32.	33.	34.	35.
Total:	Total:	Total:	Totals:

INTERPRETATION (FOR THE COACH/MANAGER)

Look at your scores in each category as one indication of the degree to which you use or are committed to this coaching philosophy, behavior, or skill.

Scores in the 12- to 15-point range indicate use of or commitment to these coaching areas.

Scores in the 5- to 8-point range indicate areas of coaching on which you may want to focus more attention.

PLOTING EMPLOYEE SCORES

To create a profile of your coaching strengths and highlight opportunities for improvement, as seen by your employees, plot the scores from each of the seven categories on the graph below. Create a plot line by connecting the circled numbers.

	Commitment toward Professional Development	Commitment toward Performance Development	Assessment, Diagnosis, Planning	Meeting Face-to-Face, Giving Feedback	Attending, Responding	Listening, Follow-Up	Implementation
MOST	15	15	15	15	15	15	15
	14	14	14	14	14	14	14
	13	13	13	13	13	13	13
	12	12	12	12	12	12	12
	11	11	11	11	11	11	11
	10	10	10	10	10	10	10
	9	9	9	9	9	9	9
LEAST	8	8	8	8	8	8	8
	7	7	7	7	7	7	7
	6	6	6	6	6	6	6
	5	5	5	5	5	5	5

You may want to plot these scores on your Self profile graph as well.

PERSONAL LEARNING JOURNAL: COACHING INSIGHTS

Use this section to analyze the results of the Coaching Inventories to identify the coaching areas in which you want to improve.

1. Look at the Coaching Inventory (Self) scores as well as the Coaching Inventory (Employee) scores. What do the score values (Self and Employee) and profile graph tell you about each category below? Also compare your self-score to your employees' scores and reflect on the possible reasons for any differences.

   a. **Commitment toward Professional Development:** This category refers to your commitment to coaching employees for career advancement and growth within the organization.

   b. **Commitment toward Performance Development:** This category refers to your commitment to coaching employees to achieving even higher job performance.

   c. **Assessment, Diagnosis, and Planning:** This category refers to your skill at assessing and diagnosing the need for coaching for each employee, as well as planning for an upcoming coaching meeting.

   d. **Meeting Face-to-Face and Giving Feedback:** This category refers to engaging in actual face-to-face coaching meetings with employees and your skill in giving them relevant and direct feedback.

   e. **Attending:** This category refers to your skill in attending to the employee's perspective, needs, and self-esteem during the coaching meeting.

   f. **Listening and Responding:** This category refers to your own skill at listening carefully to the employee and responding appropriately during the coaching meeting.

   g. **Implementation and Follow-Up:** This category refers to working with the employee to establish, implement, and monitor a development plan as a result of the meeting.

2. Look over the relative scores and plotted points from your inventories. Which categories appear to be most in need of your further attention?

12

HAVE YOUR CLIENTS UPDATED THEIR JOB REQUIREMENTS RECENTLY?

Gaylord Reagan

Overview   You may be asked to assist human resource managers conducting job analyses to identify the knowledge, skills, and abilities (KSAs) needed to perform jobs satisfactorily. This analysis consists of a detailed examination of a job (specific activities, interaction patterns, performance standards, equipment used, working conditions, supervision given and received, etc.). The resulting information provides the foundation needed to link the KSAs to specific job requirements and job performance. Job analysis is used to determine as exactly as possible what KSAs and behaviors are needed for each task in the job. Finally, this information is incorporated into tests that can be used to determine whether job candidates have the necessary KSAs to achieve success.[1]

The following sequenced activities are designed so that you can help workgroup members and their managers assess the extent to which their current tool kits, shaped and reinforced over many years of studying and working in a variety of environments, are still viable. Specifically, the model asks users first to assess the continuing viability of their *knowledge* (accumulated body of facts), *skills* (abilities or proficiencies), *attitudes* (opinions, feelings, or dispositions), and *behaviors* (observable actions or conduct), and then to develop an action plan to better align these four sets of tools with the demands of the current and emerging situations.

[1]R. Mathis and J. Jackson, *Human Resource Management*, 8th ed. West Publishing Company, St. Paul, 1997, pp.144-45, 190.

Contact Information: Reagan Consulting, 5306 North 105th Plaza, #9, Omaha, NE 68134-1209, 402-431-0279, greagan@attglobal.net

KSAB RETOOLING MODEL

This self-assessment instrument provides a framework for an individual or group development action plan.

Activity 1: What are my current KSABs?
Working on your own, identify the knowledge, skills, attitudes, and behaviors that have combined to produce your current level of success. Don't be shy—go ahead and pat yourself on the back! What has helped you get to where you are now? Be prepared to share your list with other participants.

1.

2.

3.

4.

5.

Activity 2: What are our most common current KSABs?
Share your results from Activity 1 with other participants. Then, use your group's shared information to build a master list of no more than ten of the most common factors found on individual group members' lists. Members of the group should reach consensus on which factors to include.

1.

2.

3.

4.

5.

6.

7.

8.

9.

10.

KSAB RETOOLING MODEL (cont.)

Activity 3: What anticipated challenges most concern me?
Working on your own and focusing on the next 9 to 24 months, identify five major trends, issues, concerns, demands, regulatory and technological changes, competitive efforts, emerging technologies, new competencies, or opportunities that will challenge your continuing success. Be prepared to share your list with other participants.

1.

2.

3.

4.

5.

Activity 4: What anticipated challenges most concern this group?
Share the lists that individuals developed in Activity 3. Use your group's collective results to build an integrated master list of ten of the most significant challenges that you must successfully respond to during the coming 9 to 24 months.

1.

2.

3.

4.

5.

6.

7.

8.

9.

10.

KSAB RETOOLING MODEL (cont.)

Activity 5: How do I rank and weight the common anticipated challenges?
Use the blank graphic below and work on your own to complete two related but distinct tasks, using the results produced in Activity 4.

First, rank the challenges on the top ten master list produced in Activity 4. To complete this step, please use a scale in which 10 is the highest ranking and 1 is the lowest ranking. Enter your responses in the column headed My Ranking.

Then, weight each item on the top ten master list produced in Activity 4. You have 100 points to distribute to the ten challenges in whatever way you choose. For example, if you believe that all ten challenges are roughly equal in their importance, assign each one a weight of 10 points. On the other hand, if one challenge strikes you as much more important than the others, you might give it a weight of 50 points, leaving an additional 50 points to distribute among the remaining nine challenges. Enter your responses in the column headed My Weighting.

Challenge Number	Challenge Text	My Ranking (1–10)	My Weighting (0–100)
1.			
2.			
3.			
4.			
5.			
6.			
7.			
8.			
9.			
10.			

KSAB RETOOLING MODEL (cont.)

Activity 6: What is our collective wisdom?

First, individuals share their rankings of the top ten challenges from the first part of Activity 5. Then, group members use consensus decision making to agree on a collective rank for each of the ten items. Use the blank grid to record the collective rankings (arrange the challenge statements in rank order).

Second, individuals share their weights for each of the top ten challenges from the second part of Activity 5. Group members use consensus decision making to agree on a collective weight for each of the ten items, again distributing 100 points among the ten challenges. Use the blank grid to record the collective weights.

Group Ranking (1–10)	Group Weighting (0–100)	Challenge Text
1.		
2.		
3.		
4.		
5.		
6.		
7.		
8.		
9.		
10.		

KSAB RETOOLING MODEL (cont.)

Activity 7: What KSABs must be in our tool kits to meet the challenges?

Working with other group members, carefully identify the specific knowledge, skills, attitudes, and behaviors (KSABs) that organizational members must demonstrate in order to successfully respond to each of the ranked and weighted top ten challenges examined during Activity 6.

Challenge 1: Needed KSABs

Challenge 2: Needed KSABs

Challenge 3: Needed KSABs

Challenge 4: Needed KSABs

Challenge 5: Needed KSABs

Challenge 6: Needed KSABs

Challenge 7: Needed KSABs

Challenge 8: Needed KSABs

Challenge 9: Needed KSABs

Challenge 10: Needed KSABs

Activity 8: What is my payoff?

Complete these five steps to shape the results of Activity 7 into a self-assessment and feedback instrument for use by your group:

First: Use the results from Activity 7 to write an equal number of self-assessment questions for each of the ten KSABs. A total of no more than three or four questions per KSAB is suggested. Phrase questions so they define the desired state (see example). The response format should be structured so that *Is* represents the current perceived reality with respect to the question, and *Like* represents the way the respondent wants things to be with respect to the question.

Example:

I have a strong understanding of the	**Is**	1	2	3	4	5
business aspects of this organization.	**Like**	1	2	3	4	5

Second: When the questionnaire is complete, reproduce copies for individual group members, who should then work on their own to offer Is and Like responses to each question.

Third: To process the results, group members calculate their average Is and Like responses to each question. Group members examine their own responses in comparison to two bodies of information: 1) a comparison of their individual Is and Like responses with the group's average Is and Like responses; 2) a comparison of the data developed during Activity 1 (their current KSABs) with the KSABs that the group agreed must be present in order to successfully respond to the top ranked and weighted emerging challenges.

Fourth: Individual group members share their insights and reactions with one another: Are there gaps between present and needed KSABs? If so, where are they? Do we have common gaps and strengths? What do our questionnaire results tell us about ourselves? What do group members need to get better at?

Fifth: Individual group members and workgroups prepare action plans to guide their efforts to retool their KSABs to better mesh with current and emerging challenges. Also, a date is set for members to regroup and follow up on completion of these plans.

13

ARE YOU MAKING EFFECTIVE CONTACT WITH YOUR CLIENT?

Hank Karp

Overview   Managerial effectiveness can be measured on two dimensions in most organizations. The first dimension is the manager's ability to make a substantive task contribution, and second is the manager's ability to effectively coordinate and support the work of his or her direct reports. In the technical and financial arenas of many organizations, the task contribution is frequently much more valued than the process one. The long-term result is that many managers are highly valued for their technical expertise while simultaneously creating organizational problems by badly mismanaging their people.

   The usual solution for this problem is to have a long talk with the offending manager, hoping that he or she will magically self-correct. The talk may be quickly followed by the manager being sent off to yet another leadership or human relations training program. This approach, if successful at all, yields temporary results at best. This strategy is certainly appropriate prior to, or in response to, a *first* occurrence of mismanagement, but rarely does it provide the desired long-term result after subsequent situations of mismanagement. In most cases, managers have already undergone basic leadership training and know what to do. The real problem is that they have as yet been unable to incorporate the lessons learned into their unique leadership styles.

   A much more effective approach to dealing with this widespread problem is to bring in a consultant to work directly with the manager. The consultant's main objective is to coach the manager, find new ways to use skills and capabilities that the manager already has but may not be, as yet, comfortable with. This approach is based not only on the skills of the consultant, but on data gathered from those with whom the manager interacts. While usually more costly at its inception, this

Contact Information: Personal Growth Systems, 4932 Barn Swallow Dr., Chesapeake, VA 23321, 757-488-4144, PGSHank@aol.com

strategy generally proves to be much more successful and cost-effective in the long run.

There are many unique approaches and styles for conducting this kind of consultative service. The one necessary but not sufficient condition for any of them to work is the consultant's ability to make and maintain effective contact with the manager-client. In support of this premise, the Gestalt theory base insists that the clearer the boundary between the client and consultant, the higher the probability that the contact between them will be most supportive of the desired outcome. This approach is also more conducive to dealing with Generation X managers, who are significantly more independent and autonomous than their baby boomer predecessors (Karp, Sirias, and White, 1999). One need not work or consult from a Gestalt model, per se, to use this premise to establish a stronger and clearer base for communicating with the client.

The Contact Awareness Inventory is a ten-item instrument that can be used for self-assessment or as an aid in training consultants and other support people in coaching skills. The preferred answers and their rationale are presented after the instrument.

CONTACT AWARENESS INVENTORY

Directions: Please read each statement carefully. If you agree with the statement in its entirety, put an "A" in the space next to it. If you disagree or only partially agree, place a "D" in the space.

1. Difficult clients usually do what is in their best self-interest. _____

2. You should never express anger to a client. _____

3. The client's approval of you should be of secondary importance. _____

4. The only adult you are ever responsible for is yourself. _____

5. The best way to change a client's behavior is to first change his or her attitude. _____

6. It is important to understand why difficult clients are the way they are. _____

7. The stronger you are, the weaker the client will be. _____

8. It is more important to be aware of how you are different from the client, rather than how you are similar. _____

9. There is no human characteristic that is bad in itself. _____

10. It is very important that we like and trust the clients with whom we work. _____

ANSWER SHEET

1. Difficult clients usually do what is in their best self-interest. (Agree)

   Assumption is the most reasonable one for anyone to assume, not just the client who is having problems. The point is that if you acknowledge the okayness of pursuing self-interest and helping the manager to get in with what is really wanted, it will be easier to help him or her find ways to achieve this with a more appropriate behavior.

2. You should never express anger to a client. (Disagree)

   This is like suggesting that the client should never express anger to you. If part of the problem is that the manager needs to express emotional loading more appropriately, it is important that the consultant be a model for that behavior. Expressing anger when frustrated is natural and effective, when expressed *fittingly*. Certainly one should never rage, shout, or attack a client; however, a clear expression of annoyance or frustration can be appropriate at times, as long as it falls within your expressive boundaries. It adds emphasis to a point that needs to be made and can even be seen as caring, when the client has done something self-defeating.

3. The client's approval of you should be of secondary importance to the goals of the engagement. (Agree)

   Your client's approval of you, while important, must not take precedence over your goals. There is little question that you and the client will often be in disagreement about what works best, particularly in the early stages of the relationship. What is of critical importance is that your working relationship be based on mutual respect. Once this is established, the more clearly the client can see you and where you are coming from, the more readily he or she will be able to make choices that best fit.

4. The only adult you are ever responsible for is yourself. (Agree)

   One of the problems that besets many consultants, even experienced ones, is thinking that we actually know what's best for the client. What can happen, and often does, is that when you take responsibility for what happens to the client, the client's failure or success becomes your failure or success. When this occurs, it becomes important that you give clear advice and that the client takes it, since your mutual success is at stake. This is not good consulting, because even if you are right, the client has become more dependent on you and less independent. There is always the rare exception, of course, when giving clear advice is appropriate; but these occurrences should be few and far between.

   Offering an opinion, on the other hand, is quite different and is frequently an appropriate thing to do, even while assisting the manager in generating his or her own set of alternatives. You are not only a supporter and a coach of the client, you are a fresh pair of eyes. Your job is to get the client to see what you see. Once that has been accomplished, the perception belongs to the client. It is then simply one more alternative from which the client has to choose.

---

5. The best way to change a client's behavior is to first change his or her attitude. (Disagree)

    While this approach has some validity and represents the majority opinion, it is less effective than its alternative: to change the behavior when you attack other people's attitudes telling them that they should feel other than the way they are feeling, you are assuming either that they do not have the right to feel the way they do, or that something is wrong with them for taking this position. This approach has a much higher probability of creating defensiveness and withdrawal than bringing forth a more appropriate behavior.

    A better approach is to facilitate a change in specific behavior, and let that, in turn, produce a subsequent change in attitude. For example, suppose one of the problems that a client is having is listening to her direct reports.

    Attitude: "You should appreciate what your direct reports have to say. You have to be more supportive."

    Behavior: "Maintain good eye contact when a direct report is speaking to you and take a three-count before you respond."

    Which response do you think has the higher probability of producing the desired outcome?

6. It is important to understand why difficult clients are the way they are. (Disagree)

    Getting into other people's motivation is almost always a big mistake. It doesn't matter why somebody wants something; all that matters is what they want, how available it is, and how they are presently stopping themselves from acquiring it. When you start to explore *why* somebody wants whatever it is, you are forcing the person to justify that want. This implies that there are good and bad reasons for wanting things. You set yourself up as judge and your client as defendant. Not a good working relationship, particularly when clients continue to want what they want anyway.

7. The stronger you are, the weaker the client will be. (Disagree)

    Herman and Korenich (1977) originated the "Myth of Omnipotence," which suggests that managers can see themselves as being so powerful that any statement of disapproval of the direct report's behavior would be experienced as devastating. Once in place, this myth gives rise to "Ogre Building," which holds that because the manager is tip-toeing around, treading ever so lightly, the only conclusion direct reports can come to is that the manager really is that awesomely powerful and that they had better keep a very low profile lest they be destroyed. This dual myth creates a slow downward spiral and a self-fulfilling prophesy. Some consultants can easily fall prey to the same myth. They feel that their opinion, if stated clearly, will unduly influence the clients' thinking, and therefore they should focus *only* on the process.

    The reality is that strength breeds strength. By being direct in your opinions, perceptions, and judgments, the assumption is that the client is strong enough to welcome corrective feedback or differing opinions when appropriate. This is respectful of the client and sets the stage for a stronger and more supportive working relationship. If there is any doubt about what the client prefers, you can always check it out with the client before the consultation actually begins.

    As a case in point, some years back I was competing for a team-building contract with a former client. I was the last consultant to be interviewed. I walked into the room, smiled, shook hands. The client asked, "Hank, if I ask for your opinion, will you give it to me?" I said, "Of course," and he said, "You've got the contract." My four colleagues had each refused this role, for fear of being unduly influential.

90

8. It is more important to be aware of how you are different from the client, rather than how you are similar. (Agree)

Good contact is predicated on recognizing the absolute uniqueness of each individual. The clearer you are about how you and the client respectively see things, the higher the probability that you will be able to make and maintain clear contact and contribute to the client's welfare as *only* you can do. This is so whether you are in agreement or disagreement on any given situation. Note that it is also possible to be *too* dissimilar to produce a successful outcome. However, as long as the consult falls within your boundary of acceptability, the more you can differentiate yourself from your client, the better chance you have of succeeding. Similarities are productive and important only in determining the purpose for your working together and what the final outcome of the consultation should be.

9. There is no human characteristic that is bad in itself. (Agree)

One of the traps that many managers fall into is believing there is something wrong with *who* they are, rather than with *what* they are doing. All too frequently, the client focuses on a personality change rather than on a change in specific behavior. The judgment from above generally takes the form of statements like, "You're too directive," "You're too forgiving," or, "You're too judgmental." It is easy to see that there are times when being directive, forgiving, or judgmental are exactly the correct responses, *depending on the circumstances*, just as a case can be made for killing when being bitten by a mosquito, or lying in response to the boss' demand that you state what you really *really* think of him or her.

Each and every human capacity can be justified as an asset in light of a unique situation. Furthermore, an attack on a capacity or a characteristic is an attack on the person. The key to maintaining contact with the client during coaching is always to focus on the problem behavior and its effect, rather than on the characteristic that produces that particular behavior.

10. It is very important that we like and trust the clients with whom we work. (Disagree)

The disagreement with this statement is in the word "very." There is no question that there must be a minimum level of liking and mutual trust between a consultant and the client who is being coached. Without this, it is difficult to develop the supportive working relationship that is essential for dealing with sensitive areas and painful issues. The point is that the working relationship between the coach and the client can be too close, and that is not good either. It is critical, in the effective coaching relationship, that a clear boundary and some distance be maintained between you and the person you are attempting to help. Without this, you risk losing your objectivity, taking things too personally, and confusing what would be best for you in that situation with what might be best for the client.

REFERENCES

Herman, S.M. and Michael Korenich. *Authentic Management: A Gestalt Orientation to Organizations and Their Development.* Addison-Wesley Publishing Company, Reading, MA. 1977.

Karp, Hank, Danilo, Sirias and Kristin White. "Teams: Why Generation X Marks the Spot." *Journal for Quality and Participation.* 1999.

II

HOW-TO GUIDES FOR SOLVING YOUR CLIENT'S PROBLEMS

INTRODUCTION

In this section of *The Consultant's Toolkit,* you will find 15 how-to guides for solving your clients' problems. These guides are short articles containing useful ideas and guidelines for implementing consulting initiatives.

Each guide contains step-by-step advice. Several have examples, illustrations, charts, and tables to enhance your understanding of the content. You will find that the guides are clearly organized and easy to read.

Here are four possible uses for the how-to guides:

1. guidelines for your own consulting interventions;
2. implementation advice to be shared with your clients;
3. recommendations to senior management; or
4. reading assignments prior to consultation sessions.

Feel free to download the guides to your personal computer and customize them to maximize their effectiveness.

14

HOW TO PLAN AND ANALYZE SURVEYS

David Chaudron

Overview Across the nation, organizations spend millions asking employees for their opinions about organizational culture and climate, as well as assessing their progress toward a quality standard such as the Malcolm Baldridge Quality Award or some other program of organizational development. Despite this effort, many companies do not receive all the benefits of surveying. Here are suggestions that you, as a consultant, can pass along to an organization that is serious about surveying its employees.

PART 1: PLANNING THE EMPLOYEE SURVEY

One of the major reasons organizations don't receive enough "bang for the buck" from surveys is that they don't plan them well. Planning not only makes for less stress when analyzing the survey but helps define assumptions and expectations about what you want to achieve. The following are good rules of thumb for planning your survey.

Keep the data anonymous, but communicate the actions.

Organizations often keep survey information anonymous and confidential to increase the accuracy of the data received. This rule of thumb is usually a good idea, but can also have its drawbacks. Among the drawbacks is the uncertainty of what to do with survey comments that allege illegal actions or violations of company procedures. Acting on such comments may violate the confidentiality of the respondents.

Contact Information: Organized Change, 5663 Balboa Ave. #171, San Diego, CA 92111, 858-694-8191, dc@organizedchange.com, www.organizedchange.com

Additionally, confidentiality can lead to inaction by those who need change the most, as the following story illustrates.

I conducted an employee survey for an aerospace client who had decided that accusations concerning individual behavior would be noted but not acted upon. This was done to ensure the survey would not become a witch hunt, but rather would focus on organizationwide issues. Unfortunately, in the written comments collected, there were accusations of a married manager getting a single woman pregnant and rewarding her with a promotion. This behavior would be a violation of company policy and normally such accusations would be investigated. However, as a result of the confidentiality restriction, the information was not directly acted upon.

As you can see, investigating specific accusations can be a problem. The organization can ignore the problem or try to find out more information in focus groups. These randomly selected groups of people can be asked whether certain allegations are true and what additional information they might have. Such sessions must be conducted with the utmost confidentiality by a person of good reputation who has no supervisory authority over anyone in the group.

Don't look for what you already see.

Many organizations believe they understand their problems and call in consultants only to work out the details. If an organization investigates only subject X, it will get back information only on subject X, overlooking other issues of major concern, as the following example shows.

An organization changed its telephone system and hired a consultant to determine training needs. After talking with the users of the new equipment, the consultant realized that ignorance was not causing organization's telecommunication problems. Instead, it was a management and cultural problem.

Organizations can get around this problem somewhat by using a broad-spectrum survey at the beginning of their effort, and asking specific narrow questions later. Other ways around this problem are discussed in the next section.

Use multiple survey methods.

Using multiple techniques to ask about the same kind of information is a hallmark of good information gathering. Any surveying technique has its weaknesses. For example, numerical surveys (in which survey items are rated on a scale of one to five) are easy to score. However, the specific wording of the question may not apply exactly, and may miss getting to the heart of the matter. In addition, numerical surveys, especially those that ask a narrow set of questions, only allow survey takers to be queried about a limited set of topics. An organization may miss discovering important issues because it didn't ask.

On the other hand, open-ended questionnaires use questions that are less precise, and so get richer information from the survey taker. Unfortunately, the more open-ended the questionnaire, the harder it is to score. The people who summarize written comments may inject their own opinions into the rating process, which does not happen with numerical surveys.

Focus groups offer potentially the richest source of information, in part because the leader of a focus group can ask clarifying questions. However, verbal information is harder to summarize and classify than written responses. In addition, employees in focus groups and individual interviews lose anonymity.

My recommendation is to use not one approach, but all of them if possible. Using one method just doesn't cover all bases. Focus groups and individual interviews are useful at the very beginning of the survey effort to find broad areas of concern. Open-ended survey questions and numerical surveys can pinpoint specific issues, and allow employees to express their concerns anonymously. Use focus groups again to get feedback on specific issues and allow employees to express their concerns anonymously. Use focus groups again at the end of the process to get feedback on specific issues or recommendations.

Survey information no longer has to be gathered via paper and pencil. Programs are available that allow employees to complete a survey at their own computers, whether as a stand-alone program or, if they have Internet access, via the World Wide Web. My experience has shown these methods produce more reliable results.

Decide how to analyze data before you gather it.

One manager of a manufacturing organization developed a preliminary survey to assess the effects of "delayering" of the department. He sent it to other managers, wishing to get their feedback about the questions he developed. Instead of getting feedback about the questions, he received over 50 filled out surveys! As a result of this unexpected response, he realized he had not decided what graphs, charts, and analysis he needed. It took a staff assistant many long hours to change the data into a workable form.

Whenever you create surveys, decide how you will analyze, chart, and graph the data before employees complete them. This approach avoids bias when there is no set procedure for analysis, and reduces last-minute panic when the data comes flooding in. If after developing the survey you are still uncertain about analysis, give the preliminary survey to a sample of people who are similar to the group to be surveyed. Use this sample to fine-tune questions and decide how to analyze the data.

Decide on your sampling plan and how to break out the data.

Many organizations survey their employees once a year. Two problems arise from this practice: First, because the organization surveys only once, it can't distinguish between flukes and trends. Only surveying multiple times a year, using a sampling of employees, can an organization distinguish between special, one-time events and ongoing concerns. Second, employees can behave differently just before survey time. This Hawthorne effect, whereby employees temporarily change their behavior based on expectations, can mask underlying problems. A reverse Hawthorne effect can also occur, whereby employees worsen their behavior and exaggerate their responses on the survey.

When choosing a sampling plan, decide how to break out (stratify) the data before distributing the survey. Common breakouts include how staff employees feel compared to line employees, how each department answered the survey, or how male respondents compared to female ones. These breakouts can help pinpoint employee groups that are concerned about a particular issue. However, survey authors and analysts often make the mistake of using multiple "t" tests to determine if more than two group means are statistically different from one another. Because these sample means are not independent, the level of significance cannot be easily determined or interpreted. See Hayes (1973) for a more detailed discussion of this. More appropriate statistics that avoid this problem are multiple comparisons (Kirk, 1968), discriminant analysis (Klecka, 1980) or logistic regression (Hintze, 1995).

Because these breakouts are easy to do on a computer, organizations can create graphs and charts for their own sakes. The greater the number of breakouts, the more employees must be surveyed at any given time. Otherwise, samples can be so small that the survey data are unreliable. As with any sampling method, the smaller the sample of employees, the greater the uncertainty that the sample's statistics will match population parameters. One can reduce this uncertainty by increasing sample size and using more reliable and varied methods of measurement, but probably at the cost of a more time-consuming survey. For a further discussion of sampling sizes and methods, see Kalton (1983). As with all sampling plans, survey analysts should evaluate survey statistics in light of survey results, and change their sampling accordingly.

Involve employees, especially powerful ones, in the survey effort.

Organizations can survey their employees, accurately assess their needs, and still meet with resistance to change. One way to lessen this problem is to involve, formally and informally, powerful employees in the group that develops or selects the survey, distributes and analyzes the results, develops recommendations, and implements solutions. Such employees can include management, union officials, and elected representatives of departments or job classifications. These employees act as spokespersons for the groups they represent, communicate events to these groups, and provide vital information to the survey process. One group included a vice president, a director, a manager, two engineers, two supervisors, two employees from administrative support, and two inspectors, each representing employees in a job classification.

Never survey without acting.

Management can survey employees to assess working conditions out of curiosity, or to relieve their anxieties about everything being "all right." However, surveys raise expectations in those who take them. When expectations of change remain unfulfilled, employees can become more demoralized than before the survey.

Management might ask, "What if we survey our employees and can't (or won't) do anything about their problems?" These fears are frequent when distrust is high between management and employees, or when historically, management and labor have not gotten along. On one hand, such fears can be an excuse for inaction, but on the other, they raise a point.

Management must decide what actions are possible and which are not, even before the survey authors create the survey or gather the data. When employees raise concerns, management needs to communicate that they understand the concerns. If management cannot immediately solve the issues, employees must know this. At the minimum, management must communicate survey data and their response to it. Preferably, management should answer concerns and act on them.

Include the survey process in the normal business planning cycle.

One way to allow surveys to influence an organization is to make them part of its planning cycle—its goals, objectives, and budgets. Employee involvement efforts can be integrated by scheduling survey events so recommendations are ready the month before budget planning sessions. To accomplish this, schedule backward. For example, if budgets are due in June, present survey recommendations in May and develop them in April. Analyze the survey recommendations in March, and distribute the survey (assuming a one-shot survey) in February. Determine the survey ground rules in January, and form the survey group in December. Scheduled this way, surveys deliver the maximum punch possible.

Without such planning, management can respond to recommendations from surveys and employee suggestion systems with, "That's a good idea. Where is the money to pay for it?"

Create clear, specific actions from the survey data.

"We must communicate more" and "We must change people's attitudes" are often the recommendations that come from surveys. Unfortunately, these platitudes do little to fix the problems that survey responses communicate. This table lists some possible concerns raised by employees, and a brief summary of what might be done about each issue.

Employee Concern	Possible Solution
fairness of promotions	change selection and promotion procedures, who decision makers are
fairness of pay system	gainsharing, flexible benefits plan
performance reviews	reward groups instead of individuals, change rating process
career development	create career ladders, clarify job descriptions, create mentoring systems, pay for knowledge
communication	establish bulletin boards, all-hands meetings, company videos, E-mail, focus groups
empowerment	delegate specific authority and decisions to employees
intergroup warfare, between-department communication	conduct intergroup team building, restructure by product or customer instead of functionality
management style	conduct 360° feedback, management training

Clearly communicate the survey process, recommendations, and actions.

Communication is a crucial ingredient in every phase of the survey process. Organizations must inform employees about survey planning, data collection, and implementation plans. Without this communication, employees who would otherwise support the survey become confused, frustrated, and eventually complacent. Loss of this critical mass of support may eventually doom whatever changes the company implements. Someone once said, "Whenever change takes place, a third are for it, a third are against it, and a third don't care. My job is to keep the third who don't like it away from the other two-thirds!"

Use surveys with good reliability and validity.

Validity indicates how well a survey measures what it should. Validity is enhanced by measuring each survey topic with several questions, and in several ways. This usually means at least three questions, preferably five, on each survey topic, and asking similar questions during interviews and focus groups. Evaluate the survey's validity by comparing it to existing methods of gathering information to minimize missing or unclear questions.

Reliability relates to how consistent the survey is over time, and the consistency of survey items with each other. If a survey is unreliable, survey statistics will move up and down without employee opinions really changing. What may look like a significant change over time may be due to the unreliability of the survey methods used.

If you create or change a survey, determine its reliability on groups similar to your employees. Even if you don't change the survey, check to see what reliability and validity studies have been done. It is a good idea to test the survey on a sample of your employees, even if you don't change the survey at all. It's worse than useless for your organization to hand out a survey and receive information of unknown worth.

PART 2: DEVELOPING THE SURVEY AND ANALYZING THE RESULTS

In the first part of the guide, we talked about how to properly plan and implement employee surveys, and how to integrate them into organizational change. Part 2 focuses on how to develop the survey itself, and how to make it a useful, reliable measurement tool for organizational change.

Develop questions.

It is generally best not to start out with individual items to include in the survey, but to develop broad categories (subscales) of questions. Then generate at least three questions per category. Three to five questions are needed at a minimum for consistency and reliability.

For example, suppose that the survey authors decide to measure "the effectiveness of a supervisor's listening skills." Most survey authors would simply ask one question, such as, "How would you rate your supervisor's listening skills?"

This is the equivalent of a one-legged horse: It looks funny and it doesn't stand on its own. Instead, ask three or four questions in the "effectiveness of a supervisor's listening skills" category, such as:

1. How would you rate your supervisor's listening skills?

2. How comfortable do you feel about telling your supervisor about ideas for doing your job better?

3. How often does your supervisor listen to and act on what you say?

4. Do you feel that your supervisor understands your point of view?

Repeat this exercise for every category to be measured.

Format the survey and develop instructions.

Survey formats should be as clear and simple as possible and make clear to the respondent how to answer each question. Reduce as much as possible the chance of crossover errors, whereby employees mean to answer one question but accidentally answer another. For surveys with numbers to circle, check boxes to check, etc., make sure that questions either 1) have ellipses (...) or an underscoring line from the end of the question to the numbers to circle, or 2) are formatted (bold text, italics, different type sizes, etc.) to clearly highlight what question goes with what answer.

One thing not to do, especially the first time you use a survey, is to list the survey items by group, for example, questions 1,2 3,4, and 5 all refer to a supervisor's listening skills and questions 6,7,8,9, and 10 all refer to management's responsiveness to change. Do not put headlines on the survey telling respondents how you have grouped together the survey items. This defeats the purpose of factor analysis (described later) and increases the halo effect, the tendency of employees to answer questions in the same way.

Develop survey scales.

Decide how to ask employees to react to questions. Many people use agree–disagree scales, so respondents answer questions like:

1. I like ice cream.
   - strongly agree
   - agree
   - neutral
   - disagree
   - strongly disagree
2. I hate ice cream.
   - strongly agree
   - agree
   - neutral
   - disagree
   - strongly disagree

Unfortunately, this kind of scale is problematic. First, studies have shown that these scales suffer from response set bias, which is the tendency of employees to agree with both the statement and its exact opposite, as in the case above. Second, analyzing these kinds of statements is very difficult. If I strongly disagree with the statement "I like ice cream," what does that mean? It could mean that I hate ice cream, or it could mean that I don't just like it, I love it to death. There is no way of telling what employees mean.

Instead, use frequency, intensity, duration, or need for change or improvement. Specifically, these scales would look something like this:

Frequency	1. My supervisor gives me feedback on my performance.	Never	Once or twice	Sometimes	Often	Always
Intensity	1. My supervisor actively listens to what I say.	To no extent	To minimal extent	To a modest extent	To some extent	To a great extent
Duration	1. My supervisor keeps eye contact with me during my performance review.	At no time at all	For a little time	For much of the time	For a long time	All the time
Need for improvement	1. How promotions are handled in my department	Needs no improvement	Needs a little improvement	Needs some improvement	Needs much improvement	Needs drastic improvement

Send out a sample and correct any problems.

After you've developed the initial draft of the survey, try it out on a sample of people who are similar to the ones who will ultimately take the survey. Conducting this sample satisfies several objectives:

1. It allows feedback on the clarity of questions.
2. It allows you to practice the "pitch" to survey takers.
3. It allows statistics (see factor analysis) to be produced that will tell you how reliable your survey is and how to group your questions into categories.
4. It allows practice of the step-by-step logistical sequence needed to disseminate and collect the surveys and enter the data into the computer.

Collect your data.

This is not as simple as it sounds. To maximize the rate of return, you must carefully encourage as many people as fit into the sampling plan to answer the survey. Though many organizations hope to achieve return rates of 80 to 90 percent, it is unrealistic to believe this will happen on its own. We have achieved return rates of 97 percent by 1) making the survey part of a well-organized, well publicized change effort; 2) having senior management encourage employees to answer the survey; 3) holding mandatory meetings where employees have the choice of answering the survey or turning in a blank one. Without all of these strategies, expect at best a 30 to 40 percent return rate.

Factor analyze the results, group items into categories, and test their reliability.

Factor analysis is a technique most survey authors are not aware of, but it is a critical and necessary part of survey design. Factor analysis groups items into categories to maximize the reliability and "sturdiness" of the survey.

The first step in factor analysis is to determine how many groups or categories of items to have. No matter how much experience authors may have with developing surveys, the way they group together items into categories often has little bearing on the results of factor analysis. The grouping authors performed is based in part on how they perceived the relationships between survey questions. That is a good method for developing survey questions, but not for developing reliable categories.

Factor analysis 1) defines how many statistically sound categories exist, and 2) groups survey questions into categories based upon the statistical intercorrelations between the questions, based on how all survey respondents answered your questionnaire. This statistical procedure is available in a number of statistics programs, such as SPSS, SAS, NCSS and others. I suggest that you develop a good understanding of how factor analysis works before you have to do it on a short timeline.

After factor analyzing the survey, test its reliability. Reliability is a measure of how consistently employees answer questions. There are two basic measures of reliability: internal consistency and test-retest. Internal consistency (measured by coefficient alpha) measures how well individual questions within each category measure the same thing. Test-retest reliability measures the consistency of survey answers over time. Both are important, but usually coefficient alpha is the only one used. Measuring test-retest reliability requires giving the same survey to the same people again, usually a couple of weeks later. Most survey authors don't want to make the effort to do that. However, if you are measuring organizational change over time, it is a good idea to know how much variation is due to organizational change and how much is due to the fuzziness of the questions.

Analyze and graph the data.

Now comes the fun part, analyzing the data. Two of the most common mistakes made are 1) not deciding how you want the graphs to look before you analyze the data, and 2) using survey norms inappropriately.

Imagine yourself with an immense pile of printouts with no idea of how to analyze the data. It is not a good feeling, believe me. Many a would-be survey analyst has been caught in this problem. The easiest way around this is to decide how to graph and categorize the data before this huge ocean of information drowns you. The best way to do this is to draw a few graphs of how the data might look. Develop a few scenarios with fake information and ask yourself a few questions. "If the data looked this way, what would *that* mean?" "If the data looked that way, what would *that* mean?"

Survey norms are averages of how other people have answered the survey. Established survey companies often calculate these norms. When you get reports back from them, they describe how your results stack up against these averages.

There are two problems with survey norms: 1) what norms to use, and 2) how to interpret the numbers. To be properly used, norms must come from an employee population very, very close to yours. This means they should come from the same industry, the same geographic location, the same job types, and the same size of company. Very few, if any, norms exist that are broken down this finely. To avoid comparing their apples with your oranges, use your own company as your reference point, instead of using overgeneralized norms. Do this by taking a baseline survey of your employees before (or just at the beginning of) your organizational change effort. Then, resurvey a representative, statistically valid sample of employees frequently over time. Compare these later results with your baseline to eliminate the problems associated with using someone else's norms.

Those who decide to use norms often abuse them in the following way. Let's say that according to the norms, a particular supervisor is in the twentieth percentile of listening skills; that is, compared to the norms, 80 percent scored higher than she did. You automatically conclude that this supervisor has problems with listening skills. This is a bad conclusion taken from faulty data, because you are not comparing this supervisor to those in the same industry, geographic location, size of company, and so on.

Forget all this stuff. I'll just buy a survey or use what we have.

If you find a survey you like, you can skip all this survey development stuff. The job then is to make sure that the purchased survey was developed following the above steps. In some cases they have been, but often many of the steps are either unknown or ignored by the developers of commercial surveys.

Ask about how and if they used norms, what kinds of reliability measures they used, and what those measures tell them. Ask if a factor analysis has been done, and what the results were. If the authors don't understand the questions, they probably don't know their stuff.

Another option is to customize a survey you've already bought. Customizing an existing survey still requires all the steps above. Even changing the sequence of questions has a significant effect on reliability.

If all this seems too troublesome to you, then let me ask you a question: What is the consequence of making a wrong organizational decision? If it is severe, you have little choice other than to make organizational changes on the best information possible. If the consequences of what you are doing are small, you may not need to go through the tremendous effort of surveying your employees.

REFERENCES

Edwards, Jack, Thomas, Marie, Rosenfeld, Paul, and Booth-Kewley, Stephanie.(1996) *How to Conduct Organizational Surveys*. Sage Publications.

Hayes, William. (1973) *Statistics for the Social Sciences,* 2nd ed. New York: Holt, Rineheart and Winston, Inc., pp. 478–479.

Hintze, Jerry. (1995) *Number Cruncher Statistical System User's Guide.* Kaysville, UT:NCSS, pp. 1149–1158.

Kalton, Graham. (1983) *Introduction to Survey Sampling.* Sage Series in Quantitative Applications in the Social Sciences, number 07-035. Newbury Park, CA: Sage Publications.

Kirk, Roger. (1968) *Experimental Design: Procedures for the Behavioral Sciences.* Belmont, CA: Brooks/Cole, pp. 69–98.

Klecka, William. (1980) *Discriminant Analysis.* Sage Series in Quantitative Applications in the Social Sciences, number 07-019. Newbury Park, CA: Sage Publications.

15

HOW TO MAKE APPROPRIATE USE OF FOUR ORGANIZATIONAL ASSESSMENT TOOLS

Cathleen Smith Hutchison

Overview There are a number of data collection and analysis tools that can provide information about the status of an organization. Some of these tools are:

1. a Climate Survey or Attitude Survey;
2. an Operational Audit;
3. a Culture Audit; and
4. an Organizational Scan.

Each of these tools differs in its scope and perspective. The following guide characterizes each of the four methods and identifies their key strengths and uses. The organizational assessment tools are then compared and contrasted in an easy-to-read column format for quick reference.

Contact Information: Metamorphosis Consulting Group, P.O. Box 1147, Cedar Crest, NM 87008, 505-281-4496, metamorphosis@uswest.net

FOUR ORGANIZATIONAL ASSESSMENT TOOLS

1. The Climate or Attitude Survey

This is a method of assessing the current feeling(s) and opinion(s) within the organization regarding particular topic(s), issue(s), initiative(s), or action(s). The climate survey collects data related to "what it feels like" to work in this organization. While the climate of a country reflects things like the temperature, amount of rain and sun, and the length of the growing season, the climate of an organization reflects the same type of quantifiable surface characteristics. You can experience the climate of a country at poolside in a resort hotel while sipping Mai Tais and never meet the natives. You can obtain climate and attitude information with a survey sent out from a comfortable corner office and never know there are unaddressed issues beneath the surface or relating to other issues. However, you do not raise expectations that action will be taken to address issues other than those specifically being surveyed. *If the organization is interested in what employees feel about one or more specific issues, topics, initiatives, or actions, you should conduct a climate or attitude survey.*

2. The Operational Audit

This is a method of assessing the processes, procedures, methods, and activities of the organization. The operational audit gathers data on both the actual processes and procedures that are being followed and also those that are specified and prescribed in manuals, handbooks, rules and regulations, and guidelines. It compares the two to assess the level of variance or compliance between them. This method provides a snapshot of what the organization is actually doing to achieve its results. An operational audit of a country would look not only at the laws and regulations on the books, but also at the way the citizens work around those laws and the level of consistency with which they are applied. Similarly, an organization would analyze the processes and procedures that actually occur and compare them to "the rules." This audit determines the level of consistency of procedures in actual practice throughout the organization. *If an organization is interested in the level of compliance with prescribed and documented policies, procedures, and methods, you should conduct an operational audit.*

can't do this its no written policies

3. The Culture Audit

This is a method of assessing the behavioral practices in place within the organization and the manner in which the organization conducts its business on a day-to-day basis. As with the culture of a country, the culture of an organization is comprised of how and why people in the culture behave as they do, follow the practices, dress, rituals, and have the heroes and myths, values and beliefs that they do. Understanding the culture of either a country or an organization allows the observer to understand the beliefs behind and underneath surface behaviors. It allows for behavioral understanding of an organization, and may yield the ability to broadly predict reactions and behaviors in future situations. *If the organization is interested in identifying current values, beliefs, behaviors, and practices, you should conduct a culture audit.*

4. The Organizational Scan

This is a method of assessing both what is occurring in the organization and how the organization conducts its business. This method deals with all aspects of the organization as a system. The organizational scan is, in some ways, a combination of an operational audit and a culture audit. While the breadth of the assessment is increased, the depth is somewhat reduced. The organizational scan does not usually collect data in either of the two areas to the level of detail that the individual audits do. However, a key feature is that the organizational scan does address the level of alignment between the culture and the operations of the organization and their alignment with support systems within the organization. *If the organization is interested in an overall picture of the alignment of culture and operations and how they support and interact with each other, you should conduct an organizational scan.*

	Climate/ Attitude Survey	*Operational Audit*	*Culture Audit*	*Organizational Scan*
Purpose	To determine the feelings and opinions that employees have at a given time about a given issue/initiative or set of issues/ initiatives.	To determine the processes, procedures, methods, and activities that occur throughout the organization for comparison to those that are documented and/or dictated.	To determine the values, belief systems, and behavioral practices in place throughout the organization that govern the way people behave with one another and how they get their work accomplished.	To determine what the issues are in the organization. To determine the strengths, weaknesses, values, and practices that operate throughout the organization and the level of both horizontal and vertical alignment throughout the organization on these issues.
Scope	Either limited to a specific issue or set of related issues or aimed at a broad spectrum of potential issues of "what it feels like" working within the organization. The methodology limits data collection to a surface level and makes follow-up difficult.	A broad and deep data gathering effort to identify the processes, procedures, methods, and activities the organization undertakes to achieve its results. It may be targeted at operations regarding a specific function or segment of the organization or it can address the entire organization.	A broad and deep data gathering effort to identify all behavioral aspects of *how* and *why* the organization operates as it does to achieve its results. It may be targeted at a specific function or segment of the organization or it can address the entire organization.	A very broad data gathering effort to identify not only how the organization operates, what processes and procedures it uses, but also issues around individuals or groups within the organization. The main focus is the level of alignment of all elements within the organizational system.

	Climate/ Attitude Survey	Operational Audit	Culture Audit	Organizational Scan
Methodology	Survey of questions identified prior to data collection. Usually requires choice of predetermined responses to most questions with one or more open-ended questions to elicit data broader than specified in the body of the survey.	A combination of facilitated focus groups, interviews, work site observations, review of artifacts (tools, equipment, and documents), questionnaires, and instruments. These can be modified during the process to follow up on unexpected data.	A combination of facilitated focus groups, interviews, questionnaires, and instruments. These can be modified during the process to follow up on unexpected data.	A combination of interviews, facilitated focus groups, work site observations, review of artifacts (tools, equipment, and documents), questionnaires, and instruments. These can be modified during the process to follow up on unexpected data.
Target Population	Usually the entire employee population. Sometimes a representative sample.	Key operators of specified and/or critical processes, procedures, methods, and activities. Also the users of the outputs of these processes, procedures, methods, and activities.	Either all or key representatives of the senior management group, plus representatives of all areas of the organization.	Either all or key representatives of the senior management group, plus representatives of all areas of the organization. Key operators of specified and/or critical processes, procedures, methods, and activities. Also the users of the outputs of these processes, procedures, methods, and activities.

	Climate/ Attitude Survey	Operational Audit	Culture Audit	Organizational Scan
Place in the Organizational ational System	Analyzes the feelings and opinions elicited on a given issue/ initiative or set of issues/initiatives.	Analyzes the procedural operation of the organization.	Analyzes the behavioral norms, values, and belief systems throughout the organization.	Analyzes all aspects of the organizational system and their alignment with each other.
Strengths	It collects quantifiable data that can be statistically manipulated to reflect how people feel about specific issues and initiatives.	Identifies what is actually happening within the ranks of the organization. Identifies bottlenecks, barriers, and enhancers to processes and procedures. It identifies problems and opportunities related to processes and procedures. It collects anecdotal data that can be probed as needed and can be followed up on later. Can include both quantitative and qualitative data.	Identifies values, beliefs, behavioral norms, and practices of how people interact and work with or around each other. Describes people's feelings about each other and the organization. It identifies problems and opportunities related to behaviors. It collects anecdotal data that can be probed as needed and can be followed up on later. Can include both quantitative and qualitative data.	It collects comprehensive data on the alignment of what the organization is doing and how people are doing it. It looks at both sides of the organizational alignment model and at the support systems in place to maintain them. It identifies alignment, nonalignment, and related problems and opportunities. It collects anecdotal data that can be probed as needed and can be followed up on later. Can include both quantitative and qualitative data.

	Climate / Attitude Survey	*Operational Audit*	*Culture Audit*	*Organizational Scan*
Potential Problems	It often does not collect data that is actionable. It is difficult to use as a management tool. It is difficult to follow up on unexpected data.	It does not address relevant behaviors and norms that affect how things are accomplished. It may miss barriers caused by the people side of the organization or cultural misalignment.	It does not address what processes and procedures are in place. It may miss issues around what is being done that is inappropriate for the strategy.	Ordinarily, it does not delve as deeply into issues on either side of the organizational alignment model as either of the individual audits. Because it is not as deep as the individual audits, the scan may uncover problems and opportunities that will require more detailed research or analysis for full understanding.
Uses	Identify how widespread generic feelings and opinions are held. To broadly determine if problems exist that may require additional analysis or intervention.	Determine the level of compliance with rules and regulations and if processes are adequate to achieve the strategy or if process engineering or continuous improvement interventions are needed. It can identify operational priorities for intervention.	Determine culture strength, characteristics, and strategic fit. It can identify the need for cultural change or interventions. It can identify behavioral priorities for intervention.	Determine alignment of the organization as it is operating today. Determine need for organizational alignment interventions. It can identify organizational priorities for a wide variety of potential interventions.

	Climate / Attitude Survey	*Operational Audit*	*Culture Audit*	*Organizational Scan*
Products	An academic style report of quantifiable segments of the organization and opinions about specific issues or initiatives.	A descriptive report on what processes, procedures, and activities are actually operating within the organization and a comparison to those in guideline, rules and regulations, and handbooks.	A descriptive report on how people throughout the organization interact and communicate with each other to accomplish their tasks and achieve their results and a description of the values and beliefs held by segments of the population.	A descriptive report on both what processes, procedures, and activities are actually operating within the organization and how people throughout the organization interact and communicate with each other to accomplish their tasks and achieve their results. Additionally, how the two align with each other and with the support systems in place throughout the organization.

16

HOW TO COACH EMPLOYEES THROUGH CHANGE

Nancy Jackson

Overview   Consultants need a systematic way to help clients manage change. This guide identifies stages of change that employees must go through to resolve ambivalence and change behavior. Using the model, management can apply the necessary supports to help each person discover his or her own motivation for change. The six stages are Precontemplation, Contemplation, Determination, Action, Maintenance, and Recycling. Effective coaching can help people go through the change process more comfortably and effectively by giving employees what they need when they need it.

Introduction

Over and over again we hear the charge, "Things are changing faster than ever." And our experience confirms it—changes in what we do, how we do it, and who we do it with leave us breathless and overwhelmed. Employees are faced with diversity training, TQM training, team building, and computer and skill training for jobs they never dreamed of. Quality, empowerment, work teams, reengineering, and the learning organization leave us wondering what will be the next buzzword.

What is happening to employees caught in the middle of all these changes? Stress, poor morale, attitudes of noncommitment and reactance—employees everywhere feel that teams and the zap of empowerment are just so many words to justify more work for less pay. Yet the need for change is evident. Companies have to change their focus to survive—from the mass production models of the industrial revolution to complex information systems in a global economy. We are overwhelmed and stressed; we want to go forward, but fear we are slipping back.

Contact Information: 592 S. Victor Way, Aurora, CO 80012, 303-340-8518, Nansolo@aol.com

What is needed is a systematic way to help tired, angry employees deal with the realities of the workplace of today.

The Change Cycle

Borrowing from the realm of psychotherapy, we can adopt a model of motivation for change that has been used and researched. It is readily adaptable for use in organizations to help employees and managers cope with the upheavals they face in the workplace.

The Change Cycle was developed by psychologists Prochaska, Norcross, and Diclemente watching what they called "successful self-changers." Since its development, the six-stage model has been used with thousands of changers in several countries. The results have been amazing. When changers are helped to identify their readiness and given the support they need, they are enabled and motivated to change, and they maintain the change over time. This model can be used in organizations to help employees respond more comfortably to the changes they face.

In this guide, the six stages of change and typical statements of a person who is in that stage will be described. Next, descriptions of some interventions that a coach may use to help the person resolve ambivalence and progress to the next stage will be described. To use the Change Cycle model, the coach needs to identify what stage the changer is in, to know where to begin the process. So it is important to understand what each stage looks like, and then what a person in that stage needs.

Identifying the Phases

Stage One—Precontemplation
The first stage is *Precontemplation.* A person in this stage may say, "They can't make me learn that program," "I have seniority, I'll be here forever," or, "Oh, other companies are going to TQM, but we never will." Precontemplation is denial or unawareness of the need for change. There may be rumors floating about the big move or downsizing, but the individual in the precontemplation stage denies, ignores, or avoids the information.

Stage Two—Contemplation
When individuals have passed precontemplation, they are in the second stage, which is *Contemplation.* In the contemplation stage, the individual considers the information and begins to think about it. "Someday I suppose I'll have to learn that program..." or, "Perhaps I'll have to take a class..." or, "I suppose our company will have to change

its process..." Like the government, which seems to be in a perpetual contemplation phase, a contemplator will say, "Someday we'll have to do something about inefficiency and waste." In this stage, commitment to change increases and ambivalence decreases until a decision is made and the next stage begins.

Stage Three—Determination

The third stage is *Determination*. The person has decided to change and begins to make plans and envision the future. The person begins time management strategies, scheduling, training, and other "preaction" activities in preparation for the change.

Stage Four—Action

Action is the next stage in which the individual is actually performing, practicing, or executing the change. For example, the person might be using the new program, or new teams have been formed and are meeting, or the new marketing plan is in effect. (This is usually when most change efforts begin. Unfortunately, the first two steps are frequently omitted; there is often no warm-up, only action. But without warm-up, the action is incomplete and the changes may not last.)

Stage Five—Maintenance

The change process is not over with the Action stage. The change won't really feel comfortable or "natural" for a period of months, or even years. Individual need to go through a period of *Maintenance* in which new skills may be needed to manage a new way of behaving and to handle old habits that begin to creep back. The change cycle may end here, or may go to the next step.

Stage Six—Recycling

Finally, but not necessarily, there may be relapse or *Recycling*. Perhaps there was not enough support from upper management, perhaps it was a halfhearted implementation, or perhaps the training was inadequate; for whatever reason, the individual slips back and goes through the cycle again, as in: "I've quit smoking ... ten times!"

The six steps must be gone through in succession. Too fast a progression sends the person back to "go" and he or she has to begin again. Real change takes time and commitment.

Coaching Motivation for Change

As individuals go through the Change Cycle, they need different strategies for each stage, so training for coaches is needed to identify stages in the cycle and to know how to provide what is needed at the appropriate time. Skills practice in active listening, problem solving, and effective communication can greatly enhance the process.

What follows is a brief description of the interventions required at each stage of change. These interventions or supports can be given by trained coaches, change groups, or coworkers.

Precontemplation

In the first stage, precontemplation, the individual isn't even aware of the need for change, or may be in denial. "I don't even want to think about it!" To directly insist on change at this point is an invitation for resistance. In order to help a person see the need for change, information is needed. "Why this change? How will it impact me, what will happen if we don't change?" Information about why the individual *ought* to change is not helpful, but "just the facts" to clarify the situation.

Examples of "just the facts" might be:

- ✓ "This company has adopted this policy for this reason."
- ✓ "ABC company has taken over our market share and we have to respond."
- ✓ "By next year, management's goal is that all technicians will be certified in XYZ."
- ✓ "Here's where you are now. This is the goal. What will you do?"
- ✓ "This training will benefit by…."
- ✓ "It will take three weeks to change the equipment."
- ✓ "Your speed will be increased by 40 percent after training."

When people are in precontemplation, they may be defending against change. It is best not to directly attack a defended person, but to increase trust and approach the need for change in a matter-of-fact way. "Here is the situation. What do you want to do?" It is also important to let people know that they have a choice—no matter how limited that choice may be.

Contemplation

As the recognition begins to dawn that they may want to (or need to) change, people move into contemplation. At this stage, they need someone to listen to their ambivalence, and to reinforce their motivation. What are the pros and cons of the new way? What are the pros and cons of the old way? What are your hopes and fears? As people become aware of their ambivalence and fear, there is opportunity to listen and reinforce the motivation for change. There should be no forcing of people, only the opportunity to exercise whatever control over the process they may legitimately claim, and their concerns should be listened to sincerely. It can be helpful to remember that a person does not have to be 100 percent motivated to change, just more motivated than not motivated to begin changing.

Determination

In the determination stage, people are beginning to think about the future. What will the new offices look like? How will the team meetings be conducted? Can you see yourself as a coach and not a supervisor? Again, the person in the determination phase needs to be listened to and supported. Although it may be tempting to try to tell people in this phase how they ought to proceed and what they ought to do, it has been found to be more helpful to let them construct their plans and make their own choices. Of course, individuals need to know the parameters of their empowerment—"Which training session would you prefer, morning or afternoon?" rather than "You take the afternoon training so you can get your work done first." Choices made by the employee are motivating.

Another useful tool is visualization, or the envisioning of the future state. In this stage, the person is helped to identify potential roadblocks, try to solve problems and resolve difficulties before they actually arise. "What changes do you see in how you spend your day?" or, "How do you see the new technology affecting your interaction with the customer?" or, "What problems do you think you'll encounter with the other members of the team?" As individuals visualize themselves in the change, ambivalence may crop up. It is always helpful to listen to the changers' ambivalence, and to support them in a positive way.

Action

Last is the action phase—the implementation. At this stage, the individual may need very little in the way of support, especially if the previous stages have been thorough. Perhaps occasional "how's it going" check-ups and short discussions of problem solving will be all that is needed.

Maintenance

Just because things have been smooth for awhile does not mean that the Change Cycle has been completed. Maintenance is critical. It takes a long while to truly change behavior, and the care and nurturing of a new behavior can be the difference between success and a relapse.

One great help to maintenance may be training in "soft skills" that will help individuals continue to cope with the current change as well as new changes they face. Individuals may profit from training in communication, problem solving, and other interpersonal skills that can be reinforcing for all levels. Soft-skill training gives individuals new ways to look at their jobs, and new tools with which to manage their lives. At the risk of using the overused but truly wonderful concept, soft skills are empowering, and will help people cope with the next round of changes that is sure to develop.

Recycling

Finally, sometimes recycling—a slip-up or relapse—may occur. This is not cause for despair. A relapse means that there were lapses in the commitment, the support, or the development of the cycle. The Change Cycle can be thought of as a spiral rather than a circle. Each time you go around, the trip is shorter, your ambivalence decreases, your commitment increases, and you will reach the goal.

When a relapse occurs, people need to examine their commitment. Where are they now? Probably back in contemplation—"I know I should but...." Excuses and delaying tactics appear again. People need more listening, perhaps some skill-building, and help with resolving their ambivalence. "Do I want to change? Why or why not?..." And off they go again, through the cycle. It is not uncommon for people to recycle many times. But with persistence and understanding, real, permanent change does happen.

Applying the Change Cycle to Organizations

The Change Cycle can be applied to the organization as a whole system, or on the individual level. There might be departments of a large organization in different phases of the cycle, while individuals within those departments may be at different phases, depending upon their personalities, experiences, and adaptability.

Frequently, perfectly good programs are cut because the organization seems to be in a muddle. It has often been said that many of the failures of the TQM, quality, work teams, or other programs were not caused by poor ideas, but by poor implementation. We simply did not know how to help people go through change.

Now, using the cycles of change, trainers, managers, and employees have a systematic way to diagnose the stage of change, and apply the necessary supports to help people discover their own motivation for change.

Notice that the emphasis is on the level of the individual and not the implementation of the organization. One of the important findings of the research is that people respond with resistance (reactance) when they perceive that they are being forced to change. "Push me and I push back." Therefore, people have to be helped to resolve their own ambivalence and to find their own motivation to change. These strategies are effective with heroin addicts and smokers, and will help employees who don't like the idea of teams (for example) come to terms with their ambivalence.

Summary

Organizations go through changes constantly, some of which are purposely imposed, some of which "just happen," and some of which sneak in the back door. We are engulfed by reengineering, process changes, and technological and cultural changes. It's about time that we had a method to help us cope and resolve the difficulties that change brings.

The six-step Cycle of Change used by therapists to help people change addictive behaviors can be used in organizations to relieve stress, avoid costly implementation disasters, and help motivate employees. In the long run, it is more productive and less costly to give people what they need rather than forcefully imposed new systems, structures, and technologies that leave people in the dust, tired and stressed.

REFERENCES

Miller, William and Stephen Rollnick. 1991. *Motivational Interviewing.* Guilford Press.

Prochaska, John, John Norcross, and Carlo Diclemente. 1994. *Changing for Good.* William Morrow and Company.

THE CYCLES OF CHANGE AND COACHING INTERVENTIONS

Phase	Precontemplation	Contemplation	Determination	Action	Maintenance	Recycling
Response	Denial	Ambivalence	Anxiety & Stress	Action	Vigilance	Backslide
Need	Information	Resolve ambiguity	Deal with stress	Support	Support	Reinforcement
Statement	I don't have a problem, my problem is you.	Maybe I have a problem.	I've got to do something.	I'm ready to start.	How do I keep this up?	I tried and failed.
Coach	Give information, create doubt, establish trust	Listen, identify + and – of change	Help plan, give resources	Support, affirm motivation	Support, provide skills training	Evaluate problems and obstacles, check intentions
Questions to ask	What's wrong with the way things are now?	Will it be worth it?	What will you do?	How is it going?	What helps?	What's you intention today?

17

HOW TO INITIATE AND MANAGE CHANGE

Nora Carrol

Overview   Today's combination of external and internal workplace pressure guarantees that every organization must face change. Because change represents some element of the unknown, it implies risk. The organization undergoing change can risk its human, physical, and technological resources, its collective knowledge, even its competitive marketplace position in attempting to handle change.

Risk demands that organizations plan for change, rather than waiting for it to happen and then trying to cope after the fact. This guide is a step-by-step chronology, presenting the seven key processes necessary for planning and managing change, regardless of the industry, sector, or region in which the organization operates. Because each process is addressed in question-and-answer format, the guide serves as a workbook, and the organization's stakeholders are the primary resources for providing effective, applicable answers to the questions posed.

STEP ONE: ESTABLISHING YOUR MISSION AND PURPOSE

Any organization or component of an organization must agree upon its overall mission and purpose before any change planning begins. The process of asking and answering the following questions will help lay the foundation for a successful change process.

- Do you already have a *formal* mission statement?
- If you do, does it *accurately reflect* your organization and what it offers? If not, why not? Does it need to change?

Contact Information: First Forward.com, 5836 Orchard Hill Court, Clifton, VA 20124-1072, 703-266-1266, ncarrol@firstforward.com, www.firstforward.com

- If you do not have one, *what actions are necessary* in order to formulate and approve a mission statement?
- Can you formulate a mission statement strictly within your unit, department or division, or does formulation require *participation and approval* of other parts of the organization?
- Are there *legal and institutional ramifications* to any statement you formulate?
- How much time do you think you need to formulate a statement of mission?

STEP TWO: AUDITING YOUR CURRENT ORGANIZATION

Products and Services

Your mission and purpose should be reflected in the products or services that you offer to your markets.

- Do the products or services you offer reflect your mission and purpose? If yes, how? If no, why not?
- If there is a conflict or conflicts, how can you resolve it or them? What people or processes need to be involved?

Market Identification and Development

Markets constitute your primary source of revenue, but the *type and characteristics* of the markets you serve should match your mission and purpose.

- Do you already have a *formal statement* of the markets you serve now? The markets you want to serve in the future?
- If yes, does the statement differentiate between market segments in a way that allows you to identify each segment and understand the distinctions between them?
- If you do not have a formal statement of markets, what must you do to create it?
- How many levels of authority are involved in setting market development goals?
- Do you believe that your market development expectations are realistic as related to your mission and goals?
- If not, what is necessary to make them attainable?

Unit or Organization

Your own unit's mission and purpose should relate to or reflect the mission and purpose of the organization as a whole. It is important, therefore, to compare them.

- Do your mission and purpose match, complement, or conflict with those of the organization?
- If you cannot tell, why not? If you aren't sure, what processes are needed to recognize the larger mission and purpose?

Capacities and Capabilities

Your capacities and capabilities represent what you currently can do, using existing resources. Assessing both is essential to identifying gaps that must be filled in order to handle change while respecting your mission and purpose.

- Does your unit have the capacity and capability to handle its responsibilities? If yes, in what manner? If no, why not?
- If there are gaps in capacity or capability, what are they?
- What is the impact of those gaps on your unit? What must you do to close those gaps?
- How do your unit's capacities and capabilities affect the organization as a whole? Are they complementary or in conflict?
- What must you do to achieve a maximum match between capacities, capabilities, and meeting your organizational mission and purpose?

Cost and Revenue Performance

While revenue is clearly a function and result of products or services and market development and may not be a mission in itself, it must be considered in order to determine its impact on the organization and its interaction with change efforts.

- Are there formal, enforced revenue expectations within your unit? If so, are you meeting those expectations?
- If there are no formal expectations, do you expect them to be introduced, and when?
- How often do you report your revenues to the supervising authority, and who is that supervising authority?

- Do you have the flexibility to make revenue adjustments during the fiscal year?
- Do you submit your own budget showing projected revenues and costs, with approval granted for both at once?
- If you do not get approval on revenues and costs at the same time, what process is followed?
- Are you satisfied with your budgeting process and your involvement in it?
- If you are not, what changes do you want to occur?
- Are your revenue expectations in line with or at odds with your mission and purpose?

Step Three: Scanning Your External Environment

The third phase of preparation for planned change is the conducting of an environmental or external scan. This step is particularly important in that it provides points of comparison between what you are doing, what competitors are doing, and what you want to be doing.

An external scan should explore the following issues:

- direct competition,
- indirect competition,
- concepts of competition,
- markets being served by competitors, and
- regulatory or external requirements and influences impacting your organization.

Direct Competition

Direct competitors have products or services that parallel yours and have a clearly discernible similarity in the eyes of the marketplace.

- Who are your direct competitors?
- What is it in their products or services that makes them direct competitors?

Indirect Competition

Indirect competition may exist in the form of products or services that overlap in some way with yours.

- Who are your indirect competitors and what do they offer?

- If you do not know, what resources and information do you need to find out?

Markets

The concept of markets (rather than market) is based on the belief that there are distinct differences separating markets from each other, and that those differences represent the most important characteristics for marketers to consider.

- Do you serve individual or organizational (business-to-business) markets, or both?
- Who are your markets, in descending order of importance? (If you have both individual and organizational markets, list them separately).
- What are the most important behavioral characteristics of each market you have listed?
- Which of those markets are served by direct competitors? By indirect competitors?

Regulatory or External Requirements and Influences

- What regulatory or external requirements have an impact on your organization?
- Which have an impact on your direct and indirect competitors?
- Do external influences vary by the type of organization your competitors are?

STEP FOUR: CONDUCTING MARKET RESEARCH

Before selecting market research options, it is necessary to know both the research purpose and the research stages or formats.

- Do you want to do an introductory investigation, establish patterns of behavior among markets, or confirm earlier findings?
- Does it make sense to collect quantitative (volume) or qualitative (in-depth) data, or both?

Capability

- Do you have the capability to conduct research, or should you hire an outside source?

- How much analyzed data already exist to act as a foundation for further research?

STEP FIVE: CREATING A CONTINUUM—SHORT-TERM AND LONG-TERM GOALS

You have now determined your mission and purpose, conducted your internal and external investigation, assessed your products, services and markets, and made some determinations about market research in preparation for further development. Now it's time to begin planning for change!

Planning and implementing change cannot and should not occur all at once: It makes far more sense to divide your efforts into short- and long-term activities. This strategy will enable you to test and analyze different ideas, and make refinements before investing in major long-term change.

Begin by deciding the following:

- What you want changed.
- When you want the change(s) to occur, with timetables for each.
- Who can champion those changes.
- What resources will be needed to accomplish the desired change(s).
- What processes or structural components are needed to implement the change(s).
- What is the content of what you want to change?
- What is its depth (penetration of organization) and scope (breadth of impact)?
- What is the underlying process that must support it?
- In what order of priority should desired changes occur?

Change Agents

Change is best accomplished when specific people, who have already been convinced of the need for change, take on the responsibility for planning and implementation. They are typically called change agents and champion the effort internally.

As you examine your priority list of desired changes, it is necessary to decide:

- Who will be most effective in leading everyone toward the change you want?
- What roles do those people currently serve?
- What responsibilities and authority must your change agents have to be effective in implementing the changes desired?
- Are these change agents internal (within the immediate organization) or external (outside the immediate organization)?

Organizational and Cultural Change

- What needs to happen at the organizational level to implement the desired changes? Reallocation of resources? New job descriptions? New reporting lines? New structure? Time set aside for planning, decision making, and approvals?
- What kind of organizational culture do you have, and how might it interact with change?
- Is your organization's structure formal or informal? A hierarchy, a matrix, or something else?
- Are decisions made from the top down, bottom up, or laterally? Is your decision-making process authoritative, consensus or collective, or individualistic?
- What kind of management style exists? Is it management by directive, by objectives, participatory, or other?

STEP SIX: DEVELOPING AND IMPLEMENTING AN ACTION PLAN

Implementation is the most difficult phase of an action plan, because it requires the selection, allocation, and oversight of resources to accomplish the desired changes.

Action Planning

- What are your priorities for change?
- How can you operationalize them? Can you depend entirely on internal resources and processes, or do you need assistance from external resources?
- How can you transfer the operationalized change goals into an interactive timetable?
- How can you assess and evaluate your efforts to implement and manage change?

STEP SEVEN: INTEGRATING CHANGE PLANNING INTO YOUR SYSTEM

Change planning is an ongoing, proactive process and way of thinking, not something that is done only once. As such, it is most effective when built into your organization as a permanent part of its strategic processes.

Change Triggers

There are conditions and situations under which change is most likely; these should be considered triggers that act as early warnings and can alert you to the need for heightening your analytic and planning efforts. These triggers are usually caused by:

- internal organizational change, in mission, goals, or objectives; or
- external change, in markets, technological developments, or condition and status of competitors or competitors' offerings.

Early-Warning System

It is critical to perceive triggers through an early-warning system, allowing you to recognize impending change internally and externally before changes are beyond your control.

- Who, in each of your functional or structural areas, is best able to scan the internal and external environments and report on early signals of change in that area?
- Who, in a supervisory role, is best able to authorize a response to warnings of change?
- What is the most efficient way to communicate needed changes?
- What processes need to occur to react to early warnings of change?
- When must you go outside of your immediate domain to respond to early warnings of change?
- Who can be assigned to coordinate your recommended responses to upcoming change? To implement those recommendations?
- Who is an effective negotiator and spokesperson to represent your area when response to upcoming change requires the cooperation of other organizational units?
- What can be done to recruit support among management and non-management personnel for the change(s) proposed?

Feedback System

An early-warning system will not resolve problems unless warnings are communicated to the appropriate personnel in a timely manner and then acted upon. Once you have developed your early-warning process, you are ready to construct a feedback system.

- To whom should your scanners or agents go for the greatest volume of internal feedback? The greatest depth of feedback?

- Do you currently have a mechanism for acquiring and recording market (customer) comments and responses on your products or services and organizational image? If yes, what is that mechanism? Is it actively used? If no, what do you need to do to create and approve such a mechanism?

- Do you communicate with professional colleagues at other organizations? If yes, do you have a mechanism for integrating the results into your feedback?

- Do you serve as a formal or informal communications link with other units on change-related issues? If yes, how can you integrate the effort into feedback? If no, how do you think you can establish such a link?

- At this time, can you create an organizational diagram for a feedback system that will serve your needs? If no, do you have internal resources to assist you in creating it?

- What processes need to occur for you to be able to react to early warnings of change?

- When must you go outside of your immediate domain to respond to early warnings of change?

- Who can be assigned to coordinate your recommended responses to upcoming change? To implement those recommendations?

- Who is an effective negotiator and spokesperson to represent your area when response to upcoming change requires the cooperation of other organizational units?

- What can be done to recruit support among management and non-management personnel for the change(s) proposed?

CONCLUSION

The processes of planning for and managing change impact every part of the organization, and thus require the involvement of every organizational stakeholder or interested party. It is essential that each organization be honest with itself and identify who those stakeholders are, recognizing which stakeholders:

- have a critical versus marginal impact on the organization;
- have a temporary versus permanent relationship with the organization;
- hold a stakeholder role inside versus outside the organization; and
- have direct versus indirect influence, outside the organization, on markets and competition.

Is this analysis really necessary? It cannot be underestimated in importance! There are too many cases of otherwise well-designed change efforts that have gone awry because the organization did not acknowledge, understand, or include some stakeholder group in its change planning and management initiative.

18

HOW TO INVOLVE PEOPLE IN DECISIONS THAT AFFECT THEM

Stephen Haines

Overview   The dual purpose of this guide is 1) to involve lots of employees (an unlimited number) in the key strategic and organization issues and priorities that affect them prior to implementation, and 2) to build teamwork and ownership by involving people in the creation of the strategic plan.

The process described here can be used: 1) with all types of stakeholders (internal and external) in as large a number as desired, and 2) for regular feedback on the strategic plan, change management, and entire participative leadership philosophy for your client organization.

PARTICIPATIVE MANAGEMENT

My experience with organizations has led me to focus on the dynamic tension between ownership of the strategies for change by the leadership team and acceptance or buy-in of the plan by the key stakeholders who are crucial to the successful implementation of the desired change.

Briefly, I recommend a parallel process in which real-time meetings are held with key stakeholders. The purpose is twofold: 1) to share information and provide feedback to the core leadership team in order to troubleshoot and improve the plans, and 2) to gain understanding, acceptance (i.e., buy-in), and commitment to the overall direction and implementation of the plan.

Typically, this is done in meetings held in parallel with the planning or change phases by first asking, "Is there anything fundamentally wrong with this draft document or direction?" Once the question

Contact Information: Centre for Strategic Management®, 1420 Monitor Road, San Diego, CA 92110-1545, 619-275-6528, Stephen@csmintl.com, www.csmintl.com

is clear, I ask for positive and negative comments in subgroup discussions, using an interactive approach. Each subgroup has a facilitator (chosen from the core planning and change steering teams) trained to keep the process both positive and productive.

The need to tailor the details of key stakeholder involvement is determined by the core planning team prior to beginning the actual strategic planning and change management process. This results in a much higher probability of successful implementation of your plan or major change.

PARALLEL PROCESS STEPS

1. Analyze and select all your stakeholders.

A stakeholder is any group or individual who is affected by the achievement of the organization's objectives. The groups listed in the chart below are examples of categories of stakeholders.

2. Identify the key stakeholders.

Decide whose involvement in your parallel process meetings is key, based on their importance to both the development and achievement of your strategic management (planning and change) process.

3. **Convene the leadership team.**

Decide in detail exactly how to run the parallel process meetings, by asking questions such as: How do we involve our stakeholders? When and where should we meet, and who should attend? Which documents do we gather feedback on?

4. **Conduct a short orientation and training preparation with those planning team members involved in the parallel process to ensure that they are coordinated and comfortable with their efforts.**

5. **Conduct the actual parallel process meetings as planned.**

A thorough job results in fewer implementation problems and less resistance to change. When change occurs cooperatively, people feel you're "doing it *with* them rather than *to* them." The purpose of the meetings is to:

- Explain the strategic planning and change effort and everyone's role in it.
- Understand the draft documents clearly.
- Give input and feedback to the core planning team.

Guarantee: Your feedback will be seriously considered.

Limitation: Input is gathered from many different people. Therefore, it is impossible for each person's input to be automatically placed in the final document exactly as desired.

6. **Collect feedback sheets and take them to the full planning and change team. Include:**

- Common themes and trends (as opposed to pet peeves).
- A synthesis of the flip charts developed at this meeting.
- Impressions brought back to the planning team.

7. **Have the full planning and change management team refine their plans and change process based on the parallel process feedback.**

There are two potential planning and change team problems:

- Completely rewriting documents unnecessarily (reinventing the wheel; ditching sound decisions already made).
- Replacing provocative words to make the document palatable (thus watering it down to convey meaningless or mixed messages).

8. **Provide feedback on the changes made.**

Once you have updated your plans, it is a good idea to share your input with those who were involved in the parallel process. One way is to provide a comparison of the old plan and the new plan, explaining your reasons for change. A second way is to highlight the changes on the new plans, much the same way a legal document is handled.

Note: If you need more than one round of parallel process meetings, as is often the case, simply repeat the necessary steps.

PARALLEL PROCESS MEETING OPTIONS

There are many things to consider when preparing for your parallel process meetings. Success in achieving your goals is determined by careful preplanning.

Focus first on middle managers, who are the strategic plan implementers and thus require special TLC. They must take ownership of the plan and be committed to the change process.

For best results, get on the agenda of one of the regular meetings of your stakeholders (taking care to allow enough time to adequately present your material and gain their cooperation), or schedule special small-group forums.

Take opportunities to present your plan at regular staff meetings and all employee meetings, by core planning team members. If your organization is very large, use employee focus groups to break the job down into manageable sections.

You may also need a working session with the board of directors, to get their approval and support of the entire plan and implementation process.

If you hold public meetings, proper facility setup and management of large groups are tasks to be dealt with, as well as the fact that you have less control over who will attend your meetings (e.g., lack of key stakeholders in attendance).

PARALLEL PROCESS MEETING HINTS

1. Ensure that only members of the core strategic planning team hold these meetings, as they are the only ones with the knowledge to do so. Run the parallel process in teams of two to help each other.

2. Explain the strategic plan concept or model first.

3. Explain the documents next. You will be less defensive this way. Don't just read the documents; educate the participants. They must fully understand the concepts or intent and the specific meaning of key words and phrases.

4. Make sure "draft" is written on all documents.

5. Once the stakeholders start giving feedback, make sure you prove to them that you have heard them. The best way to do this is:

   a. Repeat back the essence of their statements.

   b. Empathize with their feelings, not just the words.

   c. Write down their statements on a flip chart and check with them to ensure accuracy (or better yet, have a second facilitator do so).

6. Focus discussions on substance, on the spirit or intent of the documents.

7. If you must explain part of a document or letter, use phrases like, "The intent was..." or "What was meant was...."

8. Check stakeholders' views versus the documents you've just reviewed. Are they in fundamental agreement?

9. At the conclusion, state actions you'll take and when you will meet with them next; then, follow up!

10. Thank all attendees.

11. Go to stakeholders if at all possible; take the first step.

12. Take documents to meetings in bite-size pieces to make them digestible; don't take the full plan all at once.

13. As a general rule, don't get feedback in a large group setting; break out into subgroups with facilitators for each one (use flip charts). Begin and end the meeting with the whole group.

14. The best group size for excellent feedback is 10 to 15 people.

15. It is often useful to script each meeting. If you can't, be sure to develop a common set of overheads for all meetings, for consistency and clarity. Decide in advance whether you want everyone to have handouts of all the documents and overheads.

16. Allow enough meeting time for depth of questions and answers, or give people time for ideas and reactions to be written down and turned in later to a central point.

17. Key Success Factors (KSFs)—also called corporate goal setting—are the most difficult documents to gain feedback on. Consider asking only about the areas of success to measure first, working in the actual measurements and targets later with only the parties responsible for their approval and accountability.

18. What do you do if you don't agree with feedback or comments? Collect data. Do not comment on it unless it's a big item that is crucial to explain. This meeting is an information sharing and

feedback meeting. Decisions will be made at the next planning meeting.

19. Beware of Gestalt versus pieces: Don't let them break the plan down into isolated documents or paragraphs. They all go together and must be taken in context.

20. How do you redirect vocal people? Use a flip chart to collect their comments, check what you wrote with them for accuracy, and then move on.

SUMMARY

Good luck in your parallel process. Remember: People support what they help to create. So either involve them in parallel process during the planning and change process, or resistance will be far greater. In other words, "Pay me now or pay me later."

19

HOW TO MOTIVATE OTHERS

Brooke Broadbent

Overview Motivation generates success. If your clients are in a leadership role, chances are they're preoccupied with how to motivate others. They talk about motivation. They may have read something about motivation. But are they motivated to do anything about it? What can they do? Can they motivate others? Here is a guide that explains six easy-to-use principles for motivating others and contains two tables with specific advice.

WHAT IS MOTIVATION?

Motivation, according to the dictionary, is a noun under the word *motivate.* If you look up *motivate,* you will discover it means "to stir to action; to provide with a motive." *Motive* is defined as "an impulse that causes one to act in a particular manner." What is that "impulse" and how do we get it to work for us? Why do some people work harder than other people? Why do some strive for promotions and others reject them? What motivates people?

Many things influence our behavior and our motivation. Some of those things are: current personal situation, past experiences, present work situation, the reward system, the managerial system, group relationships, the company culture, perception, and personal values. Each of us is motivated by different things at different times.

MOTIVATION COMES FROM WITHIN

The most important thing to keep in mind about motivation is that we cannot motivate others. Motivation comes from within—people moti-

Contact Information: Brooke Broadbent, E-Learning Hub.com, 867 Explorer Lane, Orleans, Ontario, Canada, K1C 2S3, 613-837-6472, brooke.broadbent@ottowa.com, www.e-learninghub.com

vate themselves. The only thing a supervisor, a committee chairperson, an instructor, or anyone else can do is to create the conditions for people to motivate themselves.

SIX PRINCIPLES FOR MOTIVATING OTHERS

1. **Positive thoughts motivate.** What conditions motivate people? Recall the teacher, friend, or parent who motivated you to do well by telling you that you could succeed. This is an example of our first principle of motivation: Positive thoughts motivate.

2. **Enjoyment motivates.** Maybe you recollect the sheer enjoyment that came from an activity, something you did on your own or with others. You were motivated to succeed and you did. Enjoyment motivates.

3. **Feeling important motivates.** Perhaps in a wistful stroll down memory lane your mind harkens back to a time when your opinions were sought. Your ideas were important. People listened to you. Were you motivated? I bet you were! This is an example of our third principle of motivation: Feeling important motivates.

4. **Success motivates.** For many people, motivation occurs when they do something well. You feel part of a worthwhile endeavor and you work hard to ensure continued success. This illustrates principle four: Success motivates.

5. **Personal benefits motivate.** Another source of motivation is the famous radio station WIIFM—what's in it for me. When employees, course participants, or any people see how they can benefit personally, they become motivated. They tune in, an example of principle five: Personal benefits motivate.

6. **Clarity motivates.** Our sixth and last principle of motivation is best understood if you think of a situation in which you were not motivated. Chances are that the task you were to do was unclear. Instructions were ambiguous. Flip this over and we get the sixth principle of motivation: Clarity motivates.

What can you do as a leader to create situations that motivate?

There's nothing earth-shattering in our six principles of motivation. But how do you put them to work? The following table suggests common-sense ways for leaders to use the six principles. What you do in your particular situation will depend on your creativity and the context.

Principles of Motivation	What Leaders Can Do to Motivate Others
1. Positive thoughts motivate.	When the group you lead attains its goals, advertise your success. Thank individuals for the success of the group.
2. Enjoyment motivates.	Find out what people like to do and when possible, have them do the tasks they enjoy. Demonstrate your pleasure when people and the team succeed. Build in enjoyable social activities for everyone, such as having coffee or lunch together.
3. Feeling important motivates.	Ask people for their opinions. Listen intently to what they say. Consider their thoughts carefully. Give credit when you use somebody's idea.
4. Success motivates.	Set clear, reasonable goals with the group. Make certain that stakeholders help set goals, understand what the goals mean, and agree to them. Thank individuals for successfully contributing to the group.
5. Personal benefits motivate.	Identify and state how group members can personally gain from an activity. Monitor and report on success.
6. Clarity motivates.	Plan your messages, oral and written. Take time to ensure you communicate clearly. Check with others to ensure they understand your messages.

What can everyone do to create situations that motivate?

If you are not in a formal leadership position, there is still plenty you can do to heighten motivation among colleagues and fellow participants in a training session. In our increasingly participative workplace, opinions are sought. If you identify what motivates you personally and share your thoughts with an enlightened team leader, committee chairperson, or supervisor, chances are they will respond positively.

Principles of Motivation	What Everyone Can Do to Motivate Others
1. Positive thoughts motivate.	Compliment people on their success.
2. Enjoyment motivates.	Smile. Your enjoyment will be contagious. Demonstrate your pleasure when people and the team succeed. Participate enthusiastically in social activities such as having coffee or lunch together.
3. Feeling important motivates.	Ask people for their opinions. Listen intently to what they say. Consider their thoughts carefully. Give credit when you use somebody's idea.
4. Success motivates.	Set clear, reasonable goals for yourself and with others. When you attain your goals, advertise your success. Compliment individuals on their contributions to the group.

Principles of Motivation	What Everyone Can Do to Motivate Others
5. Personal benefits motivate.	Identify how you can personally gain from an activity. Keep these benefits in mind. Evaluate your level of success. If you don't succeed, determine why—so you will know what to do to succeed next time.
6. Clarity motivates.	Plan your messages, oral and written. Take time to ensure that you communicate clearly. Check with others to ensure that they understand what you say.

PERSONALIZED MOTIVATION

Each of us has motivational hot spots. We need to keep this in mind when we try to create situations that motivate others. What motivates you or me may be different from what motivates someone else. If you are motivated by clarity, you might assume that it would motivate someone else. Be careful. Don't force your motivation preferences on someone else. The safest way is to include all six motivational elements in your undertakings. That way you will connect with everyone's motivational hot spots.

DIFFERENT STROKES...

This guide is like a toolbox. The tools or ideas you find inside have to be selected—the right one for each situation. You need to learn to use these tools. How? Through structured practice. Set goals. Select techniques. Use them. Assess the results. Determine whether you hit the targets you set. If you missed a target, identify why—maybe you should consider changing tools. Give yourself feedback about how well you created conditions to motivate others. Identify what you did well and what you can improve, and map out a plan for improvements. This personal feedback will help you develop motivational techniques that energize apathetic, bored, and unmotivated colleagues, course participants, or anyone else.

A FINAL WORD ABOUT YOUR SUCCESS

We said at the outset that motivation comes from within. People motivate themselves. Since motivation comes from within, you are limited in your power to motivate someone else.

Keep that in mind when measuring your individual success. Using these six principles, you will be able to create conditions to motivate others. It may take time to motivate others. Stick with it. You will succeed. You will personally benefit from the results. Everyone else will benefit, too.

20

HOW TO MOVE YOUR CLIENT FROM TRAINING TO PERFORMANCE IMPROVEMENT

Diane Gayeski

Overview Many organizations are looking for new approaches to training and other types of communication such as documentation, policies and procedures manuals, and news updates. This guide provides an overview of how and why organizations are redesigning their training departments, describes several short case studies, and offers some conceptual foundations and practical steps to move from traditional training approaches to a more contemporary performance improvement model.

We read and hear a lot these days about moving from "training" to "performance consulting," about "reengineering" training and human resources, and about establishing new infrastructures for the dissemination of information. Why are so many organizations looking to reinvent their training and communication systems?

✓ Most training and communication systems in today's organizations were designed for old-fashioned top-down management. The traditional assumption was that there was "somebody" who had the information or knowledge to share, and it was the job of training and communication to somehow replicate that knowledge in the heads of employees. The philosophy, technology, environment, and information-dissemination practices in use today generally do not support collaboration, teamwork, or multi-way communication, which are the lifeblood of today's fast-paced and diverse organizations.

✓ Training, information, and documentation have to happen more quickly than ever to be effective and relevant. Traditional design and development paradigms generally can't keep up with changes in policies and products.

Contact Information: Omnicom Associates, 407 Coddington Road, Ithaca, NY 14850, 607-272-7700, gayeski@omnicomassociates.com, www.omnicomassociates.com

✓ Typical systems and practices often foster an "entitlement" attitude among employees with the assumption that if something is important, the company will somehow create a course and tell employees to attend, rather than continuous learning being the responsibility of all organizational members.

✓ Training and communication often don't have much credibility with management; there is little data to prove return-on-investment, and it is generally not tied to business strategy. Training courses, documentation, and manuals also are often viewed with skepticism by their audiences, who often find that the content is not current or supported by their supervisors.

Training versus Performance Improvement

Although trainers and instructional designers have continuously applied new strategies and media to their work, today's challenges demand even more radical restructuring of the conceptual and philosophical basis of learning. A popular term for this shift is "performance improvement" or "human performance technology." The core idea behind this movement is that training alone is insufficient to bridge most performance gaps, and that trainers need to develop more comprehensive interventions that include incentive systems, communication technologies, environmental redesign, selection processes, and job aids. Using many familiar theories of behavioral and cognitive psychology, translating subject matter experts' knowledge into easily understood concepts, and applying many of the same technologies being used in training, specialists in instruction can broaden their expertise and toolset to create performance improvement projects that are much more powerful.

Although it's not uncommon to hear organizations talk about "reengineering" their training systems, for many this means that they have merely replaced classroom teaching with self-paced CD-ROMs, distance education, or other new technologies. The performance improvement notion implies much more radical rethinking of the whole notion of training and learning. As you'll see in some of the short case studies below, it's not always possible or desirable to create courses of any type. Workplace performance can often be improved by other less costly and more direct methods. Moreover, faster and more collaborative communication systems can increase organizational knowledge and capabilities far more significantly and strategically.

Case Studies

Here are some situations in which organizations decided they needed to redesign their training and communication systems. They are not atypical of many contemporary organizations.

✓ A manufacturer of forklift trucks was rapidly expanding its product line, and thus was also expanding the number and size of manuals for its technicians. Technicians in the field were carrying around some 1,200 pounds of manuals (they needed to order larger trucks just to carry around the manuals, and often could not fit necessary parts on the trucks because the manuals took up so much room!). If technicians enrolled in each of the courses offered by headquarters that related to the product line, they would spend almost one-third of their first two years in the classroom rather than on the job. Despite this embarrassment of information riches, the performance of the technicians was steadily decreasing because the new computerized trucks were displaying unpredictable and complex faults that were covered neither in training nor in the documentation. Technicians were not encouraged to use the help line: The only way they were able to call in was to borrow customers' phones, and even when they called in, the staff were generally unable to come up with an answer. Customers were becoming dissatisfied with truck reliability, and technicians were becoming increasingly frustrated. Neither helped the turnover rate or customer confidence.

The solution to this dilemma was to completely abandon traditional notions that training and documentation could ever completely capture and disseminate all the information that technicians would ever need. The trucks were simply too complex to be able to teach and document everything, and there was no way that technicians could somehow memorize all the procedures and fault codes. In fact, the best information was being developed in the field itself, when complex problems were identified and somehow repaired. Unfortunately, this valuable information was never captured by the manufacturer, since technicians had no incentive to call in and explain how they figured something out. A new, interactive knowledge system was needed to replace the traditional top-down training and manuals.

The company is now building a World Wide Web site that will contain dynamic information that technicians can access in the field via a laptop computer connected via a cellular phone and modem. The information will not only provide the latest information from the factory, but will capture important knowledge from the field. Technicians and dealerships will receive incentives for sharing knowledge, and will become a community of learners, along with the training, documentation, and engineering staffs. While training classes and manuals won't go away, they will be pared down to the basic concepts—while details of troubleshooting will increasingly be built into the trucks themselves and shared via the Web site.

✓ A large international bank found that tellers were actually performing *worse* after going through the basic teller training course than before it. They were apparently being loaded down with so much information that they literally "froze" when they returned to work and faced customers. This classroom training was not only ineffective, it was expensive and cumbersome: The bank's 34,000-person workforce spanned over 4,000 miles, from branches in major cities to remote locations with only one or two employees in part-time jobs. On top of rapidly changing policies and bank products, the bank was completely restructuring its workforce in an initiative that would eventually eliminate tellers' jobs and upgrade them to customer service representative positions. Their new CEO launched initiatives to foster diversity, teamwork, and a customer orientation.

The training department realized that a redesign of not only teller training, but of their entire training philosophy was in order. They commissioned an analysis of their training methods and materials, resulting in a document that defined new philosophies and practices for the training department. These policies aligned the training department more closely with the bank's mission and values, and oriented it to performance improvement rather than teaching. The consulting team not only worked with the training department, but also involved advertising and employee communication professionals on the implications of communicating messages and customer expectations. These crucial inputs provided important links among the various communication providers in the company. As a model of the new philosophy, the former training courses were replaced by a series of short magazine-like training modules, each of which contained opportunities to observe and participate in the actual work and to be mentored by the branch manager and experienced colleagues. "Feature stories" for these manuals were based on actual incidents contributed by tellers within the bank and highlighted teamwork and diversity. A number of job aids were developed to minimize dependence on memorization. This new approach has fostered not only better technical performance, but a new and more consistent culture within the bank.

✓ An insurance company was faced with having to continually update coverage manuals. The manuals had gotten so large that they could not figure a way to number the pages, and could not fit the manuals horizontally on the desks. Training had risen to 10 weeks in length before a customer service rep could ever perform any actual work, and often managers sent new employees back to training because their performance was not up to expectations. The training classes were so long that it was almost impossible to fill customer service vacancies in a prompt fashion, and many individuals left the job even before they had gotten through basic training.

It was obvious that the training and documentation systems needed to be redesigned. If the manuals could be designed to be easier to use and more accurate, training would not need to be so lengthy. A first, rather obvious "fix," was to convert the print manuals to an on-line hypertext form which was easier to search and update. However, more fundamental changes in the concept of training and performance were necessary. The notion that employees had to be "fully trained" before doing any work was questioned and abandoned. Short coaching modules were developed that allowed trainees to go onto the floors and observe, and then practice, simple skills under the supervision of an experienced representative. Self-instructional modules allowed individuals to learn certain concepts at their own pace, and to review complex material once they were on the job. Even more fundamentally, the selection process for customer service representatives was analyzed and changed; skills that were easily taught, like typing, were given less weight than a candidate's ability and enjoyment of explaining complex material to customers. Recruiting and interviewing procedures were changed so that applicants got a better picture of the job requirements, and this resulted in better qualified employees who required less training and supervision. Once the manuals are totally converted to an on-line performance-based system, the training is expected to be reduced by almost half, resulting in significant savings as well as an improvement in trainee morale.

✓ Restaurant managers in a U.S. national chain reported that they were spending almost two hours a day responding just to e-mail updates and announcements—in an organization that demands a high level of contact with customers for its managers. The three-day training course for wait staff had gotten so detailed that many servers left the job before they ever waited on a customer, thinking that they could never learn so complicated a job. Fewer employees were interested in management positions, because it meant having to spend 10 to 12 weeks away from home at company headquarters to go through management training.

This organization is in the process of creating communication guidelines to try to eliminate information overload and help individuals make better decisions about using various media such as memos, e-mail, and voice mail. The basic task requirements for servers and food preparers are being examined, such as the traditional requirement that they memorize a complex system of two-letter codes for all the menu items. Prototype electronic "knowledge banks" are being created that will allow trainers to download continuously updated manuals, and will enable managers to easily sort through and summarize daily news updates. A "pull" rather than "push" strategy for communication is being developed which will focus on enabling employees to maximize their time spent with customers rather than with new information.

✓ The training subsidiary of a European automobile and truck company faced declining requests from internal clients for training. In a period of about two years, their revenue had decreased some 30%, as customers looked for newer and faster solutions to their performance problems. Line managers in factories began to contract for training themselves instead of going through headquarters, or just dropped training altogether. In order to try to maintain their jobs and budgets, the training staff was increasingly recommending more expensive and elaborate courses to their clients, but this strategy backfired completely as they priced themselves out of the market.

In order to remain a relevant and competitive resource to their clients, they refocused their service as "performance improvement consultation." They reorganized their staff to align them directly with business lines and content specialties, and added skill sets in performance analysis and in organizational communication support, such as meeting planning and presentation media and documentation. A major program of staff development was initiated, including bringing in industry experts as mentors and workshop leaders. The staff also began to energetically participate in international associations in training and performance improvement, such as the International Society for Performance Improvement. They are now becoming the experts in knowledge acquisition and management for the company's entire international operations, and are enjoying renewed support from their clientele and management. Moreover, they have become leaders in Europe in fostering the performance technology approach.

✓ The staff development department for a regional healthcare system was so occupied doing time management and sexual harassment training that it had no time left to even consider courses on the new economic realities of managed care and capitation that were necessary to the organization's survival. Not surprisingly, this department received little support from management, and became less and less involved in strategic decisions. Employee morale throughout the company was declining, both because of the uncertainty of the environment, and also because of a perceived lack of credibility of management messages and training.

To remain competitive, it was clear that the organization needed to foster continuous learning not just about new medical technologies, but also about management and economics. The CEO formed a strategic planning team, including representatives from human resources, information technology, media production, staff development, corporate communications, and finance, to develop a plan to implement concepts of the "learning organization" and performance technology. After a four-month period of meetings, study, and mentoring by external consultants, they have received approval to reorganize themselves into a "human and organizational development" team that will provide integrated solutions to performance problems in the organization, identify the skills that the company will need to survive in the new marketplace, and implement individual development plans for all members of the organization, from groundskeepers to the executive team. However, staff reorganization and new projects are only the surface changes that are occurring: A philosophy of valuing diverse opinions, appreciating alternative approaches, acknowledging everyone as a learner and a mentor, and celebrating mistakes as well as successes is being promoted. New infrastructures that will make it easier for employees to collaborate and to communicate with management are being implemented, and methods of performance appraisal and compensation are being redesigned.

Key Concepts

There are several key concepts that provide the framework for all of these new designs:

- ✓ integrating the various "islands of communication" (Gayeski, 1993) in the organization so that training, employee communications, external communications, human resources, and other key message sources all speak with "one voice" for the organization;
- ✓ improving the selection and integration of training and communication interventions so that clients aren't ordering a two-day course when a simple job aid or a redesign of incentive systems would be a better solution;
- ✓ developing methods to analyze return-on-investment for communication and learning projects, and making them part of the organization's strategic plan, rather than a form of "entertainment";
- ✓ building a fast, multi-way, collaborative information infrastructure that makes it easy to share, store, and index knowledge;
- ✓ forming a new image and structure for training—one that often integrates trainers with employee communications specialists, human resources professionals, media producers, and even advertising and marketing departments; and
- ✓ ensuring that the basic philosophies and practices of training and communication are aligned with the organizational culture, goals, and values.

How to Get Started

If you are interested in moving your client from training to performance improvement, here are some specific steps to take.

1. First, define the current gaps and opportunities that exist. Some of the symptoms of a training and communication system that don't work include the following (circle those that describe situations in your organization):
   - ✓ Courses and manuals are getting too long and are difficult to keep current.
   - ✓ People complain of "information overload."
   - ✓ There is no return-on-investment data for training and communication projects.
   - ✓ Communication and training aren't currently part of the organization's strategic plan.
   - ✓ People feel that organizational information in training, manuals, policies, or employee communications is confusing or not credible.

- ✓ People don't act as if learning and teaching are part of *everybody's* job.

- ✓ There are few standards for "exemplary" performance and analyses of the costs for not achieving exemplary performance for specific jobs.

- ✓ Training, technical publications, employee communications, information systems, and external communication and marketing do not work together regularly to focus and integrate core messages.

- ✓ Training and communication are "event"-based (like entertainment) rather than performance-based; they are measured by audience satisfaction.

- ✓ When managers notice substandard performance, they assume that training will fix it, and they "order" a course.

- ✓ Trainers and developers are rewarded for how much material they produce, rather than for how much time or money they save.

2. Get management endorsement to form a study team or task group. This should be a cross-functional group with representatives from training, HR, employee communication, information systems, and media production. In many organizations, the marketing and advertising departments should also be included. This team should look at what each department is doing to promote performance improvement, and how the various teams could work together more closely. Establish a firm but simple goal and an aggressive time schedule.

3. Execute a prototype intervention. Take a significant organizational performance gap, and with the team, develop an intervention that includes a wide range of coordinated performance improvement activities. Examples of this might be:

- ✓ a prototype intranet (an internal World Wide Web server) that integrates a short training module, company news, and continuously updated news about your industry, linking all these facts and issues into a comprehensive context

- ✓ a new employee selection and orientation system for a certain job, including more appropriate ways to describe the job, interview and select applicants, give them an accurate picture of the job even before they accept it, and then provide a firm context of the organizational culture and mission

✓ a system to reduce waste, including some employee awareness, incentives, and training in the new ways to operate more efficiently

✓ a new computerized sales tool that includes presentation materials that can be customized, along with a coaching guide and product knowledge tutorials and quizzes

Evaluate the return-on-investment of this prototype, and document what you learned that will help you create more powerful projects in the future. Don't be discouraged if this project takes a long time and leads to a lot of infighting and frustration. You will just be learning new skills and interacting with a new team. It's natural to get defensive and to stumble over new ground. Don't give up.

4. Spread the word of your study and prototype undertakings. Gradually make others aware of these new approaches by highlighting courses or professional meetings and by publicizing the success of your intervention. Consider writing up your case study and presenting it at a conference or publishing it in a trade journal.

Although these recommendations may sound ambitious, numerous consultants have applied just these steps to redesign and renew training departments and individual careers. Although no two results are (or should be) the same, this process has been demonstrated to produce quick and dramatic improvements. As one professional who participated in a four-month intensive strategic planning committee and prototype intervention said, "There's no going back—I'll never do my job the same way again."

REFERENCES

Gayeski, D. and Williams, D.V. (1994) *Tools for Reengineering Training.* Ithaca, NY: OmniCom Associates.

Gayeski, D. (1993) *Corporate Communication Management: The Renaissance Communicator in Information-age Organizations.* Woburn, MA: Focal Press.

Robinson, D.G. and Robinson, J.C. (1995) *Performance Consulting: Moving Beyond Training.* San Francisco: Berrett-Koehler Publishers, Inc.

21

HOW TO DEVELOP STRATEGIC PLANS BASED ON STRATEGIC VISION

Marlene Caroselli

Overview Are your client's strategic plans worthless? They are if they are written without a strategic vision in mind. Failing to be "externally aware" can result in incomplete plans. And failing to articulate a vision can create a hole in the fabric of those plans. Here is a guide that provides step-by-step instructions for developing strategic plans based on these two important elements.

The United States Office of Personnel Management has developed a list of succession competencies, which move from the most basic to the highest level of "knowledge, skills, and abilities." Only two requirements are cited for executive-level managers: vision and external awareness. Without attending to these critical elements, the integrity of strategic plans is compromised and the solidity of future-orientation is jeopardized.

The very phase "strategic planning" can be daunting: Managers typically think of themselves as controllers, directors, and even planners—but not "strategists." Yet the process, when broken down, affords an opportunity to marshal the strengths of the present in order to diminish the impact of weaknesses in the future. Basically, there are five steps involved in the process.

1. Begin by Asking Questions

Peter Drucker, the father of modern management science, says of outstanding leaders: "They know how to ask questions—the right questions." From questions come ideas, which Mark Van Doren advises us to bring in and entertain "...royally. One of them may be the king." In similar fashion, experienced strategic planners begin with a series of questions. They provide the framework within which critical decisions

Contact Information: Center for Professional Development, 324 Latona Road, Suite 1600, Rochester, NY 14626, 716-227-6512, mccpd@aol.com, http://hometown.aol.com/mccpd

are made. The more questions, the greater the likelihood of finding those that will point the way to the best ideas, from which the best decisions can be made.

Here are but a few to stimulate thinking in the first step in the planning process. These questions can be used for strategic planners at any level of the organization.

✓ What substantive issues face us today?

✓ What will face us tomorrow?

✓ How has technology effected change thus far in the way we do business?

✓ How might technology effect change in the way we will conduct business in the future?

✓ What are we doing and doing well?

✓ What are we doing and not doing well?

✓ What do we need to enhance?

✓ What measurements will tell us how well we are doing?

✓ What should be eliminated?

✓ What are we doing for the community and world of which we are part?

✓ Has our ethical stance been clearly defined?

✓ Are we thinking globally and acting locally?

✓ What are we not doing that we should be doing?

✓ What kind of training will we need to plan for?

✓ What demands are customers likely to make?

✓ What opportunities are we missing?

✓ What mistakes have been made recently by those in our same industry?

✓ What resources are we wasting by defending the past?

✓ What wheels have already been invented?

✓ What customer complaints could lead to innovative products or services?

✓ How would we define our existing culture?

✓ What might our culture become?

✓ What makes us unique?

✓ Do we have morale problems?

✓ What potential profit areas are we overlooking?

✓ What are we doing to encourage creativity?

✓ What kind of uniqueness will we need in the future?

✓ What can we do to shape that outcome?

✓ By what standards or terms do we wish to be known?

✓ What demands might employees make?

✓ How can we involve them more?

✓ What will future customers want?

✓ Does mission drive us?

✓ What is our existing vision?

✓ How cognizant are employees of it?

✓ How familiar are customers and suppliers with our vision?

✓ How can we improve the way the adjusted vision and new strategic plans are communicated to those who matter most to us?

✓ What barriers prevent optimization of resources?

✓ How much and what are we willing to commit?

✓ What safety issues should concern us?

✓ What is the ideal workplace?

✓ Who is the ideal leader?

✓ What is the ideal company?

✓ What is the ideal product or service?

✓ Who is the ideal employee?

✓ What messages are we sending?

✓ What distinctions are beginning to blur?

✓ What form will future competition take?

✓ What market trends should we be paying attention to?

✓ What is our competitive edge?

✓ What gaps need to be filled?

✓ Which risks are worth taking?

✓ How can we expand our markets?

✓ What basic principles can we agree upon?

✓ What myths surround our efforts?

✓ What are the realities?

✓ What combinations might spell improvement or greater profits?

✓ Have we imagined every possible negative eventuality?

✓ Do we have plans in place for dealing with them?

✓ What are our priorities?

✓ What are our values?

✓ What philosophy has survived the years since the organization was started?

✓ How much credence are we willing to give to author Warren Bennis' prediction: "The factory of the future will have only two employees, a man and a dog. The man will be there to feed the dog. The dog will be there to keep the man from touching the equipment"?

2. Determine the External Events Impacting the Vision, Taking Care Not to Be Overly Influenced by "The Brilliance of Transient Events"

Prussion military strategist Karl von Clausewitz warned of the danger of paying too much attention to transient events, especially brilliant transient events. What makes strategic planning difficult is the challenge of determining which events are transient and which will have profound effects upon the organization's future. The title of "manager" does not confer omniscience. And so, the best we can do is forge ahead with planning yet be prepared to adapt as necessary.

One of the most valuable and yet most frequently overlooked elements of strategic planning can be found in daily news reports—and not merely those emanating from Wall Street. Whenever an event shatters walls we have erected around traditional thinking, it is time for leaders to review existing policies and make provisions for future eventualities. This is especially true of crises. The Oklahoma bombing should have made every organizational leader ask, "Could it happen here? If so, are we prepared?" Such scrutiny leads to basic planning: "Is there an evacuation plan in place?"

Realistically speaking, the odds of disaster striking are slim. Nonetheless, with a minimal expenditure of resources, contingency plans can be established. This is true of safety and security issues (violence in the workplace, sexual harassment, drugs, alcohol, disasters) as well as financial matters (interest rates, mergers, health care costs) and technological advances. (The number of telecommuters is growing—nearly 15 percent of the existing workforce works at home instead of in an office for part or all of the workweek. How do such statistics impact supervision, for example? Office space? Schedules? Compensation?)

Sometimes we relay on intuition to help us prioritize which of the many possible influences impinging upon our operations are the ones most deserving of inclusion in our plans. Sometimes we rely on the

158

advice of others. So, in developing a strategic plan for his or her department, a supervisor may confer with other supervisors to obtain a general sense of priorities or organizational emphases.

Resources are limited, however, and so choices must be made. The vision remains the definitive core. If safety is indeed part of the vision, then decisions and plans will be made to ensure it. If profits are over-riding concern, then efforts are clustered around that focus. If coevolution ("the development of new markets via collaboration among competitors, customers and vendors") appears to be the most promising direction in which to head, then initiatives are begun to attain such unity. If technology seems to offer the best hope for the future then we plan accordingly.

3. State the Vision

Vision has been described as the art of seeing the invisible. It requires idealism, imagination, and courage to face the darkness of the unknown, to distinguish the outlines of possibilities, and then to reify barely visible shapes. Those shapes, of course, emerge because of the context whose definition permits them to develop.

Just as we see what we want to see, we create the ideal in our mind's eye. Motivational speakers encourage us to write 100 goals for our lives and to experience the thrill of achieving them one by one. By extension, we as individuals and as leaders can use a wide array of hopes, aspirations, and intentions to formulate our plans for the future. We can use the answers to questions raised in Step 1 as a starting point. We can include the external events needed for thorough, comprehensive thinking. Only then can we formulate the broad concepts that will lead to the vision, and from there, to the plans that will realize it.

The Fishbone Diagram will help, as shown in Figure 21.1. The most salient questions and corresponding answers that were raised in Step 1 would be placed in the appropriate categories shown. (Occasionally, a given point will appear in more than one place.) These are illustrative categories; many other stratifications could be used instead.

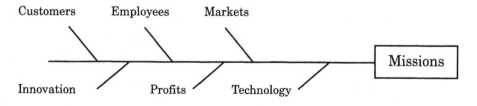

Figure 21.1

Assume six people are part of the strategic planning committee. The questions raised in Step 1 are divided into six broad areas. Each person would take one area and the questions that comprise it and work to obtain answers, measurements, and opinions prompted by the questions raised. Next, each person formulates a statement of importance or value for the area to which he or she is assigned. From the broad concepts, the vision will emerge. This vision must always precede planning.

Here is a sample and simple workplace vision, written by a first-line supervisor to define her aim. It evolved from the process of asking numerous questions, stratifying them into six categories with multiple questions and answers in each. Once the broad picture has been narrowed like this, the essentials needed for maximum effectiveness can be ascertained.

Provide a safe, functional work environment to accomplish required tasks.

Because the essentials are generally stated, planners can next move to the specifics of procedural planning, the "how's" that will accomplish the "what." In this subsequent stage of planning, we move from the overarching umbrella of generalization to the specific spokes that support its wide frame. We consider the means that will yield the end.

Examining the first adjective, "safe," leads to further questions, some of which should be answered by employees themselves. A survey, with room for open-ended responses, would provide information regarding the degree of safety employees currently experience in the workplace. Eliciting suggestions for improving safety would no doubt yield valuable ideas. (In *Kaizen,* author Masaaki Imai points to Toyota of Japan, which receives over a million employee ideas each year, 95 percent of which are implemented fully or partially.)

A focus group could be established to benchmark, to learn what other organizations are doing to improve upon basic safety guidelines. Armed with such knowledge, the group could then make recommendations that in time will be incorporated into the strategic plan. As author Gary Hamel observes, though, strategy has to be "subversive." He asserts that if it is not challenging existing practices, it is not strategy. So the vision-staters, the plan-developers, the plan-implementers must proceed with caution through each step of the process.

The second adjective, "functional," calls its antonym to mind: "dysfunctional." Are work units functioning at optimal levels of efficiency or are they divided by internal strife? What barriers prevent them from operating at peak proficiency? What stressors plague them and which can be eliminated or reduced? How much cooperation do they extend to both internal and external customers? Do they have the tools and training they need to perform as they should? Are they aware of the mission?

These and numerous other questions must be asked and answered if the vision of a functional and well-functioning workplace is to be realized. Such a workplace does not happen naturally; leaders must plan its emergence. (In the words of the sage Peter Drucker: "The only things that evolve by themselves in an organization are disorder, friction, and malperformance.")

Definitions of the verb "accomplish" will help the strategic planner as he or she moves from the clearly stated vision to its realization. Accomplish with what degree of quality? Within what time frame? According to what regulations or standards? With what degree of rework? For which customers? With what resources? The transformation from vision to strategy lies embedded in a network of questions and answers, definitions and provocative scenarios. Challenges are part of that network; employees and the strategists to whom they report are, ideally, advocates of continuous improvement. As such, they seek new and better, quicker and cheaper means of fulfilling their respective duties.

The work "required" should prompt the same kind of speculation. It stimulates thinking about who the "requiring" bodies might be in the future and what kinds of expectations we may have to face from them. Segments of the population that may have been voiceless in the past are now standing up and asserting their rights, as seen in recent scandals (Tailhook, Aberdeen, Texaco) involving women and minorities. In books like Walter Bogdanich's *The Great White Lie,* for example, we find patients and family members making demands that institutions like hospitals must respond to.

Finally, the concept of "tasks" calls forth reengineering prospects, the opportunity to imagine that we could design a process, system, or operation "from scratch" and then proceed to do exactly that. Such mental meandering forces us to juxtapose the real with the ideal and specify the steps that will lead us to the latter. It also forces us to determine which tasks are redundant or wasteful, too time-consuming, or unsatisfying to customers.

Being externally aware means being attuned to possibilities of both kinds—the injurious and the opportunity-laden—and making provisions for them in the vision statement itself.

4. Develop Plans Based on That Vision

Having analyzed the process that must be put in place if the ideal is to become real, we move from visionary, concepts-based strategic planning to operational planning, the practical, logistically-based "skin" that meshes with the support system in place for the vision. Less glamorous than the vision, more functional than the procedure, operational planning examines the incremental steps that eventually lead to the accomplishment of the visionary goal. Operational planning focuses on routine decisions that face us day-by-day, quarter-by-quarter, and even year-by-year.

Measurable objectives are part of that plan, as are the actions to be taken in prioritized order. The plan anticipates problems and specifies how they will be solved. It is what we arrive at after several contractions and expansions: The range of questions and external events led to narrowed categories and concepts which led to the even more narrowly-stated vision. The vision is then expanded via strategic decisions regarding the procedures that will accomplish the aim of the vision. Those procedures are opened wide once again to include the multiple steps that will accomplish the aim of the procedural planning.

To achieve greatest effectiveness, operational planning must be easily understood by employees at any and all levels of the organization. Directions must be clear and concise. The reporting vehicles must be carefully and fully depicted. Problems that arise as the operations are executed are solved at the lowest possible level. This may be the individual worker or the team assigned to a project. If decisions cannot be reached here, the problem is turned over to first-line supervision. If the problem to be solved or decision to be made is of sufficient magnitude to involve middle management, it is turned over to that level. But always, those closest to the process are the first (and ideally last in the majority of situations) to become involved, thus freeing senior management to engage in the activities for which they were hired.

When operational issues are ignored, vision remains in the realm of potential. When long-term strategy is ignored, future growth becomes a haphazard possibility rather than a planned-for objective, pursued with determination along a deliberate course of action.

5. Implement the Plan, Communicating It as Often as Possible

Inadequate implementation planning will nullify the strategic plan and the correlative plans that can transform strategy from potential to reality. Effective leaders repeatedly communicate both the "spirit" and the "letter" of the new "law" that will govern individual and institutional behaviors in the years ahead.

The manager making strategic plans, whether for a microcosmic work unit or the macrocosmic corporate body, attempts to establish the relationship between his or her scope of control and the "big picture."

Change is integral to such planning. Without it, the manager is simply maintaining the status quo rather than preparing for the future. The possibility of such change has led Graham Briggs, vice president of Charles River Data Systems, to declare strategic planning "damn scary." He acknowledges it's easier to simply declare, "Next year's going to be better" and leave it at that. Of course, improvement evolves from more than mere wishful thinking. It evolves from present planning.

As the work unit or the organization itself stretches to meet demands, new opportunities will open up. But without planning, we make ourselves deaf to opportunity's knock. We remain unattuned to possibilities and unaware of the potential impact of external events, events with long-term implications. In the words of master strategist Peter Drucker, "Long-range planning does not deal with future decisions, but with the future of present decisions."

HOW TO IDENTIFY PERFORMANCE PROBLEMS IN AN ORGANIZATION*

G.M. (Bud) Benscoter

Overview   How many times have you heard it said that one of the biggest challenges faced by American business is finding or developing people to solve problems effectively? A fact that's often ignored, though, is that problem **identification** and **analysis** are critical first steps to good problem **solving,** since successfully solving the wrong problem is worse than not addressing the real problems at all.

This how-to guide presents a format for identifying which problems to attack and how to analyze the impact they are having on your client's organization. The approach used is a six-step process called **PRIAM,** for **PR**oblem **I**dentification and **A**nalysis **M**odel. While the model can be used by an individual consultant, it is also very effective with intact working groups who sometimes find it difficult to sort out the "trivial many" from the "critical few" issues on their plates.

By following this six-step process, your clients should discover that they're working on the problems that have the greatest impact on their business and that they're laying a foundation for selecting the appropriate solution that will yield measurable results.

The PRIAM Model

Figure 22.1 is a graphic representation of the model, which looks at four areas:

✓   Impact on the business in terms of business metrics

✓   Impact on business processes

*Note: A special thanks to James and Dana Gaines Robinson and to the late Thomas F. Gilbert for the inspiration their work provided in formulating the PRIAM approach.

Contact Information: The Vanguard Group of Investment Companies, 100 Vanguard Boulevard, Malvern, PA 19355, 610-669-6647, bud_benscoter@vanguard.com

✓ Impact on worker performance

✓ Obstacles to top performance

Gap Analysis

A "Gap" is the difference between what IS happening and what SHOULD or COULD be happening.

For each of the impact areas, you'll be asked to think about the following:

✓ The "should" vision of the area of the model under investigation: What results should be happening that aren't?

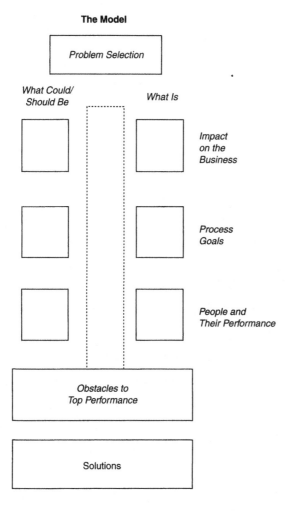

Figure 22.1

✓ The "is" of the issue: In terms of results, what is actually happening? What adverse impact is it having on business results?

You should find the model to be useful for not only improving conditions that are currently deficient, but also those that meet your standards today but will need to improve to meet the challenges of tomorrow. You can enter the model at different places and move back and forth depending on where your analysis leads you.

Applying the PRIAM Model

Step #1: Select an Issue

The first step in the model is to identify an issue. Your group may want to brainstorm potential issues and list them on a board or flip chart. When selecting an issue or a problem from the list you've developed, consider how you can separate the "critical few" from the "trivial many." The questions listed under Step #1 get to the heart of what's causing "pain" in the organization, how the pain is measured, the benefits to solving the issue, and how "solvable" the problem is.

Step #2: Analyze the Issue in Terms of Impact on the Business

Look at the impact of your group's issue on the business (e.g., lost revenue, reduced productivity, cost overruns, turnover). Issues that have greater impact are likely to deserve attention. From there, describe what the situation should (or could) be if the issue were resolved to everyone's satisfaction.

Step #3: Analyze the Process Issue

Process seems to be everyone's focus since the advent of Business Process Reengineering. Recognize the impact that a poor process can have on our operations. To analyze the process issues, identify process goals, which are the gaps between desired and actual process results, and any "disconnects" (gaps) in the current process flow.

Step #4: Analyze the People and Their Performance

Describe what worker performance looks like now, then what it should or could look like if performance dramatically improved. Focus on performance and its outcomes as well as on behavior, attitudes, and morale.

Step #5: Analyze the Obstacles to Top Performance

More problems are caused by deficiencies in the work environment than by people in the workplace. The key to investigating problems within a process is measurement. A series of core questions in step #5 are designed to identify obstacles to top performance. The questions relate to what is expected of people on their jobs, whether they're receiving timely, appropriate, and relevant feedback on their performance, and any incentives or disincentives to perform that may exist in the workplace. For each question, answer "yes" or "no." The questions that you answer "no" to should be areas of opportunity for improvement.

Step #6: Select Solution Criteria

You now have the information you need to identify possible solutions to the issue you selected in Step #1. Before doing so, ask yourself what requirements (such as cost, practicality, or cultural impact) any final solution must meet.

STEP #1: SELECT AN ISSUE

✓ Is the issue causing pain in the organization?

✓ How do I know it's a "problem"?

✓ Who else sees this issue as a problem?

✓ How are business metrics impacted by this issue?

✓ What would happen if I did nothing about this issue?

✓ What will be the benefits to the company and/or the business unit if the issue is successfully addressed?

✓ Is the problem "leverageable"; i.e., can a significant improvement be made with a minimum of effort?

STEP #2: ANALYZE THE ISSUE IN TERMS OF IMPACT ON THE BUSINESS

Describe, in economic terms, the current situation:

Describe what the situation should (or could) be if the issue were resolved to everyone's satisfaction:

STEP #3: ANALYZE THE PROCESS ISSUE

✓ What are the goals of the process?

✓ If the goals are not being achieved, what is the gap between desired and actual process results?

✓ Can you "map" both the current and desired processes and identify the critical differences in terms of process efficiency, effectiveness, cost?

✓ Are there "disconnects" (gaps in process flow) in the current process?

✓ Is the process being managed cross-functionally?

STEP #4: ANALYZE THE PEOPLE AND THEIR PERFORMANCE

Describe what worker performance looks like now, then what it should or could look like if performance dramatically improved or changed. Try to focus on performance and its outcomes as well as on behavior, attitudes, and morale.

Current Performance

Desired Performance

STEP #5: ANALYZE THE OBSTACLES TO TOP PERFORMANCE

(Answer "yes" or "no" to each of the following questions. The ones you answer "no" to should be examined more closely.)

1. Are the goals and objectives of the work unit/process/job clear and well communicated to everyone?

2. Do people know what's expected of them in their jobs? For example, are there job descriptions that include job expectations and performance standards?

3. Do people receive relevant, timely, and appropriate feedback on their performance?

4. Do people have the tools and resources needed to achieve top performance?

5. Do people have good work processes?

6. Do people have relevant and effective incentives for doing their jobs?

7. Are incentives contingent on job performance?

8. Is good performance rewarded?

9. Is poor performance punished?

10. Do people have the necessary skills and knowledge to do their jobs?

11. Do people have the mental, emotional, physical, and psychological capacity to do their jobs?

12. If other obstacles were removed, would people want to do well in their jobs?

STEP #6: SELECT SOLUTION CRITERIA

What criteria must your proposed solution meet for it to be acceptable?

1.

2.

3.

4.

HOW TO INCREASE THE VALUE OF PERFORMANCE IMPROVEMENT INTERVENTIONS

Warren Bobrow and Kammy Haynes

Overview Whether acting as an internal or external consultant to an organization, one of the toughest challenges is convincing top management to implement performance improvement initiatives. They are often leery of spending time and money on interventions that cannot be directly tied to meeting bottom-line objectives. That is, they are concerned that the performance improvement intervention will not yield a sufficient return on investment. This guide presents a framework for linking performance improvement initiatives to business objectives that will improve the likelihood of your intervention producing the desired results.

INTRODUCTION

What is the purpose of performance improvement interventions? While the immediate answer is, "To improve the skills and performance of employees and managers," that is only part of it. The big-picture answer is, "To improve the performance of the organization." All consulting success stories end with "...and the company succeeded in achieving its objectives." Yet how many times have we seen projects that ended with everyone being happy about what was done, while the organization did not achieve any substantial gains in productivity or performance? This guide outlines how to design interventions that have a greater chance of yielding the desired results.

Contact Information: Warren Bobrow, The Context Group, 5812 W. 76th Street, Los Angeles, CA 90045, 310-670-4175, warrenb@contextgroup.com, www.contextgroup.com
Kammy Haynes, The Context Group, 2073 Lake Shore Drive, Suite A, Chino Hills, CA 91709, 909-591-2848, kammyh@contextgroup.com, www.contextgroup.com

How Performance Initiatives Support Strategy

While the model above does not encompass all possible performance improvement activities, it shows the relationships between some of the major ones. When we consider what we can do to maximize the value of a company's employees, we should start with the business strategy. The strategy should clearly outline the goals and objectives of the company. Once we know the company's objectives, we are in a better position to provide value by devising programs and processes that support those goals. A sample business strategy statement for a company might read:

To provide our consumers with the highest quality products, our partners and consumers with the highest customer service, and our shareholders with the highest possible return. We will accomplish this as a team and while being exemplary corporate citizens in our communities.

To carry out the strategy, the company may choose the following tactics:

- Implement a new quality program in our own facilities and work with our suppliers to do the same.

- Survey our partners (suppliers and customers) and consumers regarding customer service issues. Commit resources to address any problems or areas for improvement.

- Implement a program to reduce overhead and administrative costs by 10 percent.

- Transform the culture into one that fosters teamwork by increasing upward and cross-functional communication.

- Establish community awareness of the corporation by participating in community events and sponsoring charity events.

With this information, we have a clearer picture of where the company is going and how it plans to get there. We can now plan performance improvement initiatives that can help the company carry out its strategy and meet its business objectives.

IDENTIFY CORE COMPETENCIES

One of the first steps is to develop a list of the core competencies (CCs) that individuals need to possess in order to carry out the company's strategy. For a manager, the CCs could include:

- Communicates effectively and directly with customers, team members, and direct reports.

- Provides effective coaching to others in order to improve their performance.

- Budgets resources in order to establish priorities and maximize value.

- Understands and accepts team decision making while taking responsibility for outcomes.

- Anticipates and solves problems.

- Understands and balances customer concerns with business needs.

- Is willing and able to act as liaison with the community and promote the company.

Note that the CCs are directly related to the business strategy statements on the previous page. Once we understand the CCs for a particular job, we are in a position to pursue activities designed to improve performance in that job.

While this model is helpful in explaining your intentions to top management and will help keep you focused on your task, it is built on the premise that your organization has a relatively clear strategy that can be articulated to employees at all levels. Without this clarity, your task takes on added complexity. However, working under the assumption that you have a strategy, the next important step is the definition of the core competencies. These definitions will drive many of the subsequent interventions.

Keys to Success:

In order to be useful, the CC definitions must be:

- written in terms that employees can understand;
- tailored to the job and level of responsibility (e.g., supervisor CCs are not a carbon copy of manager CCs);
- observable;
- measurable; and
- relevant to current and future business needs.

CAREER DEVELOPMENT

We know that many companies want to develop the skills of existing employees so they can move up in the organization. However, these development efforts must be directly linked to reaching strategic business objectives. Without this connection, skill development efforts will not result in any significant changes in the company's performance.

For instance, let's say that a motivated engineer wants eventually to become a manager. This situation provides the organization with an excellent opportunity to promote someone who already understands the company and shares its values. However, the CCs required of a manager are considerably different from those required of an engineer, so some development will be necessary. The company can either promote the engineer and hope that he or she develops into the job (trial by fire), or it can construct a development plan (or career path) to prepare the engineer for a manager's position when it becomes available. Obviously, the latter option is more likely to result in success for both the engineer-manager and the company, because the employee already has many of the required skills for the manager position. By shortening the learning curve (through prior training and preparation), the company is able to realize an immediate return on investment rather than waiting for the newly appointed manager to grow into his or her responsibilities. An example of a development plan for two of the CCs is shown here.

Sample Career Development Plan

Core Competency	Does the person possess the CC?	What can the person do to gain competence?	Time to acquire the skill
Budgets resources in order to establish priorities and maximize value.	No	1. Complete Budgeting Basics class at Anytown Community College. 2. Attend quarterly budget discussion meetings. 3. Assist the current manager in developing the next budget.	6 months
Understands and balances customer needs with business needs.	Yes	N/A	N/A

By showing the engineer the relationship between the CCs and the manager's job, we can demonstrate the importance of the skill development. At the same time, we provide the employee with a roadmap for acquiring the necessary competencies. By showing top management the direct link between the development initiative, the CCs, and the business strategy, we can more easily justify the training expenditure, because the engineer is going to learn skills that will help the company succeed.

Keys to Success:

Successful career development requires:

- support from top management;
- clear connections between the training courses and the CCs;
- an easy-to-follow roadmap for development that assists the employee in getting to the position that she or he wants;
- motivated employees;
- rewards and recognition for skill acquisition; and
- constant updating of the catalog to anticipate future trends.

SELECTION

When we understand the CCs required for a position, we can make better hiring decisions by assessing candidates on each of the CCs.

Assessments can take several different forms, including interviews, tests, role plays, and reviewing the candidate's previous experience. By gaining a good understanding of the CCs, we are able to identify the most effective way to measure the CCs in order to determine the candidate's skill level. In many cases, this understanding leads to the creation or implementation of non-traditional assessment tools (e.g., interactive role plays or computer simulations, stand-up presentations, multiple-exercise assessment centers). Regardless of the assessment method selected, if the CCs are directly linked to the business strategy, the performance of the chosen candidates can be validated against clear business objectives (for example, reduced errors by 5 percent).

As we review the CCs for a manager, you will see that there is no one best assessment method to measure them all. Careful consideration should be given to matching the assessment tool to the CCs (although some tools can measure more than one CC). For example, the following assessment methods might be used for the manager position:

	Selection Technique		
Core Competency	Interview	Test	Role Play
1. Communicates effectively and directly with customers, team members, and direct reports.	X		X
2. Provides effective coaching to others in order to improve their performance.	X		X
3. Budgets resources in order to establish priorities and maximize value.		X	X
4. Understands and accepts team decision making while taking responsibility for outcomes.			X
5. Anticipates and solves problems.	X	X	X
6. Understands and balances customer concerns with business needs.	X		X
7. Is willing and able to be liaison with the community and promote the company.	X		

It is important to note that, the CCs (derived from the business strategy) drive the recruiting, staffing, and selection processes. We need to have the proper tools to identify the individuals (internal and external to the organization) who possess the CCs that will help the company be successful. By combining the CCs and carefully chosen assessment tools, we are able to fill the job openings with the best candidates. The assessment process also allows us to identify training and development needs (of both successful and unsuccessful candidates).

Keys to Success:

In order for a selection system to be successful, you must:

- Prioritize the CCs (if you cannot measure them all).
- Use the CCs to drive your recruiting efforts and the design or choice of assessment methods.
- Use the right assessment method for the CC you are measuring.
- Provide a realistic job preview (e.g., working conditions, chances for promotion, amount of overtime).
- Make performance expectations clear to candidates (e.g., you will be held accountable for coaching your employees and for their productivity).
- Use the assessment information to create training and development plans.

TRAINING

Training is a critical component of an organization's success. The company needs its employees to acquire new skills in order to stay competitive. However, to be effective, training must be linked to business needs. Many companies put together catalogs of training courses and allow people to sign up on their own. There is often no thought or explanation given to the connection between the course offerings and the business strategy. As a result, employees may sign up for training that has no direct impact on their performance. Consequently, training is perceived as adding little or no value to the organization's bottom-line objectives.

Training has the greatest value when it improves the performance of existing employees, helps them meet changing business needs, and positions them to face the challenges of the future business environment. Therefore, training dollars should be focused on improving or acquiring those CCs that contribute to the company's current and future success.

Keys to Success:

In order for a training program to be successful, you must:

- Offer training courses in areas that directly impact the business strategy or bottom-line productivity results.

- Provide training in areas that are needed currently and anticipated in the future.

- Update your training offerings and courses to accommodate changes in the business environment.

- Include training opportunities for all levels of the organization (from the front line to senior management).

- Recognize and reward employees for learning and applying new skills.

- Provide opportunities to practice new skills without fear of reprisal for "failures."

- Offer refresher courses or updates as new information or techniques are identified.

PERFORMANCE MANAGEMENT

Performance management is probably the most difficult process that can be used to improve organizational success, and yet it offers the largest potential return for the company. Performance management systems are hard to change despite the fact that, in many cases, they are recognized as being dysfunctional. In addition to being labor-intensive and threatening to users, most performance appraisal systems are not directly linked to business strategies or objectives. While some of them use terms or statements that look like CCs, scores are often based on a few numbers (for instance, making budget). Here is an example of how good measures and standards can be applied to a manager's performance expectations:

- Take steps to implement a new quality program to reduce errors by 5 percent.
    - ⇒ Attend two seminars on quality.
    - ⇒ Participate in cross-functional quality teams.
    - ⇒ Implement ideas to improve quality.

These performance objectives are directly linked to the business strategy and can be objectively measured within a certain time frame. By basing these measures on the business strategy, you can measure success and reward those who are adding value to the organization. Just as important, if these performance expectations are not met, the managers need to understand what training and development opportunities are available to help improve their performance. The evaluation process also allows you to document the efforts made by management to assist in improving performance, so that those employees who consistently fail to meet expectations can be disciplined or terminated.

Keys to Success:

In order for a performance management system to be effective, you must:

- Make whatever changes are necessary to bring your system into alignment with your business objectives.
- Train managers and supervisors on how to use the system and explain how they benefit from using it correctly.
- Make the process and forms easy to understand and easy to complete (e.g., checklists, places for comments).
- Hold managers and supervisors accountable for practicing good performance management:
  ⇒ Make effective performance management part of their performance plans.
  ⇒ Provide specific, timely, and constructive feedback.
  ⇒ Keep employees informed; use continuous feedback so there are no surprises at the review meetings.
  ⇒ Recognize and reward good performance while taking appropriate actions to remedy poor performance (e.g., coaching, discipline, termination).

CONCLUSION

Using this strategic approach to performance intervention allows you to close the loop between them and business strategy, because you are consistently linking your activities to core competencies that are required for business success. By taking the time to ensure a direct connection for each of your interventions to the business strategy, you will gain support from top management and increase the impact of your efforts on the company's bottom line.

24

HOW TO LEAD EFFECTIVE MEETINGS

Laura Bierema

Overview Meetings are messy affairs. It has been said that a meeting is an event where people speak up, say nothing, then all disagree; or a place where you keep the minutes, but throw away the hours. Meetings are the most costly communication activity in the business world. Many professionals find themselves in meetings for over half of the workweek. With all the time spent in meetings, one would expect meeting processes to be near-perfect in this modern, technological age. Yet, there seems to be a collective unconsciousness about the wastefulness, inefficiency, and dysfunction of most meeting processes. What is a frustrated meeting attendee to do? Effective meetings begin with good planning, get better with active facilitation and troubleshooting, and continuously improve with reflective evaluation.

   This guide offers tips for improving meeting processes, from planning to evaluating meetings. This tool will be most useful to meeting facilitators and teams concerned with improving their meetings.

Contact Information: Human Resource Education and Training Center, School of Labor and Industrial Relations, 425 South Kedzie Hall, Michigan State University, East Lansing, MI 48824, 517-432-2798, bierema@pilot.msu.edu

QUICK GUIDE TO EFFECTIVE MEETINGS

MEETING PLANNING

QUESTIONS TO ASK *BEFORE* MEETING:
1. What is the purpose of the meeting?
2. What are the desired outcomes?
3. Is a meeting really necessary to achieve the purpose and outcomes?
4. What alternatives exist to meeting?
5. Who should attend the meeting?
6. What is the chemistry of the invitees?
7. What is the meeting plan?
8. What unexpected issues might arise?

Creating a POP: Purpose, Outcomes, Plan
The **purpose** should state why a meeting is needed. Write one by finishing this sentence. *"The purpose of the meeting is to _____."*
Outcomes focus the meeting by indicating what information is to be shared and what decisions or actions need to occur.
The **plan** is the actual agenda that accounts for the leaders, content, sharing, processing, and timing of the meeting.

ACTIVE FACILITATION STRATEGIES

Set ground rules to create a team contract of how people will behave. It keeps the meeting focused. Example:
⇒ All participate.
⇒ Challenge ideas instead of individuals.
⇒ Start on time/Stop on time (SOT/SOT).
⇒ One conversation at a time.
⇒ Confidentiality.
⇒ Evaluate the meeting.

Appoint roles to formally share meeting ownership. Examples:
Facilitator: Objectively leads meeting.
Cofacilitators: Support facilitator.
Scribe: Notes actions/decisions on flip chart.
Note Taker: Records decisions/actions, shares.
Process Observer: Ongoing/postevaluation.
Timekeeper: Monitors time, focuses group.
Others: Designated by group as needed.

The parking lot is a *visible* space to scribe items that are important, but not relevant to the issue at hand. The Parking Lot is analogous to a car in the parking lot. It is important for moving to the next destination, but irrelevant to the moment at hand (or immediate meeting's purpose). Designate a scribe and note issues on a flip chart.

Involve participants at the start by spending a few minutes checking in. This invaluable communication period sets the tone for the entire meeting. Try:
⇒ 5-minute informal conversation period.
⇒ Paired interviews on predetermined topics.
⇒ Roundtable sharing of business concerns & good news.

Premeeting assignments are tasks done by participants in advance of the meeting. If you assign them, abide by these rules:
⇒ Explain why it is important.
⇒ Give adequate lead time.
⇒ Provide clear instructions (read, analyze...).
⇒ Emphasize need to complete it in advance.
⇒ Assign it *only* if you intend to use it.
⇒ Plan a process for using assignment at meeting.

Presentations can be time wasters if they are not planned and facilitated well. Follow these ground rules to ensure quality and critical thinking:
⇒ Separate presentation from discussion.
⇒ Allow clarification questions *only* during presentation.
⇒ Give participants reflection questions:
What points did you agree/disagree with?
How could the proposal be improved?
What new questions does it raise?

Meeting breakouts work for 10 or more participants and are effective at reducing meeting cycle time and maximizing results.
⇒ *Determine space requirements.*
⇒ *Decide size of breakout teams.*
⇒ *Plan composition of breakout team.*
⇒ *Determine supplies/materials needed.*
⇒ *Plan breakout team process.*

Breakout team process options:
⇒ Buzz teams.
⇒ Small teams on same task; report outs.
⇒ Small teams on varied tasks; report outs.
⇒ Focused, short report outs.
⇒ Time for silent reflection.
⇒ Process for action on team information.
⇒ Process for making decisions.

Flip charts are invaluable for:
⇒ Keeping meeting focused.
⇒ Freeing participants from notetaking.
⇒ Catching up latecomers.
⇒ Depersonalizing ideas.
⇒ Helping notetaker.
⇒ Retaining the process visually & emotionally.
Get some colored markers and a scribe, and you are ready to create a meeting mind map!

Flip charting tips:
⇒ Write the words that people say if possible.
⇒ Share scribe role among multiple members.
⇒ Keep all information visible (hang charts).
⇒ Clarify with team when you add your ideas.
⇒ Seek permission to paraphrase ideas.
⇒ Establish and use a Parking Lot.
⇒ Use color.
⇒ Print clearly.

Helping Behaviors
Proposing *"How about ..."*
Building *"To build on Diane's idea ..."*
Information Seeking *"Please describe ..."*
Opinion Seeking *"How do you feel, Kenny?"*
Information Giving *"Here is my report ..."*
Opinion Giving *"My opinion is ..."*
Disagreeing *"I disagree with Ron because ..."*
Summarizing *"To recap the issue ..."*
Testing Comprehension *"I heard you say ..."*
Consensus Testing *"How many agree?"*
Encouraging *"Say more about that idea ..."*
Harmonizing *"What do we agree on?"*
Performance Checking *"How close are we?"*
Standard Setting *"We need to decide by ..."*
Tension Relieving *"The humor in this is ..."*
Paraphrasing *"What I heard you say was ..."*

Processing Conflict
Acknowledge feelings. Feelings cannot realistically be left outside the meeting. Get them into the open.
Remain neutral. Respect people's right to have their feelings and encourage expression.
Seek first to understand, then to be understood. Model and expect this behavior.
Process feelings by:
• Observing silence (reflection time).
• Taking a break.
• Silently brainstorming issues on cards.
• Round-robin sharing of concerns.
• Buzz team discussion and sharing.
• Identifying areas of conflict and commonality and ideas for bridging gaps.
• Suggesting ways of resolving conflict.
Refocus conversation on original topic/goals.

Hurtful Behaviors and Strategies
Late Arrivers Start on time, don't update.
Side Conversations Stop, look at offenders. Ask them if they would like to share their idea.
Dominators Ask them to scribe; use ground rules; seek input from all participants.
Quiet Members Periodically draw them in without putting them on the spot.
Rambling Stay focused on agenda, use Parking Lot if point is relevant.
Negativity Ask group to comment on negative opinions. Check for agreement/disagreement.

Dealing with Unruly Behavior
- Establish ground rules before problems occur. Refer to them often.
- Confront unruly behavior.
- Expect all participants to share responsibility for meeting process.
- Communicate nonverbally.
- Recognize helpful behavior.
- Meet privately with repeat offenders.
- Create group signals for confronting behavior (3-knock rule, Koosh balls, periodic process checks).

Consensus Building
Consensus is a psychological state of supporting an action for decision that the group decides to pursue.
Formula: C=A+S (**C**onsensus=**A**greement+**S**upport)
Test for consensus by verbal polling or a written vote.
Use consensus to determine team functions (meeting frequency, ground rules, roles, etc.); agree on team projects; agree on key implementation points of projects.
Recipe for consensus:
I've heard and understand your position.
You've heard and understand my position.
The decision does not compromise my values or ethics.
I can support the proposed decision.

Recognize Symptoms of Conflict
- Ideas get attacked before they are fully stated.
- Comments are personal attacks.
- Suggestions don't build on previous ones.
- Win-lose pressures.
- Victim mentality (versus proactive).
- Members take sides.

Act to Resolve Conflict
- Recognize that conflict is a natural, inevitable aspect of team process.
- Mutually agree resolution is desirable.
- Empathize with each other.
- Move from problem identification to solution.
- Seek a variety of opinions on issue.
- Listen.

Seek closure by summarizing and generating conclusions and/or action items throughout the meeting. Record them on a flip chart. This makes reaching conclusions and minute writing easier.
Reflect on:
What actions have been decided?
What decisions have been made?
What are agenda items for next time?
What issues remain open?

Post Mortem The only way to improve meetings is to strengthen what works and eliminate or change what doesn't.
Here are a few ideas:
Take action on Parking Lot items at end.
Review outcomes, decisions, and actions.
Highlight items for next agenda.
Critique session: Open conversation, written survey, combination.

25

HOW TO CONDUCT A PERFORMANCE ANALYSIS*

Allison Rossett

Overview Performance analysis is the first step in any problem-solving or performance improvement effort. While many consultants speak favorably about study prior to action, those words do not typically translate into practice. This guide will help by providing information about how to encourage analysis in your client's organization and how to choose the best performance analysis strategy.

*Adapted from A. Rossett, *First Things Fast*, Jossey-Bass, 1998.

Contact Information: Department of Educational Technology, San Diego State University, San Diego, CA 92182, 619-594-6088, arossett@mail.sdsu.edu, www.jbp.com/rossett.html

WHAT IS PERFORMANCE ANALYSIS?

Performance analysis involves gathering formal and informal data to help customers and sponsors define and achieve their goals. Performance analysis uncovers several perspectives on a problem or opportunity, determines any and all drivers toward or barriers to successful performance, and proposes a solution system based on what is discovered. This table lists types and descriptions of drivers and possible solutions.

Type of Driver	Description	Solutions
Lack of skill, knowledge, or information	People don't because they don't know how, they've forgotten, or there's just too much to know.	Education/training Information support (job aids) Documentation Coaching/mentoring Clarity re standards Communications initiatives
Weak or absent motivation	People don't because they don't care, don't see the benefits, or don't believe they can.	Education/training Information support (job aids) Documentation Coaching/mentoring Participatory goal setting Communications initiatives
Ineffective environment, tools, or processes	People don't because processes or jobs are poorly designed or necessary tools are unavailable.	Reengineered work processes New or improved tools, technologies, or work spaces Job design or redesign Job enrichment Participatory decision making
Ineffective or absent incentives	People don't because doing it isn't recognized, doing it is a hassle, or doing it is ignored.	Improved appraisal/recognition programs Management development New policies New and shared goal setting

WHAT DOES A PERFORMANCE ANALYST DO?

Here is a list of some of the things you might do as part of a performance analysis:

- Interview a sponsor or randomly selected representative.
- Read the annual report.
- Chat at lunch with a group of customer service representatives.
- Read the organization's policy on customer service, focusing particularly on the recognition and incentive aspects.
- Listen to audiotapes of associates with customer complaints.
- Lead a focus group with supervisors.
- Review the call log.

- Read an article in a professional journal on the subject of customer service performance improvement.
- Chat at the supermarket with somebody who is a customer and wants to tell you about his or her experience with customer service.

RESPONDING TO CUSTOMERS, EXPERTS, AND PERSONNEL

Because analysis consumes time and resources, some will doubt the need for it. It is not unusual to encounter skeptical customers, disinterested personnel, and resistant experts during performance analysis. This table provides examples of customer resistance and analyst strategies.

CUSTOMERS' PERSPECTIVE	ANALYST STRATEGIES
"I've got no time for any assessment. I know what I need."	Ask questions related to the value to the effort: "Are the employees eager for this change? Do they know why we're moving in this direction? Has RAM increased? Are managers on board?" Focus on defining the change they want to put in place, on the functions that will be improved as a result of the change, on what will drive the effort to success.
"I've never seen any benefits in all this study. It's analysis-paralysis. Action is my middle name."	Respond with action. Don't argue. Instead seek the minutes of meetings that launched the rollout. Examine contracts with technology vendors. Point to interviews and focus groups that revealed important directions for prior efforts. Collect examples of the power of data to improve decisions.
"Thank goodness you're here. I've got to go to Singapore and I need you to bring this to fruition while I'm on the road."	If the executive is disappearing, who'll play his or her role in the project? The work of the analyst needs to be done under the aegis of an executive or sponsor. Push back here. This sponsor or another leader must be involved. The trick is to define a "reasonable" amount of executive involvement or to find a substitute sponsor.
"This is a tough one and I'll want to see everything before it goes out. In fact, maybe we should meet daily."	This is the micromanaging exec. Why is she or he concerned? What's tough? Put some energy into gathering data on his or her views of the situation and then negotiate a close relationship that isn't oppressive.
The executive expresses concern that your interactions with employees will "stir things up in the field."	You are asking about drivers and barriers, about organizational consistency and messages. Explain why it is important to raise these issues and how you're going to use the data. Cite past efforts that were unitary and thus unsuccessful. Brief the executive about the solution system that will emerge. Offer the opportunity to review questions prior to meeting with people in the field.
The customer wants to know why a training gal or a technology guy is talking about processes and strategy and organizational climate.	Explain that you expect to be doing some training, but that you want to customize and tailor the effort. That involves getting into the organization. Does the executive want training events or improvements in the performance of employees?

Performance Analysis for Different Challenges

Think about the challenges you confront and select the performance analysis that matches your situation. This table provides examples of the types of opportunities and the rationale.

Example	Type of Opportunity	Rationale
The organization commits to a new computer operating system and every employee must be supported in the shift.	Rollout	The challenge here is to help people understand, appreciate, and use a new system or way of doing business. Note that rollouts are about more than technology.
"I went to a dinner party and the two people sitting next to me complained about the service they got from us. What's up here? What are we going to do?"	Performance Problem	Something is wrong and the executive needs to know two things: a sketch of the nature of the problem, and the drivers associated with each aspect of it.
"Our sales are down 11 percent, while the industry trend is up 2 percent. Something has to change here."	Performance Problem	The focus here is on finding out why, prior to figuring out what to do. What should that "something" be? In this case, the nature of the problem is clear, but the cause is in doubt.
Hospital administrators must be able to thrive in an environment that is changing rapidly. How can we prepare for that?	People Development	The focus here is on the position and the people who hold it. The challenge is to anticipate future challenges and skills.
"What I envision is HR helping us with a program to get everybody on the same page here. We need a shared vision, I think."	Strategy Development	No specific problem. No new technology or philosophy. No focus on one position or another. This is about broader planning issues.

26

HOW TO DEVELOP AND IMPLEMENT AN EVALUATION STRATEGY

Susan Barksdale and Teri Lund

Overview In today's world, there is much focus on continuous improvement, knowledge management, and linkage of performance solutions to business objectives. One cannot be successful in orchestrating these initiatives without deploying evaluation tactics that serve as navigational tools for the initiative implementation. In today's competitive environment, it is essential that organizations use resources in the most cost-effective and efficient way. Knowledge management programs and learning solutions need to be linked tightly to business needs and clearly provide the outcomes that were advertised.

But what should be evaluated? How? When? Why? What will be done with the results of an evaluation? An evaluation strategy begins by answering these questions and providing the linkage to the overall business strategies and tactics. An evaluation strategy will:

1. Provide information about the effectiveness of the solution for the individual enrolled in the solution, the manager of the individual, and the business itself.

2. Provide an "effectiveness scorecard" that will identify improvement opportunities for the design and delivery of performance solutions.

3. Identify the barriers present in the workplace that inhibit the transfer of the knowledge gained through the learning activity back to the job or business.

4. Assist in identifying "what we know" in an organization and "how we use (or don't use) what we know."

Contact Information: Susan Barksdale, PMB 412, 25 NW 23rd Place, #6, Portland, OR 97210, 503-223-7721, sbbfle@msn.com

Teri Lund, 4534 SW Tarlow Court, Portland, OR 97221, 503-245-9020, tlund_bls@msn.com

IDENTIFICATION OF LEVELS OF EVALUATION

To provide the business linkage, it is important for evaluation to be viewed holistically. An evaluation that emphasizes either quantitative or qualitative indicators may not provide key information needed to determine the effectiveness of learning solutions or manage how knowledge is used within an organization. To ensure a balanced evaluation, a combination of two models is recommended. These models are Kirkpatrick's four levels of evaluation and the Balanced Scorecard developed by Robert S. Kaplan and David P. Norton.

Kirkpatrick's four levels are defined as:

✓ *Level 1—Reaction.* As the word implies, this measures how those who participate in the learning solution react to it.

✓ *Level 2—Learning.* This measures the extent to which those who participate in the learning solution change their beliefs, improve knowledge, or increase skill as a result of the learning solution.

✓ *Level 3—Behavior.* This is defined as the extent to which behavior has changed back on the job because of participation in the learning solution.

✓ *Level 4—Results.* Measuring results quantifies the impact to the business as a result of the individual's behavior change. Final results can include Return on Investment (ROI), increased production, improved quality, decreased costs, reduced inventory, increased new product development, etc.

The Balanced Scorecard is based on four perspectives and places more of a business emphasis on evaluation than Kirkpatrick's four levels do. The Balanced Scorecard's four perspectives are defined as:

✓ *Customer Perspective:* Did the solution meet the need or expectation? Was it delivered using the right method at a time when it was needed? Are the users or customers satisfied with the end product?

✓ *Learning Perspective:* Did the participant gain skills or knowledge that he or she did not have before? Has there been an improvement in the methods used? Can the difference be measured (using pre- and post-testing or baselines)?

✓ *Business Perspective:* Has there been an impact "back on the job" as a result of the intervention? Has productivity increased? Is job behavior different? Has cost improved? Is technology being used where it was not before? Are results occurring back on the job as planned?

✓ *Financial Perspective:* Did the program have a financial payoff or benefit to the company? Did the program assist in increasing revenue, decreasing costs, or providing some type of Return on Investment (ROI) or financial impact?

An evaluation strategy is not limited to Kirkpatrick's Four Levels of Evaluation or the Balanced Scorecard. It is critical that this type of strategy encompass a broad view of what is important to measure in order to meet the evaluation objectives. Therefore, an evaluation strategy can also include:

✓ Benchmarking the comparison of one's own practices against identified best practices to identify opportunities for improvement.

✓ Completion of an audit against a solution or training program to ensure a process was followed or preestablished criteria were met.

✓ Peer analysis whereby peers use agreed-upon criteria to evaluate others' work or results to identify strengths and opportunities for improvement.

✓ Subject matter experts observing or reviewing results to ensure credibility and accuracy.

✓ Completion of a cause and effect impact analysis using leading indicators to predict or validate lagging indicators.

✓ Establishing criteria and measuring the extent to which an individual is meeting the criteria for certification.

✓ Using preestablished standards (Standard Analysis) to act as guidelines for performance.

There are a variety of different approaches that can be used to provide information regarding the performance impact or areas of improvement for programs, solutions and interventions or departments as a whole.

EVALUATION PROCESS

Establishing a process to develop an evaluation strategy will ensure that timely, cost-efficient, and consistent methods are used to define the evaluation components most useful in an organization's culture.

The following process is recommended for determining the components that should be included in an evaluation of knowledge management or the effectiveness of a learning solution.

Step 1: Determine the business need and the objectives of the evaluation strategy.

Step 2: Align the business worthiness of the evaluation strategy with the organization's goals.

Step 3: Determine the mechanics of the evaluation strategy.

Step 4: Determine the resources needed.

Step 5: Define the implementation plan.

Step 6: Pilot the methods, tools, or process.

Step 7: Define maintenance triggers.

The remainder of this guide focuses on these seven steps and provides tools to more clearly define the activities involved in the process.

Step 1—Determine the Business Need

In this step, the business need is identified (from the big picture viewpoint). Then evaluation strategy objectives are defined (the outcome of the evaluation itself). Each stakeholder may have a different need for the evaluation strategy and these needs drive the evaluation tactics, methods, and tools that should be developed. Therefore, key business information must be determined prior to kicking off an evaluation strategy.

Tool 1 is provided to assist in determining the questions to ask key stakeholders regarding the evaluation strategy. Each question in the tool relates to a component of the Strategy Implementation Plan (which is defined in Step 5) listed in the second column.

The next step in the process is to synthesize the information gathered in Step 1 and align the evaluation objectives with the business objectives to ensure congruence.

Step 2—Align the Business Worthiness of the Evaluation Strategy

During Step 2, the information regarding mission or purpose and the key measures are analyzed and matched against the organization's business drivers (organization in this context may be at a corporate, department, or team level, or at all levels). Examples of typical business drivers that an evaluation strategy may align with include:

- *Market or Customer Drivers.* Changes in customer demographics, definition, and needs that place demand on products or change product design. Increased competition or other changes in how the organization views the marketplace in which it competes.

- *Technology Drivers.* New innovation and technology that creates opportunities or needs for change in information keeping and processing.

- *Change in System, Process, or Key Policy Drivers.* Changes in work processes, systems, or key policies that change employee skill or behavior requirements.

- *Shareholder or Financial Drivers.* Responses to Wall Street or bank demands for higher profits or lower costs reflected on the balance sheet.

Tool 1—Key Stakeholder Questions

Question	Question's Relation to Evaluation Strategy
1. What do you see as the purpose of the evaluation strategy?	Mission/Purpose
2. What business objectives are most likely to be impacted by the program(s) or solution(s) to be evaluated?	Mission/Purpose
3. What value would evaluation provide to the business if it supplied the needed information?	Mission/Purpose
4. What information gained from the evaluation would be of "value"? How would it bevaluable to you or how would you use this information?	Mission/Purpose Key Measures Evaluation Tools
5. What are the key quality indicators that should be part of the evaluation strategy (competitive advantage, best-in-class, improvement against baseline, etc.)?	Key Measures Evaluation Tools
6. What information do you use today that could be enriched by a more comprehensive approach to evaluation? How would it be enriched?	Key Measures Evaluation Tools
7. What information is missing from the methods and tools being used today?	Key Measures Evaluation Tools
8. From your viewpoint, what are the objectives of the evaluation strategy?	Mission/Purpose
9. From your viewpoint, what should *not* be part of the evaluation strategy?	Mission/Purpose
10. From your viewpoint, what methods, processes, or information gathering techniques have been especially successful in the company's environment today? Why?	Evaluation Tools
11. What has not been successful in the past? Why?	Evaluation Tools
12. How will the data from the evaluation strategy be used?	Key Measures
13. Who will own the evaluation system that is identified in the strategy?	Roles & Accountabilities
14. Who will be responsible for what components (data collection, reporting, managing, etc.)?	Roles & Accountabilities
15. Who are the key players in the evaluation strategy, implementation, and pilot?	Roles & Accountabilities
16. Who should own the data?	Roles & Accountabilities
17. Who should have access to this data? How?	Roles & Accountabilities
18. What tools do you think would be appropriate for the external evaluation – client survey, focus group surveys, learner surveys, instructor surveys, or other tools?	Evaluation Tools
19. What tools do you think would be appropriate for the internal evaluation – peer assessment, certifications, benchmarking?	Evaluation Tools
20. Is there an automated system that the data collected via these tools will need to reside on or be integrated with?	Evaluation Tools

The level of evaluation is determined as part of the alignment process. Tool 2 is recommended for use when deciding if evaluation of a learning solution should take place and at what level. Each decision criterion relates to one of the four levels of evaluation and its alignment with the business objectives. Read each criterion and determine whether or not the information for the course is key to long- or short-term business goals. If the majority of items for each level are answered with "yes," that measurement level should be considered for the learning solution.

Tool 2—Determining the Business Worthiness of the Evaluation Strategy

LEVEL	DECISION CRITERIA	YES/NO
1. Reaction or Customer	Is it important to gather opinions regarding content usefulness, instructor ability, timing, and other factors regarding this learning solution to support continuous improvement objectives of the organization?	
	Is the course brand new? Should customer reaction be collected for at least a short period of time to support customer satisfaction?	
	Is there some potential problem with the course that needs to be monitored (instructor, facility, delivery method, etc.)?	
2. Learning	Is it critical that the individual learn the content in the course (safety requirements, governmental requirements, job performance, certification, etc.)?	
	Is it politically important to demonstrate that there has been knowledge acquisition or skill development as a result of the solution?	
	Is it important to determine how effective the learning solution was (for example, a new delivery method is being used)?	
	Is it important to determine what has *not* been learned for another intervention (coaching, other coursework, etc.)?	
	Is it important to capture objectives or content that most of the participants are either gaining or missing as a result of this course (for example, effectiveness of particular content, need for follow-up module, effectiveness of a guest instructor for Module 3)?	
3. Business	Was the launch of this learning solution based on the business results it would provide?	
	Is it important to determine *what* in the work environment is a barrier to the transfer?	
	Is it important to determine what skills, knowledge, or behavior changes have *not* occurred?	
	Is it of value to management to determine whether what has been taught is being used?	
	Is it important to determine the *degree* of skill or knowledge transfer?	
4. Financial	Is this solution critical to the of business and will the results be valued by management, therefore justifying the time and expense by a required Level 4 evaluation?	
	Is the cost of delivery method or the solution high?	
	Is it important to determine which skills or knowledge taught have the biggest payoff in results?	
	Is this program a pilot that will be far-reaching, and therefore are financial results required for implementation?	

Once the objectives and process have been identified, the tools and methods can be selected. This is done in Step 3.

Tool 3—Data Collection Identification

LEVEL	DATA NEEDED	POTENTIAL APPROACH	EFFECTIVENESS MEASURED
1.	Student's overall impression of the learning solution Is the individual confident with what was learned via the solution so that she or he believes it is possible to apply it back on the job? The effectiveness measured at this level is perception-based. Does the individual perceive the learning solution to be effective?	Survey Interviews Attitudinal Survey Confidence Rating	1. Did the learning solution meet the individual's expectations? 2. Are the format, content, and delivery method effective? 1. Did the learning solution provide content and practice time to enhance an individual's confidence in his or her skill? 2. Does the course promote assurance in one's ability or knowledge?
2.	Did the individual acquire new knowledge or skill from the learning solution? The effectiveness measured at this level is learning-acquired. Was the learning solution effective in transferring learning to the individual? Was learning in a skill or knowledge base increased?	Pre- and post-assessment for knowledge development (increase in knowledge level) Pre- and post-observation of skill development (increase in skill level) (To identify the effectiveness of learning, a baseline of knowledge and skill must be established.)	1. Were the learning activities provided in the learning solution conducive to acquiring skills or content? 2. Was the content that was delivered accurate? 3. Were there barriers to learning and if so, what were the barriers?
3.	Can the individual apply what was learned on the job? The effectiveness measured at this level is whether, as a result of the learning solution, the individual is more effective back on the job.	Pre- and post-intervention job-related measures that track job performance (increased productivity, decreased error rate, increased idea generation, etc.)	1. Were the learning activities provided in the learning solution conducive to transferring skills or knowledge back to the job? 2. Did the individual gain too much information, too little information, or just the right amount to apply back on the job? 3. Has the individual's performance improved as a result of the learning solution? 4. Were there barriers to transferring the learning and if so, what were the barriers?
4.	As a result of using the knowledge or skill acquired in the solution, did the desired business impact occur? The effectiveness measured at this level is the actual business result or impact on the business itself.	Pre- and post-intervention financial and nonfinancial related measures that track business results (ROI, decrease in inventory levels, decrease in time to market, cost decreases)	1. Were the desired business objectives met as a result of transferring what was learned? 2. Did the actions the individual deployed as a result of the learning solution affect the business environment as predicted? 3. If the business indicators did not change, was that a result of the learning solution or were other barriers present?

Step 3—Determine the Mechanics of the Evaluation Strategy

During Step 3, the types of methods, tools, and processes to be used to conduct the evaluation are identified; for example, an assessment, an observation checklist, collection of baseline data, determination of best practices. Tool 3 demonstrates the relationship between various evaluation components and the levels of evaluation information desired.

When the methods and tools have been chosen, resource requirements can be determined in Step 4.

Step 4—Determine the Resources Needed

In Step 4, it is time to determine what resources will be needed to conduct the evaluation using the tools defined in Step 3. In this step, it is determined if there are budget requirements or human resource requirements, or if other departments need to be involved (for example, Information Services, to build a Web page). Developing a budget for evaluation may be part of this step. Tool 4 provides a list of resources that may need to be deployed to support evaluation.

Once the business purpose, mechanics, and resources have been identified, it is time to determine how the Evaluation Strategy will be implemented.

Step 5—Define the Implementation Plan

In Step 5, what has been decided upon in steps 1 through 4 is documented, and how the evaluation methods and tools will be implemented is determined and published. At this point, the communication plan, the resources needed, the timeline, and the milestones for implementing the tools, methods, or processes are identified and documented.

An outline of the implementation plan for an evaluation strategy is provided in Tool 5.

Once the implementation plan has been created, developing a pilot of the tools, methods, and processes of the evaluation strategy is the next step.

Step 6—Pilot the Methods, Tools, or Process

By using a trial audience to determine if the evaluation tools, methods, or process identified in the strategy will meet the goals and provide the data required, the risk associated with evaluation can be limited.

Prior to implementing the entire plan, it is important to ensure that the tools, methods, and processes that have been created actually provide the evaluation data that is required. The pilot also targets

Tool 4—Potential Resources for Evaluations

TYPE OF RESOURCE	PURPOSE OF RESOURCE
Human Resource	• Project leader or manager for the evaluation program itself. This may be the individual who owns the program(s), department, or component. This individual is responsible for identifying the components to be measured. • The evaluator. It is suggested that this person not be the individual who is responsible for the components being measured, as the results may be biased. This person is responsible for tool design (or modification), implementation, analysis, reporting, and recommendations. • Stakeholders also have a role. They will receive the report and determine what actions will be undertaken.
System Requirements	• This is the system(s) that will be used to collect, analyze, and report the information. There may be a need for several systems, such as a survey writer and reporter, a data spreadsheet tool (such as Excel) and a database management tool.
Technology Resource Requirements	• New technology may be used for the data collection or reporting, such as a Web page or a chat room. Resources outside of actual equipment or software are identified here.
Budget Requirements	• The budget requirements for the evaluation should be identified or estimated. A typical evaluation project (from design to implementation) costs between $25,000 and $50,000, depending on the complexity. A project is defined as a specific component, such as benchmarking or measuring Level 3 results of a learning solution.
Capital Expense Requirements	• If any capital expense requirements are necessary, they should be identified here. An example of this is the need to purchase new computers.
Interface or Other Process Owner	• Other process or interface owners and their time requirements need to be identified. Other process owners typically included are: managers of participants, participants in the learning solution, instructors, financial analysts, accountants, etc.

where the methods, tools, and processes may need to be tweaked. In some cases, the pilot can also be used to provide initial measurement data that can influence others to jump on the evaluation bandwagon.

Once the final methods, tools, and processes have been implemented and are in place, it is time to plan how to maintain the evaluation strategy and, in a sense, begin the process all over again!

Step 7—Define Maintenance Triggers

As with anything else, if an evaluation strategy is not kept up to date with the business, it soon will not provide the data and information needed. The final step in the evaluation strategy is to identify the triggers that will initiate the need to change the tools, methods, or processes. Tool 6 will help you identify events that may trigger the need for evaluation strategy maintenance.

Evaluation Strategy Implementation Plan Components

Mission/Purpose Definition
* The primary organizational needs the evaluation will fill (no more than 5).
* How the evaluation strategy will support these needs (technologies, process, tools).
* The primary focus of the evaluation strategy.
* The core competencies the evaluation strategy supports for the organization as a whole.
* The goals of the evaluation strategy.
* The organization's evaluation philosophy and its importance to its final deliverables.

Key Measures/Metrics/Result Indicators
* The key metrics for the organization that will be gathered and reported through the evaluation system, including knowledge gain, customer satisfaction, ROI for the customer, etc.
* The measures that will determine the value of the evaluation system itself, including use of data, number of process improvements identified as a result of the data, etc.

Evaluation Structure/Scope/Definition
* What the evaluation system will include: What products, services, and deliverables will be considered part of the evaluation system? What levels will be included in the evaluation system? How will the organization determine what program to evaluate at what level? At what frequency will each level be used? What standards will be used at each level?
* What elements will be included in each level?
* Who will make the decision about the components that will be included in the evaluation strategy (benchmarking, Levels 1 to 4, etc.)?
* What activities, technologies, or processes will be part of the evaluation strategy?
* Who are the customers of the evaluation strategy?

Integration with Other Processes
* The processes that will be included in the evaluation strategy data gathering and reporting.
* How the processes will be integrated.
* The methods and processes used to gather data for the strategy.
* The information that will be captured in each process (Level 1 survey vs. Level 2 test).
* The analysis and reporting requirements for the process.
* Any dependencies for integration.

Roles and Accountabilities
* Who is responsible for what components?
* Who are the key players?
* Who are the stakeholders?
* What are the roles (evaluation owner, project leader, data provider, partner, user, customer, consultant)?

* What are the responsibilities and accountabilities for each role?
* Who owns the data?
* What data can be accessed and by whom?
* Do different levels of evaluation have different owners?

Evaluation Tools/Systems/Processes

* A clear definition of what is and what is not included in the evaluation strategy.
* Prototypes, process flows, and design requirements for each of the levels and functions that will be supported by the evaluation strategy (such as instructor evaluation).

Reporting Requirements

* Identification of each standard report, its contents, and its distribution.
* The data available through reporting, how the data is collected, the data source, any potential data bias.
* Collection and reporting of quantitative versus qualitative data (comments).
* System requirements for reporting (ad hoc, etc.).
* Data requirements for reporting.
* Distribution requirements.

Resource Requirements

* Human resources requirements.
* System resources requirements.
* Technology resources requirements.
* Budget requirements.
* Capital expense requirements.
* Other requirements.

Maintenance Plan

* The owner of the maintenance plan.
* Frequency of review for maintenance.
* Events that will trigger maintenance needs.
* How maintenance will be budgeted and managed.

Communication Plan

* The owner of communication of the evaluation strategy.
* The methods for communicating the strategy.
* The audience(s) for communication.
* Ongoing communication needs or communication points.

These questions can be modified or added to depending on the purpose of the evaluation strategy. Once the original information is gathered, you are ready to begin planning the strategy.

Tool 6—Identifying Maintenance Triggers

EVALUATION STRATEGY QUESTIONS	POTENTIAL TRIGGER
What key changes to the business goals might impact the evaluation strategy (change in competition, products, customers, economy)?	
How likely is it that change will occur in the methods, tools, or processes currently in place to deliver performance solutions? (Emphasis shifting from classroom to Web-based training, for example.)	
How stable is the organization? (Are reorganization, large management shift, merger, acquisitions, etc. likely?)	
Will new information become available that would be important to include in the data being used for evaluation? (For example, updated bench-marking statistics, new data-gathering system such as SAP that makes new learner information available, change in financial reporting.)	
What is the likelihood that organizational metrics may change? (Errors counted differently, new equipment that eliminates scrap, etc.)	

CONCLUSION

In today's business environment, gathering information that will be truly useful for making business decisions is critical. An evaluation strategy can be developed quickly and can provide the structure necessary for designing methods and tools to gather crucial information. An evaluation strategy provides information that proves the effectiveness and value of training programs and performance solutions and can be used for long-term planning. When an evaluation strategy is aligned with the key business strategies and performance needs, commitment is gained and management recognizes the value you bring to the organization.

REFERENCES

1. Bennis, W., *Organizing Genius*. Reading, MA: Addison-Wesley, 1997.

2. Edventure Holdings at http://www.edventure.com

3. Edvinsson, I. and Malone, M. *Intellectual Capital*. New York: HarperCollins, 1997.

4. Evans, P. and Wurster, T., "Strategy and the New Economics of Information." *Harvard Business Review*. September-October 1997.

5. *Forbes* Magazine at http://forbes.com

6. Hagel, J. and Armstrong, A. *Net Gain*. Boston: Harvard Business Press, 1997.

7. Kaplan, R. and Norton, D., *The Balanced Scorecard*. Boston: Harvard Business Press, 1996.

8. Lev, B., "The Old Rules No Longer Apply." *Forbes ASAP*, April 7, 1997.

9. Stewart, T., *Intellectual Capital: The New Wealth of Organizations*. New York: Doubleday, 1997.

10. Thurow, L., "Needed: A New System of Intellectual Property Rights." *Harvard Business Review,* September-October 1997.

27

HOW TO MOVE A TEAM FROM STAGE TO STAGE

Phil Lohr and Patricia Steege

Overview   Teams, like individuals, progress through various stages in their life cycles. Each stage of development holds its own unique relationships and demonstrated behaviors. The stages of team development must be understood by team members and leaders in order to recognize the signals that indicate normal team growth and development. Furthermore, the degree to which the leader interacts with the team varies from stage to stage. The combined efforts of leaders and team members to appropriately nurture the team will increase the probability of the team remaining intact and reaching its full potential.

Use the following guide to help a team identify which stage it is at and what team needs and leadership styles are most appropriate for maintaining it or progressing to a new stage.

Contact Information: Phil Lohr, Bristol-Myers Squibb, P.O. Box 5400, Princeton, NJ 08543, 609-818-3589, philip.lohr@bms.com

Patricia Steege, Unisys, Township Line and Union Meeting Rds., P.O. Box 500, Blue Bell, PA 19424, trsteege@worldnet.att.net, 215-986-5659

STAGES OF TEAM DEVELOPMENT

Forming

The initial forming stage is the process of putting the structure of the team together. Team members enter with ambiguous feelings and attitudes. Conflict is avoided at all costs because of the need to be accepted into the group. Team members reflect not only on the tasks at hand, but also about each other.

Feelings and Thoughts	Observable Behaviors	Team Needs	Leadership Style Required
Excitement, anticipation, and optimism	Politeness	Team mission and purpose	**Directing:**
	Guarded; watchful		Telling
Suspicion, fear, and anxiety about the job ahead	Sporadic participation	Team membership	Guiding
	First agreements	Team goals and objectives	Establishing
Pride in being chosen for the group	Attempts to define tasks and decisions on how it will be accomplished	Measurement and feedback	High task and low relationship involvement
Tentative attachment to team	Attempts to establish acceptable group behavior	Definition of roles and responsibilities	Manager makes decisions, tells group what to do, when, where, how, with whom to do it
Why am I here?	Abstract discussions of concepts and issues	Team member expectations	
Why are they here?		Team operational guidelines and procedures	Clear boundaries
What is expected of me?	Discussion of symptoms and problems not relevant to the task; difficulty in identifying relevant problems	Behavioral norms and values	One-way communication from leader to follower
How much influence will I have?		Effective meetings and facilitation	
How much am I willing to give?	Complaints about the organization		
	Decisions on what information needs to be gathered		
	Impatience with discussion		

Storming

This stage is characterized by competition and conflict among team members. In the process of organizing tasks, interpersonal conflicts will begin to surface. Leadership, structure, and power issues dominate. The team must grow from this testing mindset to one of problem solving in order to progress in its development.

Feelings and Thoughts	Observable Behaviors	Team Needs	Leadership Style Required
Resistance to task	Arguing among members	Interpersonal relationships	**Coaching:**
Fluctuations in attitude about the team	Defensiveness and competition	Identification of style differences	Provides guidance
What are the job-related risks and benefits of sharing information?	Polarizations and pecking orders in team	Effective listening	Clarifying
	Power struggles and clashes	Giving and receiving feedback	Persuading
What are the risks and benefits of being open or closed?	Lack of consensus-seeking behaviors	Conflict resolution	Explaining
Do I agree with the team's purpose?	Lack of progress	Leadership clarification	High directing and supporting behavior
Do I agree with the team's approach to accomplishing the task?	Establishing unrealistic goals	What position does the team take when people don't get along?	High task and high relationship involvement
How do I feel about my personal influence and freedom in the team?	Concern over excessive work	How should the team deal with violation of codes of conduct?	Leader consults but makes final decision
	Attacking the leader	What should we do if team gets stuck?	
	Confusion, loss of interest; opting out		
	Code-of-conduct violations		
	Poor attendance		
	Questioning wisdom of other members of the team		

Norming

In this stage, team members are breaking from paradigms of preconceived ideas and opinions. As the group develops cohesion, leadership is shared and team members are trusting one another. Interpersonal conflicts give way to sharing of feelings and creative thinking. The group operates in cohesion and members are glad to be a part of the team.

Feelings and Thoughts	Observable Behaviors	Team Needs	Leadership Style Required
Sense of belonging to team	Procedures established and practiced in problem solving, leadership, resolving conflict	Decision making	**Supporting:**
Personal accomplishments		Problem solving	Committing
I understand how I contribute effectively	Open, honest communication; practicing communication skills	Management coaching	Participating
I have freedom to be myself and express my ideas	Effective conflict resolution	Leadership skills	Encouraging
I can trust my teammates and they trust me	Sincere attempts to achieve consensus decisions		Listening
Ability to express criticism constructively	Free participation and risk taking		Collaborating
Acceptance of membership in the team	Productive; steady progress		High relationship and low task involvement
Relief that it seems that everything is going to work out	Shared decision making		Minimal influence in decision making
	Develop routines		Promotes discussion
	Unified mission and purpose		Asks for contributions from followers
	Focused problem solving		
	Sets and achieves task milestones		
	Members honoring code of conduct		
	Strong team identity		
	Healthy balance of power		

Performing

True interdependence is the mainstay of this stage of group development. The team is highly flexible as individuals adapt to meet the current needs of the team. There is high productivity in task and personal relationships. A team operating in this mode is unique and a value added to its organization.

Feelings and Thoughts	Observable Behaviors	Team Needs	Leadership Style Required
High commitment	Constructive self-change	Coaching and counseling	**Delegation:**
Trusting; friendships	Flexibility, versatility, and midcourse corrections	Measuring performance	Observing
Fun and excited		Customer focus	Monitoring
High personal development and creativity	Tries new way of doing things		Fulfilling
Involvement with team inspires the best in me	Excited participation, enthusiasm, and volunteerism		Low relationship and low task involvement
Understand other's strengths and weaknesses	Attachment to team, connectedness and unity		Provides little direction
	High level of mutual support		Leader sets goals; team accomplishes
	Humor		Low amounts of two-way communication needed
	Satisfaction at team's progress; celebrating successes		
	Expressions of pride in team's unique accomplishments		
	Ability to work through group problems; confronting with support		
	Ownership of results		
	True consensus decision making		
	Management and creative use of team's resources		
	Momentum maintained		
	Smooth task and process flow		
	Purpose and mission basis for action		
	Goal attainment		

REFERENCES

Hersey, P. 1984. *The Situational Leader.* New York: Warner Books, Inc.

Tuckman, B. W. and M. A. C. Jensen. 1977. Stages of small-group development revisted. *Group and Organization Studies,* December, 419–427.

28

HOW TO IMPLEMENT PERFORMANCE IMPROVEMENT STEP-BY-STEP

Anne Marrelli

Overview   Improving performance within an organization requires careful planning and a methodical approach. The time your client invests in planning and implementing a well-designed improvement process will be richly rewarded with gains in productivity, quality, efficiency, revenue, or cost savings.

The performance improvement process includes six phases:

1. Identify the areas to improve.

2. Analyze performance improvement needs.

3. Design interventions to produce the needed improvements.

4. Develop the interventions.

5. Implement the interventions.

6. Evaluate and sustain the interventions.

This guide outlines the six phases of the process and details the steps for successfully implementing a performance improvement process.

PHASE ONE: IDENTIFY THE AREA FOR PERFORMANCE IMPROVEMENT

In the first phase of the performance improvement process, you will identify the specific improvement need, you will focus on and work with stakeholders to create a project plan.

1. Identify the area you will improve. In any organization, there are many areas that could be improved, but you need to focus your

Contact Information: American Express, 3 World Financial Center, Mail Drop 32-14, New York, NY 10285, 212-640-1974, anne:f.marrelli@aexp.com

improvement effort on a specific procedure, process, system of several processes, work role, work group within a function, function, or operation.

2. Obtain the support of executives and senior managers. Before you embark on a performance improvement effort, it is essential that you secure sponsorship of the organization's leaders. They will need to actively champion the project and provide resources and influence.

3. Communicate the purpose of the performance improvement project to stakeholders. Talk with members of affected work groups, leaders, customers of the work group, and others as appropriate, and enlist their support and help. Emphasize the benefits they will derive from the improvement effort. From this point on, communication with all stakeholders will be a continuing feature of the performance improvement process. As you make progress in each phase described here, you will communicate this progress as well as expectations for the next phase to stakeholders.

4. Work with stakeholders to develop a project plan. Include these elements in your plan:

    ✓ roles, responsibilities, time constraints, and expertise of the people who will participate in the project

    ✓ project tasks and deliverables

    ✓ deadlines and schedules

    ✓ funds available and any restrictions on these funds

    ✓ information already available and its reliability and validity

    ✓ resources available for use in the project

    ✓ potential risks and pitfalls

5. Train everyone who will be participating in the improvement process. Be sure all persons working on the improvement process, including support staff, understand the objectives of the process and their individual roles in it. Provide detailed training as needed for those assisting in collecting or recording data.

PHASE TWO: ANALYZE PERFORMANCE IMPROVEMENT NEEDS

In the second phase of the performance improvement process, you will compare current performance with desired performance in the area of focus and establish specific improvement objectives.

1. Describe current performance.
   a. To understand current performance in the target area:
      - ✓ Become familiar with terminology and tools, reference manuals, and training materials.
      - ✓ Map the current procedures and processes as appropriate.
      - ✓ Define the current organization of the relevant work group, their work roles and responsibilities, and the relationship of the target area to other work groups, processes, and procedures in the organization.
      - ✓ Identify environmental and organizational constraints on current performance such as regulations, resources, available talent pool, competitors, organizational structure and culture, etc.
   b. Meet with employees and leaders to discuss:
      - ✓ How are we meeting our customers' needs today?
      - ✓ What products and services are we providing?
      - ✓ What value are we adding to the organization?
      - ✓ What processes are we using to accomplish work?
   c. Measure current work accomplishments, when appropriate, to provide a baseline for later comparisons.

2. Define desired performance.
   a. Work with leaders to articulate how the goals, strategies, and objectives of the business are connected to the target area.
   b. Work with staff and leaders and collect data from customers to answer these questions:
      - ✓ Who are our customers?
      - ✓ What do our customers like and not like about what we are providing now?
      - ✓ What do our customers need and expect from us?
      - ✓ How are our customers measuring or evaluating our products and services?
      - ✓ Why do our customers want our products and services?
      - ✓ How can we help our customers serve their customers?
      - ✓ How can we improve our work?

3. Determine the causes of the performance problems (discrepancies between desired and actual accomplishments).

a. Examine each of the elements of effective work performance: Information, Environment and Tools, Competency, and Motivation. Ineffective job performance can be traced to the absence or inadequacy of one or more of these elements. (Please see the Performance Analysis Model following the last step of this process for more detail.)

b. If exemplary performers can be identified, compare their accomplishments and work behaviors with those of typical performers.

c. Use these tools to collect data:

   ✓ Observations

   ✓ Interviews

   ✓ Focus Groups

   ✓ Surveys

   ✓ Process maps

   ✓ Knowledge maps (identify tasks required to accomplish work, and the information needed and produced during each task)

   ✓ Performance support maps (identify the support and resources needed for specific tasks or decisions)

4. Estimate the cost of the performance problem in dissatisfied or underserved customers and wasted time, resources, and opportunities.

5. Estimate the improvement potential for the target area. Decide whether the benefits of the expected improvements will outweigh the costs of improving performance. In most, but not all, cases, they will. If so, proceed with the performance improvement process. If not, terminate the process for the target area.

PHASE THREE: DESIGN INTERVENTIONS

In Phase Three of the performance improvement process, you will define specific objectives for improvement, describe the requirements for the interventions to achieve the desired improvements, and select and design the intervention most likely to be effective and sustainable within your organization.

1. Define specific objectives for performance improvement. Each objective must meet these criteria:

   ✓ Describes the desired result in explicit, measurable terms.

   ✓ States any qualifying conditions.

   ✓ Specifies the standards for acceptable performance.

   ✓ Is meaningful, i.e., an important benefit is to be gained if the objective is achieved.

2. Define specifications for the interventions to achieve the defined objectives.

   a. Solicit requirements from stakeholders including sponsors, leaders, employees, and technical experts.

   b. Research the applicable literature and collect benchmark data, when appropriate.

   c. Prioritize requirements.

3. Describe effective and efficient interventions for the identified problem that meet the defined specifications. (Please see the table of Performance Improvement Interventions at the conclusion of this article.)

4. Estimate the design, development, and implementation requirements of each appropriate intervention.

5. Select the interventions most likely to be effective and sustainable within environmental constraints including:

   ✓ Organizational culture, values, and history,

   ✓ Likely acceptance of and support for the intervention,

   ✓ Organizational and individual capabilities,

   ✓ Practicality,

   ✓ Cost, and

   ✓ Time.

Note: Because most performance problems are complex and multidimensional, a combination of interventions is usually required to solve the problems. For example, improving performance in a single functional area may require revising selection criteria for work role incumbents, creating job aids, and revising the work process and policies.

6. Design (or select for purchase) the interventions in accordance with the defined specifications.

   a. Create detailed specifications.

b. Prepare the design.

c. Document the design and obtain stakeholder approval.

d. Revise the design as needed.

PHASE FOUR: DEVELOP THE INTERVENTIONS

In Phase Four of the performance improvement process, you will develop and test the interventions you designed in Phase Three.

1. Develop the interventions and the support mechanisms required to ensure their sustainability. In many cases, you will need to develop job aids, training, procedures manuals, help lines, coaching programs, or other support products and processes to assist people in implementing and sustaining the intervention.

2. Pilot test the interventions. Pilot testing is a crucial task in developing interventions. You cannot assume that an intervention, no matter how well designed, will work in your particular environment.

3. Revise the interventions as needed. Pilot testing will highlight the components of the interventions that require revision.

4. Produce the interventions and support mechanisms.

PHASE FIVE: IMPLEMENT THE INTERVENTIONS

In the fifth phase of the performance improvement process, you will communicate the planned changes, initiate the training or other support needed before the intervention can be implemented, and begin the interventions.

1. Communicate to all stakeholders the implementation schedule and the changes it will bring. This communication is a continuation of the information you have been sharing with stakeholders about the progress of the improvement effort. Full and widespread communication is especially important, however, as you are ready to implement the interventions. Create a process for people to ask questions and have them answered so that everyone is comfortable with the planned interventions before they are implemented.

2. Provide training or other support mechanisms as needed before implementation. Preparing people for the new interventions is a

crucial element of the entire process. If the people who will implement the changes are not fully prepared through changes in incentive programs, policy and practice changes, training, supervision, job aids, or other needed supports, all the work you have invested thus far can be wasted.

3. Implement the interventions. As you implement the interventions, remember you may have to move slowly for people to become comfortable with and accepting of the changes. The support mechanisms you designed must be carefully deployed. Expect objections and questions and be prepared to answer them. Also allow time to resolve problems that were not apparent in the small-scale pilot test.

PHASE SIX: EVALUATE AND SUSTAIN THE INTERVENTIONS

In the last phase of the performance improvement process, you will evaluate the effectiveness of the interventions and work to ensure their success.

1. Evaluate the effectiveness of the interventions in achieving the objectives specified in Phase Three. Your key focus in evaluating the interventions is on how well they are achieving the defined objectives, not on how popular the interventions are.

2. Revise the interventions as needed and evaluate the revisions. Most interventions will require some revisions. Make these as soon as possible to gain the full benefit from your improvement effort.

3. Sustain the full effectiveness of the interventions over time. You will need to continuously monitor the interventions to ensure their effectiveness is maintained. Changes in the work environment over time may require changes in the interventions. Also, it is possible that after an initial enthusiasm for the new interventions, people may return to former work habits. To avoid a relapse to the former routine, you may need to implement periodic refresher training, group meetings to discuss progress and problems with the new interventions, supplementary job aids, and so on.

PERFORMANCE ANALYSIS MODEL

Performance improvement needs can be identified by examining each of the four elements of effective work performance: Information, Environment and Tools, Competency, and Motivation. Ineffective job performance can be traced to the absence or inadequacy of one or more of these elements at the Individual, Process, Work Group, Business Unit, or Enterprise levels. The table below lists examples of components of these four elements.

Information	Environment and tools	Competency	Motivation
Business strategy	Organizational structure	Knowledge	Emotional perceptions
Goals	Culture/Values	Skills	Career stage
Objectives	Management	Abilities	Life Stage
Accountability	Coworkers	Behaviors	Consequences to performer
Policies	Support staff	Values	Prerequisites
Job Design	Expert systems	Attitudes	Appraisal system
Schedules	Reference materials	Selection criteria	Promotional system
Performance standards	Job aids	Authority	Compensation
Measurement	Computer systems	Training	Monetary incentives
Feedback	Software	Learning opportunities	Nonmonetary incentives
Assignment parameters	Voice mail	Professional affiliations	Expectations
Project history	E-mail	Keeping up with one's discipline	Recognition
Reference materials	Funds	Access to the right people	Visibility
Handbooks	Processes and methods	Opportunity to apply training	Peer pressure
Regulations	Workload		Job titles
Internal communications	Temperature		Challenge
Workflow	Light		
Meetings	Air quality		
	Office layout (private, cubicles, open designs)		Interesting, meaningful work
Legislation	Location		Recruitment to match reality
	Supplies and materials		Career path
	Equipment		Work preferences
	Workstation ergonomics		Inspirational leadership
	Hand tools		Work group/ team ties
	Safety hazards		Amount/rate of change

PERFORMANCE IMPROVEMENT INTERVENTIONS

Sample interventions that may be implemented to improve work performance are organized in the table below according to the elements of performance they are designed to improve. The range of possible interventions is almost limitless.

Information	Environment and tools	Competency	Motivation
Identify goals and objectives	Use conflict management tools	Revise selection criteria	Redesign how employees are measured
Establish performance standards	Install new software	Provide training	Redesign compensation systems
Institute mesurement	Create job aids	Assess competency	Recognize employee contributions
Revise policies	Revise work process	Provide self-study programs	Make consequences personally meaningful
Document unwritten policies and practices	Provide new tools	Require participation in professional associations	Managers walk around work areas
Create a knowledge architechture	Upgrade equipment	Install certification programs	Team building
Provide continuous feedback	Change physical layout	Create employee development programs	Establish organization rituals
Hold manager-employee dialogs	Improve light, heat, air conditions	Reassign employees	
Assign accountability Create handbooks	Remove safety hazards	Provide needed authority	Tailor rewards to individuals
Hold more frequent or more efficient meetings	Reduce workload	Provide access to people	Provide more employee participation
Provide more written communication	Give employees more control over pace	Offer mentoring	Provide personal counseling
Hold open forums	Revise production schedule	Offer job rotation programs	Change job title Publish criteria for promotion
Begin cultural transmission programs	Employ flexible work schedules	Offer structured on the job training	Enforce negative consequences of poor performance
Share business strategy with employees	Change work flow	Allow safe practice	Allow employees to partially define their own jobs
Tell employees the truth	Provide more reference materials	Provide for transfer of learning	Revise performance management system
		Institute a knowledge management system	
Clarify functions and tasks	Install expert system		Allow employees to claim credit for their work
Change information reporting channels	Create more attractive environment	Allow employees to claim credit for their work	Create work-life balance
	Improve workstation ergonomics	Create work-life balance	

INTERVENTION ACTIVITIES TO INCREASE YOUR CLIENT'S EFFECTIVENESS

INTRODUCTION

In this section of *The Consultant's Toolkit*, you will find seventeen intervention activities to expand your clients' effectiveness. They are designed to:

- Introduce consultation topics.
- Practice skills.
- Promote attitude change.
- Increase knowledge.
- Stimulate discussion.

All the activities featured here are highly participatory. They were designed in the belief that learning and change best occur through *experience* and *reflection*. As opposed to preaching or lecturing, experiential activities place people directly within a concrete situation. Typically, participants are asked to solve a problem, complete an assignment, or communicate information. Often, the task can be quite challenging. Sometimes it can also be a great deal of fun. The bottom line, however, is that participants become active partners in the learning of new concepts or in the development of new ideas.

The experiences contained in the activities you are about to read can also be of two kinds: *simulated* and *real-world*. Although some may find them to be artificial, well-designed simulations can provide effective analogies to real-world experiences. They also have the advantage of being time-saving shortcuts to longer, drawn-out activities. Sometimes, of course, there is no substitute for real-world experience.

Activities that engage your clients in actual, ongoing work can serve as a powerful mechanism for change.

Experience by itself is not always "the best teacher." Reflecting on the experience, however, can yield wisdom and insight. You will find that the activities in this section contain helpful guidelines for reflection. Expect a generous selection of questions to process or debrief the actual activities.

All the activities have been written for ease of use. A concise overview of each activity is provided. You will be guided, step-by-step, through the activity instructions. All the necessary participant handouts are included. For your photocopying convenience, these handouts are on separate pages. Any materials you need to prepare in advance have been kept to a minimum. Special equipment or physical arrangements are seldom needed.

Best of all, the activities are designed so that you can easily modify or customize them to your specific requirements. Also, time allocations are readily adaptable. Furthermore, many of the activities are "frame exercises"... generic activities that can be used for many topics or subject matters. You will find it easy to plug in the content relevant to your team's circumstances.

As you conduct any of these activities, bear in mind that experiential activity is especially successful if you do a good job as facilitator. Here are some common mistakes people make facilitating experiential activities:

1. *Motivation:* Participants aren't invited to buy into the activity themselves or sold the benefits of joining in. Participants don't know what to expect during the exercise.

2. *Directions:* Instructions are lengthy and unclear. Participants cannot visualize what the facilitator expects from them.

3. *Group Process:* Subgroups are not composed effectively. Group formats are not changed to fit the requirements of each activity. Subgroups are left idle.

4. *Energy:* Activities move too slowly. Participants are sedentary. Activities are long or demanding when they need to be short or relaxed. Participants do not find the activity challenging.

5. *Processing:* Participants are confused or overwhelmed by the questions posed to them. There is a poor fit between the facilitator's questions and the goals of the activity. The facilitator shares his or her opinions before first hearing the participants' views.

To avoid the pitfalls, follow these steps:

I. Introduce the activity.
   1. Explain your objectives.
   2. Sell the benefits.
   3. Convey enthusiasm.
   4. Connect the activity to previous activities.
   5. Share personal feelings and express confidence in the participants.

II. Help participants know what they are expected to do.
   1. Speak slowly.
   2. Use visual backup.
   3. Define important terms.
   4. Demonstrate the activity.

III. Manage the group process.
   1. Form groups in a variety of ways.
   2. Vary the number of people in any activity based upon that exercise's specific requirements.
   3. Divide participants into teams before giving further directions.
   4. Give instructions separately to groups in a multipart activity.
   5. Keep people busy.
   6. Inform the subgroups about time frames.

IV. Keep participants involved.
   1. Keep the activity moving.
   2. Challenge the participants.
   3. Reinforce participants for their involvement in the activity.
   4. Build physical movement into the activity.

V. Get participants to reflect on the activity's implications.
   1. Ask relevant questions.
   2. Carefully structure the first processing experiences.
   3. Observe how participants are reacting to the group processing.
   4. Assist a subgroup that is having trouble processing an activity.
   5. Hold your own reactions until after hearing from participants.

29

PROBING TEAM ISSUES BEFORE THEY BECOME PROBLEMS

Brenda Gardner and Sharon Korth

Overview
Many quality teams and long-term task forces or committees struggle with similar issues over extended time periods. This exercise is designed to help such teams address many of the common events that occur in the beginning, in the middle, and near the end of a project. By participating in these case exercises, team members have the opportunity to deal with these issues proactively and to voice their concerns and attitudes in a nonthreatening, neutral environment. The exercise will also help teams develop a list of team norms that can help them monitor their own behaviors.

Suggested Time
40 to 50 minutes for each round of cases

Materials Needed
For each team member:

✓ A copy of Form A (for the first round at the beginning of the team's development), Form B (for the second round at some point after the fourth meeting or first month of the team's development), and Form C (for the third round after the midpoint of the team's life-cycle).

✓ For the third team meeting, a copy of the team norms developed at the second meeting of the team.

Procedure
1. As a facilitator for an intact team that is just forming, discuss with team members the value of discussing issues that oftentimes occur when teams have to work closely together in problem-solv-

Contact Information: Brenda S. Gardner, Xavier University, 3800 Victory Parkway, Cincinnati, OH 45207-6521, 513-745-4287, gardner@xu.edu
Sharon J. Korth, Xavier University, 513-745-4276, korth@xu.edu

ing, task, or ongoing advisory situations. Depending upon your objectives, you might want to provide them with an overview of a team development model such as Tuckman's (1965) "Forming, Norming, Storming, Performing," Francis & Young's (1992) "Testing, Infighting, Getting Organized, Mature Closeness," or Schutz's (1958) theory of group norms of "Inclusion, Control, Affection."

2. At the end of the first meeting, distribute Form A to each team member. Ask them to read the case and be prepared to discuss their responses to the questions for the next team meeting. Suggest that the issues raised in the case may not necessarily occur in their team but that discussing what reactions or solutions members have about the points raised in the case may help them learn about how members feel about these behaviors and situations. Reassure members that the cases are fictitious and were not written based upon any previous experience with a specific team in their organization or setting. Tell team members that this fictitious team will be followed through a lifecycle similar to theirs.

3. At the next meeting of the team, facilitate a discussion of the members' responses to the case questions. Depending upon the size of the team, you might want to break up the team into smaller teams of 4 to 6 members who can report back to the total team. During the discussion, be sure to steer comments away from members naming specific people in the organization who may exhibit similar behaviors. The goal of the discussion is for the team to air any concerns that they may have about teamwork and to develop a list of team norms that may be used throughout the team's lifecycle. Be sure to keep notes during the discussion so that you can facilitate discussion about team norms.

4. After the general discussion is over, ask members if you can summarize the issues the team discussed and their general consensus about the situations so that the team will have a list of norms that they can use to monitor their own behavior as their time together progresses. Post on a flip chart the major issues that may have surfaced:

Attendance
Consensus
Role Clarity
Minutes
Agenda
Conflict Management

Disruptive Behavior
Appropriate Leadership
Commitment
Goal Agreement & Clarity
Participation Patterns
Constructive Feedback Mechanisms
Achievement Orientation
Follow-Up Mechanisms
Problem-Solving Techniques
Decision-Making Techniques

Be sure that members agree with your summarization and understanding of how they perceive the situations. Volunteer to have the team norms typed and distributed at the next meeting. You might ask members if they'd like to have a large poster of the norms available at each of their meetings for reference and review.

5. At the next meeting of the team, distribute copies of the norms to all team members and leave time available to discuss any new thoughts/concerns that may have surfaced since the original discussion.

6. Depending upon how long the team will be in existence, distribute Form B to each team member at about the fourth team meeting (or after the first month) for discussion at the fifth team meeting. Remind members that the goal of the case is to help members voice concerns about how team norms are followed and how they suggest such situations be managed.

7. At the fifth team meeting, lead a discussion of the new issues that have surfaced in this case. Lead the discussion to a review of their team norms and how the case dealt with revisions/adjustments/observance of their own norms.

8. Depending again upon the length of the team's experience, distribute Form C to each team member after the midpoint of their time together or after the midpoint of a project they've been working on. Again, tell the team that this fictitious team has been dealing with a number of issues that may or may not have occurred in their own team and that the goal of following this case is to build a more effective and efficient team by addressing issues that commonly impede this process. Ask them to discuss their responses to the case and take the opportunity once again to review the team norms they developed/revised since the first team meeting.

Variations

✓ You might want to rewrite the cases to reflect common issues that occur in your client's organization. Don't make the cases too realistic, however, or members will think that you are identifying "problem" team members, not fictitious people. Examples of other common issues in organizations may be supervisor–subordinate roles in the team, changing deadlines, inappropriate membership, union–management relations, and individual versus team recognition or rewards.

✓ If the team has a major project it is working on, you might revise the cases to reflect milestones, and time the distribution and discussion of the cases according to these identified milestones.

✓ Instead of distributing the cases at the end of a meeting and having the team members discuss the questions at the next meeting, you could pass out the case, have the team read it, and have them discuss the case immediately.

✓ If the issue of changing membership (i.e., someone leaving the team due to promotion, leaving the organization, changed roles, etc.) will be part of the team, you might want to add this character to either Case B or Case C to substitute for Ambitious Ann:

Substitute Sam

____ 30-year-old male

____ 6 years' experience with the organization

____ has reported to Ambitious Ann for 3 years

____ is aware that Ann has played a leadership role with the team

____ concerned about how his facilitative style will be received by the team

____ feels much pressure to be successful

REFERENCES

Fisher, C. D., Shaw, J. B., and Ryder, P. (1994) Problems in project teams: An anticipatory case study. *Journal of Management Education, 18,* (3), 351–355.

Francis, D., and Young, D. (1992). *Improving Work Teams,* rev. ed., San Diego: Pfeiffer & Co.

Osgood, T. Forming, norming, storming & performing: A card sort exercise. In M. Silberman, ed., *The 1996 McGraw-Hill Team and Organization Development Sourcebook* (pp. 5–10). New York: McGraw-Hill.

Schutz, W. C. (1958) *FIRO: A Three-dimensional Theory of Interpersonal Behavior.* New York: Holt, Rinehart & Winston.

Tuckman, B. (1965) Developmental sequence in small teams. *Psychological Bulletin,* 63, 384–399.

CASE A   FORM A

Read over the case, answer the questions individually, and be prepared to discuss your responses with your team members.

The team in the following case is being formed and will be working together for an extended period of time. During this time, the team will have responsibility for certain decisions, recommendations, or products and must report to their sponsors as requested. The team members in the case are fictitious and were not written based on any previous team in your organization or setting. Although the issues raised in the case may not necessarily occur in your team, discussing reactions and possible solutions for the case team may help your team learn how members feel about certain behaviors and situations throughout your team's life cycle.

The team consists of:

Intuitive Ike

____ 35-year-old male

____ 2 years with this organization; owned and managed a small business for 10 years

____ likes thinking about the "big picture" and looking at connections between various organizational systems

____ very well read on leadership and interpersonal issues

____ gets bored with the details of projects

____ thinks that this team should meet after hours into the evening

____ works best under pressure from a close deadline

Planful Pat

____ 27-year-old female

____ 8 years of experience in this organization; recently promoted

____ feels anxious about the pressure that comes with her new position

____ likes handling the details of a project; likes to plan and organize things

____ favors completing work comfortably ahead of the deadline

____ prefers to meet often, during work hours, to make sure that things are getting done

____ cannot stay after hours without prior planning due to child care arrangements

Ambitious Ann

_____ 40-year-old female

_____ 10 years of work experience with this organization; 10 years elsewhere in a similar function

_____ often takes over the work of others to make sure that it meets her standards

_____ is not particularly concerned with "people issues"

_____ is impatient with people who do not make decisions quickly

_____ has excellent project management skills

_____ prefers to have lengthy meetings once a week, after work hours because it is more efficient

Supportive Sue

_____ 26-year-old female

_____ 3 years of experience with this organization

_____ feels honored to be a part of this team, with her limited work experience

_____ will do anything to help the team, especially behind-the-scene tasks

_____ very quiet in team meetings; reluctant to speak in front of large teams

_____ wants to make a good impression

_____ afraid to admit that she does not understand something

_____ uncomfortable with conflict; likes harmony

Political Paul

_____ 50-year-old male

_____ 25 years of experience in the organization

_____ hoping that being on this team will help him get the promotion he thinks he deserves

_____ wants to be involved in the roles that provide greater visibility in the organization

_____ overlooks his responsibilities to the team if something else would benefit him more

_____ his work experience gives him valuable information that will help the team succeed

_____ is reluctant to set a regular schedule for meeting; likes to call impromptu meetings when needed

Questions for Discussion

Case Team

1. What are the positive elements about this team that could help it be successful?

2. What issues are likely to limit the team's success?

3. What can the team do to get off to a strong start?

Your Team

1. How can you relate the issues of the case team to your current team?

2. What might your current team be able to do to enhance its ability to work together?

3. What are some norms that your team could develop that would help deal with these issues?

CASE B FORM B

Read over the case, answer the questions individually, and be prepared to discuss your responses with team members.

It is now about a month after the team was formed and the first big milestone is coming soon. Ambitious Ann has been acting as the informal leader of the team and Planful Pat has been scheduling the meetings and keeping minutes. When Supportive Sue offered to take a turn with the minutes, Ann quickly told her that Pat has been doing that task very well and will continue throughout the project.

Whenever the team seems close to a decision on an item, Intuitive Ike offers several other options which throws the team back to the beginning. Both Ike and Political Paul have expressed that they think the team spends too much time on details and not enough on strategic issues. Over the past month, Supportive Sue has been very quiet in meetings, rarely speaking. The one time she offered a suggestion, Ann told her that the decision had already been made.

Political Paul has missed several meetings. Sue contacted him to see if he was planning to come to the next meeting and to ask about the progress on his portion of the project. After talking to Paul, Sue started doing the behind-the-scenes work for Paul and speaking on his behalf at the meetings.

As the deadline for the first milestone approaches, Ike has not completed his part of the project, but assures the team that he will have it by the deadline. Sue is working on both her part and Paul's. Ann volunteers to pull the whole project together, with the help of Pat. The team agrees to meet again one hour before their deadline to make sure that everything is ready.

Questions for Discussion:

Case Team

1. What issues have surfaced with this team?

2. How would you describe the situation from the perspective of each team member?

3. What suggestions do you have for this team to improve its effectiveness?

Your Team

1. How do the issues raised in the case team relate to your team's norms?

2. What are ways to revise, adjust, or observe your team norms that will help make your team more effective?

CASE C FORM C

Read over the case, answer the questions individually, and be prepared to discuss your responses with team members.

It is now after the midpoint of the team's time together. The feedback from the sponsors has been generally positive, especially for Political Paul's part. Intuitive Ike's portion, completed at the last minute without feedback from others, was not consistent with the other parts of the project, which upset the other team members.

There is a significant amount of work yet to be completed by the team. Although they have had successes and continue to receive support and encouragement from the sponsors, the team has lost momentum. Ambitious Ann has been focusing her energy on another big project and she has missed the last two meetings. Pat has tried to take over the team leadership but her attempts to run the meetings do not seem to have the backing of Paul and Ike. Supportive Sue is becoming more confident in her role with the team because of Paul's support.

Pat is very worried that the team does not have the energy and commitment to meet the upcoming milestones and is frustrated because her attempts to make things happen have been to no avail. She leaves messages with each of the members expressing her concerns.

Questions for Discussion:

Case Team

1. What has happened to this team?
2. How have the roles changed?
3. What can they do to salvage the team?

Your Team

1. Has your team been following the norms it has developed?
2. How might you apply learning from the case team to your own team?
3. What can your team do to keep focused, healthy, and productive?

30

DISCUSSING ORGANIZATIONAL CHANGE

Scott Simmerman

Overview Most organizations fail to recognize that ideas for improvement already exist in the workplace. They generally lack good tools for generating ideas and possibilities, especially when line managers are to lead discussions. Using Square Wheels*, consultants can:

✓ generate a high level of creativity and discovery and capture the benefits of diversity of thinking and perspective;

✓ generate a high degree of interactivity and action learning;

✓ confirm that current systems and processes are generally less than optimal;

✓ stimulate a discussion on change or continuous quality improvement;

✓ identify new ideas and solutions to solve difficult problems;

✓ focus on learning organization approaches and change the language of organizational improvement—a powerful approach to change management;

✓ challenge existing beliefs about how the organization really works.

Suggested Time 60-90 minutes

Materials Needed

✓ Form A (Square Wheels Worksheet) for each participant

✓ Form B (Square Wheels Background and Facilitation Details)

*Square Wheels® is a registered servicemark of Performance Management Company. All materials copyright Performance Management Company, 1993-2000.

Contact Information: Performance Management Company, 3 Old Oak Drive, Taylors, SC 29687-6624, 800-659-1466 (U.S. only), 864-292-8700, Scott@Square Wheels.com, www.SquareWheels.com

Procedure

1. Make a few introductory comments about discovering a model of organizational behavior or change (whatever is most appropriate) and say that you will share the model for discussion.

2. Give each person one copy of Form A (the worksheet with the image below) in a *suggested* setting of round tables with 6 seats (with no limit on overall session size).

© Performance Management Company, 1993. Not for Reproduction.

3. Then, with a handout in hand, say something like: *"Take a minute or so, working alone, or generate as many ideas as you can about this illustration and your reactions. Then, begin to discuss it with the people at your table. We'll take about five minutes for this."* In reality, give them enough time to generate a good deal of content or until you perceive the energy level of the group begin to wane.

4. After a few minutes, mention that you would like each table to select one person who will serve as spokesperson for the group.

5. As they complete their table discussions, have each group share their thoughts and ideas about the illustration with the others. Responses will generally be quite varied and many will be humorous. Allow the group to have fun. Some probable responses are detailed in Form B, which is not a handout but a guide for your facilitation.

6. Summarize the discussion and make any key points you would like about the general theme of your presentation. Again, utilize Form B for suggestions.

7. Have the groups now discuss some of the possible Square Wheels that may operate within the organization.

8. Have the groups select a few of these Square Wheels (maybe one per table) and have them generate a list of potential Round Wheel solutions to those specific Square Wheels.

9. Discuss what the groups might be able to do to test and/or implement Round Wheel solutions. Recognize that the best approach to implementing one of these solutions will often parallel the successful implementation of another idea in the past.

SQUARE WHEELS WORKSHEET FORM A

Square Wheels®

by **Scott J. Simmerman, Ph.D.**

Performance Management Company   Taylors, SC 29687 USA   864-292-8700   FAX 864-292-6222   email: Square Wheels.compuserve.com

This is how things really work in many organizations:

Your Name:

SQUARE WHEELS BACKGROUND AND FACILITATION DETAILS   FORM B

This tool is a proven and engaging approach to identifying alternatives to the way things are done. The illustration links neatly to issues of change and quality and you can link it to your own preferred change model. Square Wheels also change the language of performance, and thus work subliminally to impact long-term development. This cartoon metaphor also works to generate Action Learning-type perspective and objectivity and is a much better interactive alternative than traditional lecture techniques for team building, communications, and leadership development.

Over 200 points about the illustration have been accumulated. To give you some idea of the more obscure ones, how about:

Square Wheels are better because they are biodegradable.

You can't cook good hot dogs on round rubber tires.

Square Wheels were obviously designed by (someone of the opposite sex).

We're not like that—we push our wagon uphill.

Most round wheels aren't usable because they have no rims.

Square Wheels are better for going downhill.

The rope is about to: choke the leader / come loose so the pushers will fall on their faces.

Once people have shared their ideas, you should summarize and then provide anchor points to your key themes for the session. Recognize (and reinforce) the similarities and differences in thinking among participants. Some groups will go off in one direction while others will have a much different set of beliefs and discoveries.

In your review, you will probably want to include links to what might be represented by:

✓ the person in front   ✓ the people in back   ✓ the body of the wagon
✓ the rope   ✓ the square wheels   ✓ the round wheels

Consider your own perceptions about how things work and the beliefs you can add based on the main themes of the session and your thoughts on the illustration.

Your debriefing points might include:

The person in front can represent leadership, top and middle management, or others focused forward (and seldom backward). Leaders get insulated by their ropes from the bumps and thumps of many realities of the journey forward. They work hard to pull the organization ahead.

The rope may be so long that the leaders lose touch with what actually happens. After all, *"A desk is a dangerous place from which to view the world."* Leaders can implement bad changes with good intentions; most leaders *do* have good intentions but little current "hands-on reality."

The people in back represent the front-line employees and supervisors who cannot see far ahead and feel every bump and pothole in the road. They push but have to trust the leadership to steer the course of the journey. They have no "big picture" of where the organization (the wagon) is headed, but work hard to do what is expected of them. They lack perspective and vision. Intentions are positive.

The body of the wagon: The body itself is well made and sturdy, much like the basic core of any organization. It will do the job for which it was designed. Its nature makes changing direction quite difficult, but it works like it always has. New wagons are also quite expensive!

The Square Wheels: These represent the traditions of the organization, the way things have always been done, the old ways, the systems and procedures to respond to quality and service initiatives or other issues of relevance to the group. In some organizations, they might represent interdepartmental conflicts and the common experience of an organization that does not move smoothly forward.

The Round Wheels: These represent new ideas for innovation or improvement, generally coming from within the organization itself. Round Wheels already exist in the wagon and are used by the exemplary performers!

Overall, the visions are difficult to effectively communicate to everyone in the work group and continued motivation is necessary to keep pushing forward. People generally trust leadership to lead the journey. But after pushing for a long time, people in the back may lose interest in where the organization is going or needs to go and can become resigned to the fact that the Square Wheels are a way of life. The organization clunks along, and everyone knows it.

31

DEALING WITH MANAGEMENT RESISTANCE

Sharon Wagner

Overview Unless facilitated properly, otherwise effective presentations can be derailed by audience resistance. Personal agendas, differences in values and interpersonal styles, and competition for organizational resources can all contribute to resistance in group settings. This exercise simulates a meeting in which members of the audience challenge the presenter to deal with resistance in a constructive way. Use it as a tool to develop your client's abilities.

Suggested Time Approximately 75 minutes

Materials Needed
- ✓ Form A (Role 1)
- ✓ Form B (Role 2)
- ✓ Form C (Role 3)
- ✓ Form D (Role 4)
- ✓ Form E (Role 5)
- ✓ Form F (Role 6)
- ✓ Form G (Observation Sheet)
- ✓ Form H (Nikkison Products Organizational Chart)

Procedure 1. Introduce the exercise by stating:

Each of us has probably witnessed an otherwise useful presentation that was derailed by its audience. Personal agendas, differences in values and interpersonal styles, and competition for

Contact Information: Quantify Consulting, 101 Soquel Ave. #47, Santa Cruz, CA 95060, 877-465-7031, slw@quantifyconsulting.com, www.quantifyconsulting.com

organizational resources can motivate people to block, resist, or sabotage presentations. Today's exercise simulates a meeting in which members of the audience challenge the presenter to deal with resistance in a constructive way.

2. Assign or ask for volunteers to play each of the following roles:

   Role 1: Presenter, Vice President of Human Resources

   Role 2: Member of Management Team, Plant Manager

   Role 3: Member of Management Team, First-Shift Supervisor and Union Representative

   Role 4: Member of Management Team, General Manager

   Role 5: Member of Management Team, Vice President of Finance and Operations

   Role 6: Member of Management Team, Vice President of Marketing and Sales

   Role 7: Observer A

   Role 8: Observer B

   Role 9: Observer C

   Note: Although the presenter role is essential, the facilitator may choose to eliminate one or more of the management team roles or one or more of the observer roles when working with a small group. Alternatively, the role play may be videotaped and replayed for participants, eliminating the need for all observer roles.

3. Provide the individual playing role 1 with Form A, the Nikkison Products Organizational Chart (Form H), flip chart paper, and markers. Provide the individuals playing roles 2 to 6 with the appropriate role information sheets (Forms B, C, D, E, and F) and the Nikkison Products Organizational Chart (Form H). Provide each observer with an observation sheet (Form G).

4. Ask each participant to work silently to prepare for his or her role. If possible, provide the presenter (role 1) with a separate room during preparation time.

5. The presenter (role 1) will deliver his or her presentation to the management team. All participants should act in accordance with their roles.

6. Before debriefing the activity, present the following guidelines:

   • Remind participants that all individuals were playing assigned roles.

- Remind participants that in a real-life presentation, possible sources of resistance can often be anticipated.
- Allow participants to acknowledge any frustration or anger they felt during the role play.
- Ask observers to guess the roles the management team members were playing. How was their resistance manifested?

7. Use the following steps to guide the debriefing:
   - Ask the presenter to describe his or her reactions to the role play. Were there any surprises? What were the emotional reactions? Did the role play seem realistic? Familiar? Was he or she tempted to take the resistance personally? Was he or she able to finish the presentation in the time allotted? What was the outcome?
   - Ask the presenter to assess his or her own performance. What was done well? What could have been done differently?
   - Ask the management team: Were your concerns addressed? Did you buy into the presenter's plan?
   - Ask the observers to assess the role play. Was it realistic? What did the presenter do well when confronted with resistance? What could he or she have done differently?
   - Ask all participants and observers: What was the importance of perceptions in this role play? Did role players attempt to understand each other's perceptions? Values?
   - Ask all participants and observers: Did status differences among participants affect the outcome of the role play?
   - Ask all participants and observers: What would have been an ideal outcome for this role play? A consensus-based decision? Buy-in for the training program? Stopping the discussion to review the organization's strategic plan?

ROLE 1: PRESENTER, VICE PRESIDENT OF HUMAN RESOURCES FORM A

"The key to this company's survival is cutting costs through standardized operator training."

Nikkison Products, a family-owned business, has a 42-year history of producing pet foods and supplies in the northeastern United States. According to the folklore of the company, S. Peabody Nikkison experimented with pet food formulations in his garage on weekends, then employed friends and relatives to start the fledgling business. "Old Sandy," as he is fondly called, ran the business himself until 12 years ago, when he retired at the age of 70 and handed over the role of General Manager to the former Vice President of Operations. Although the company always had a small market share, it managed to turn a profit until recently, when four straight years of losses were recorded. In an attempt to ensure the company's survival, the new General Manager has recently reduced or eliminated several product lines, expanded others, and in an unprecedented move for Nikkison, downsized 18 positions, and eliminated the third shift.

As Vice President of Human Resources, you strongly believe that antiquated machinery and a lack of standardized training for operators contribute to Nikkison's lack of competitiveness. You have asked for ten minutes at the monthly management meeting to explain your position. Your goal is to convince the group that a minimal investment in operator training will positively impact product quality and reduce downtime. Because there are different theories about why the company is doing poorly, you expect some resistance to your plan.

Prepare a 10-minute presentation for the management team. The main points of your presentation are:

- Historic and current practice for training operators consists of poorly supervised on-the-job training.
- After years of this practice, operators have developed various idiosyncratic techniques for operating and maintaining the machines.
- Operators' techniques are contradictory, leading to malfunctions, downtime, and large variations in the quality of output.
- Across the two shifts, operators' techniques are particularly different. Operators tend to blame the other shift when machines malfunction.
- The long-term goal should be to replace the antiquated machinery. This solution, however, is cost-prohibitive at this time.
- Standardization in machine operation should be the current goal.

   Identify the top operators.

   Develop a hands-on training program based on their knowledge.

   Train them to deliver the training through a behavior modeling approach:

   Trainer explains the steps in a particular work process.

   Trainer demonstrates the work process for the trainee.

   Trainer observes while the trainee performs the work process.

   Trainer provides immediate corrective feedback to the trainee.

   Trainer positively reinforces the desired behavior when it is demonstrated on future occasions.

You have been given a 20-minute slot at the beginning of the management meeting for presentation and discussion.

(Please do not share your role with anyone.)

ROLE 2: PLANT MANAGER   FORM B   DOWNLOADABLE

"We've moved away from our roots as a family-owned business."

Nikkison Products, a family-owned business, has a 42-year history of producing pet foods and supplies in the northeastern United States. According to the folklore of the company, S. Peabody Nikkison experimented with pet food formulations in his garage on weekends, then employed friends and relatives to start the fledgling business. "Old Sandy," as he is fondly called, ran the business himself until 12 years ago, when he retired at the age of 70 and handed over the role of General Manager to the former Vice President of Operations. Although the company always had a small market share, it managed to turn a profit until recently, when four straight years of losses were recorded. In an attempt to ensure the company's survival, the new General Manager has recently reduced or eliminated several product lines and expanded others.

As Plant Manager, you are dismayed about Nikkison's recent problems. For the first time in its history, Nikkison was forced to make cutbacks in its personnel last year. The third shift was eliminated, and you had to decide which 18 employees would be fired. You are a 26-year veteran of the company; many of the employees who lost their jobs were people whom you considered friends. This downsizing episode has left you depressed and somewhat defensive. You are aware that the VP of HR plans to propose some kind of training program during today's meeting. You strongly resent and will angrily challenge any implication that Nikkison is failing because of operators' performance. On the other hand, if it appears that the training program will ultimately help employees, you will support it.

(Please do not share your role with anyone.)

ROLE 3: FIRST-SHIFT SUPERVISOR, UNION REPRESENTATIVE FORM C

"This is not the time for some half-baked 'program' from HR."

Nikkison Products, a family-owned business, has a 42-year history of producing pet foods and supplies in the northeastern United States. According to the folklore of the company, S. Peabody Nikkison experimented with pet food formulations in his garage on weekends, then employed friends and relatives to start the fledgling business. "Old Sandy," as he is fondly called, ran the business himself until 12 years ago, when he retired at the age of 70 and handed over the role of General Manager to the former Vice President of Operations. Although the company always had a small market share, it managed to turn a profit until recently, when four straight years of losses were recorded. In an attempt to ensure the company's survival, the new General Manager has recently reduced or eliminated several product lines and expanded others.

As First-Shift Supervisor and union representative, you are dismayed about Nikkison's recent problems. For the first time in its history, Nikkison was forced to make cutbacks in its personnel last year, and the third shift was eliminated. You know that the VP of HR plans to propose some kind of training program. In the past, you have had negative experiences with human resources personnel, who in your opinion tend to dream up new "programs" in order to justify their own careers. During the meeting, you will state this point of view and remind participants of your role as advocate for the operators. You will vociferously oppose any new training program on the grounds that it will create extra work for already overworked employees.

(Please do not share your role with anyone.)

ROLE 4: GENERAL MANAGER
FORM D

"It's time we stopped coddling our employees—some of them need a swift kick in the pants."

Nikkison Products, a family-owned business, has a 42-year history of producing pet foods and supplies in the northeastern United States. According to the folklore of the company, S. Peabody Nikkison experimented with pet food formulations in his garage on weekends, then employed friends and relatives to start the fledgling business. "Old Sandy," as he is fondly called, ran the business himself until 12 years ago, when he retired at the age of 70 and handed over the role of General Manager to you, the former Vice President of Operations. Although the company always had a small market share, it managed to turn a profit until recently, when four straight years of losses were recorded.

As General Manager, you are dismayed about Nikkison's recent problems. In an attempt to ensure the company's survival, you have recently reduced or eliminated several product lines and expanded others. You were also forced to make the unprecedented move of downsizing (18 positions) last year, and eliminating the third shift.

Throughout your 14-year association with Nikkison Products, you have been less than satisfied with the skills and attitudes of the employees. Your management philosophy differs considerably from that of your former boss, Sandy Nikkison, who in your opinion tended to coddle his employees. You have remarked to your spouse that Nikkison "raised nepotism to a new level." Lately, worker attitudes seem to be worsening.

You know that the VP of HR plans to propose some kind of training program. If the training program is focused on improving workers' motivational levels, you are in favor of it. If the employees can't improve their attitudes, then maybe "new blood" is needed anyway.

(Please do not share your role with anyone.)

ROLE 5: VICE PRESIDENT OF FINANCE AND OPERATIONS FORM E

"It is imperative that we improve efficiency."

Nikkison Products, a family-owned business, has a 42-year history of producing pet foods and supplies in the northeastern United States. According to the folklore of the company, S. Peabody Nikkison experimented with pet food formulations in his garage on weekends, then employed friends and relatives to start the fledgling business. "Old Sandy," as he is fondly called, ran the business himself until 12 years ago, when he retired at the age of 70 and handed over the role of General Manager to the former Vice President of Operations. Although the company always had a small market share, it managed to turn a profit until recently, when four straight years of losses were recorded. In an attempt to ensure the company's survival, the new General Manager has recently reduced or eliminated several product lines and expanded others. He also made the unprecedented move of downsizing (18 positions) last year, and eliminating the third shift.

As Vice President of Finance and Operations, you are dismayed about Nikkison's recent problems. The General Manager has charged you with cutting the fat and improving efficiency. You have been working 70 to 80 hours a week for the past month, and wearing both the finance and operations "hats" during these difficult times has become overwhelming. You know that the VP of HR plans to propose some kind of training program at the meeting today. Your preoccupation with other things, however, will be evident from your body language at the start of the meeting. Sit with your arms folded, and do not make eye contact with the presenter. You may even take some work with you, or doodle while the presenter speaks. If the presenter succeeds in engaging you, however, and especially if he or she makes the case that the training program will increase efficiency, you will become the presenter's most ardent supporter.

(Please do not share your role with anyone.)

ROLE 6: VICE PRESIDENT OF MARKETING AND SALES   FORM F

"The key to this company's survival is devoting our resources to marketing."

Nikkison Products, a family-owned business, has a 42-year history of producing pet foods and supplies in the northeastern United States. According to the folklore of the company, S. Peabody Nikkison experimented with pet food formulations in his garage on weekends, then employed friends and relatives to start the fledgling business. "Old Sandy," as he is fondly called, ran the business himself until 12 years ago, when he retired at the age of 70 and handed over the role of General Manager to the former Vice President of Operations. Although the company always had a small market share, it managed to turn a profit until recently, when four straight years of losses were recorded. In an attempt to ensure the company's survival, the new General Manager has recently reduced or eliminated several product lines and expanded others, and in an unprecedented move, downsized 18 positions, and eliminated the third shift.

As Vice President of Marketing and Sales and a newcomer to the company (less than one year on staff), you are dismayed about Nikkison's recent problems. You are convinced that Nikkison's current problems result from the lack of a coordinated marketing plan. You also believe that this is the wrong time for new human resources programs, especially because any budget allocations for training would be better spent on marketing. You will repeatedly suggest that the presenter's plan be tabled so that more important matters can be discussed.

(Please do not share your role with anyone.)

OBSERVATION SHEET   FORM G

Role:	Plant Manager	Supervisor, Shift 1	General Manager	VP Finance	VP Sales
What did he or she say and do?					
How did the VP of Human Resources respond?					
How effective was the response?					
Suggestions for improvement:					

SOLVING A TEAM PUZZLE

Sivasailam "Thiagi" Thiagarajan

Overview
This activity requires teams to solve a logic puzzle. In the process, they learn to trade off among time, money, and information. You can use the activity to focus on many aspects of team dynamics, such as leadership, collaboration, inclusion, and so forth.

Suggested Time
45 minutes

Materials Needed
✓ Form A (Team Conference: A Logic Puzzle)
✓ Form B (A Dozen Questions and Answers)
✓ Form C (Cross-Check Matrix)
✓ Form D (How to Play Time, Money, and Logic)
✓ Form E (Solution Table, for facilitator's use)
✓ An Envelope with $20,000 in play money for each team

Procedure
1. Divide participants into teams so that each team has 3 to 7 members.
2. Distribute one set of Forms A, B, and C and an envelope of $20,000 in play money to each team.
3. Explain the rules of the game. Walk participants through the set of instructions on Form D, How to Play Time, Money, and Logic.
4. Begin the game. Announce the time limit and start the timer.
5. At the end of each minute, collect $1,000 from each team.
6. Whenever any team comes with a question, collect the required fee first. Secretly check with the solution table and give a "Yes" or "No" response.

Contact Information: Workshops by Thiagi, Inc., 4423 East Trailridge Road, Bloomington, IN 47408, 800-996-7725, thiagi@thiagi.com, www.thiagi.com

7. If a team comes with a completed solution table, secretly check it against your solution table. If the team's solution is not correct, send them back to work on the correct solution. Do not give any additional feedback. If the team's solution is correct, congratulate them and tell them to keep the rest of the money.

8. Stop the game at the end of 20 minutes or when all teams have correctly solved the problem. Identify the winning team, the one with the most money.

9. Debrief participants by using the *What? So What? Now What?* sequence: Ask participants to share what happened to them during the game. Next invite participants to ask themselves, "So what?" What does the activity reveal about how they work together in their own teams? Finally, ask participants to consider, "Now what?" and list steps they can take to apply what they learned from this game.

TEAM CONFERENCE: A LOGIC PUZZLE
FORM A

Dr. Glen Barker is organizing a conference on high-performance teams. He has invited five prestigious researchers (Dr. Armstrong, Dr. Bennett, Dr. Collins, Dr. Dalton, and Dr. Edwards) from the departments of Business, Anthropology, Sociology, Psychology, and Political Science. These researchers (from MIT, Stanford, Yale, Harvard, and Princeton) are presenting their latest findings in the areas of goal setting, conflict resolution, trust building, decision making, and leveraging diversity among team members.

Review the Dozen Questions and Answers handout. Using the information given on that handout, correctly complete this solution table:

Name	Department	University	Topic
Armstrong			
Bennett			
Collins			
Dalton			
Edwards			

A DOZEN QUESTIONS AND ANSWERS
FORM B

1. **Question:** Is Dr. Collins making the presentation on conflict resolution?
   Answer: Yes!

2. **Question:** Is Dr. Armstrong from the Political Science department?
   Answer: No!

3. **Question:** Is Dr. Dalton from the Psychology department?
   Answer: Yes!

4. **Question:** Is Dr. Armstrong's presentation about decision making?
   Answer: No!

5. **Question:** Is Dr. Edwards from Yale?
   Answer: Yes!

6. **Question:** Is Dr. Dalton from Stanford?
   Answer: No!

7. **Question:** Is the Anthropology professor making a presentation on decision making?
   Answer: Yes!

8. **Question:** Is Dr. Edwards from the Anthropology department?
   Answer: No!

9. **Question:** Is the Princeton professor from the Sociology department?
   Answer: Yes!

10. **Question:** Is the MIT professor from the Anthropology department?
    Answer: No!

11. **Question:** Is the professor from MIT making a presentation on goal setting?
    Answer: Yes!

12. **Question:** Is the professor from Stanford making a presentation on building trust?
    Answer: Yes!

CROSS-CHECK MATRIX
FORM C

How to Use This Matrix:
Enter the information from A Dozen Questions and Answers in the appropriate boxes in the matrix. Use an "X" to indicate a definite "No," a dot to indicate a definite "Yes." After placing a dot, place X's in the other four boxes in the same row and in the same column in that section of the matrix.

For your convenience, the information from the first two questions and answers has already been entered in this matrix.

	Conflict	Decision Making	Diversity	Goal Setting	Trust Building	Harvard	MIT	Princeton	Stanford	Yale	Anthropology	Business	Political Science	Psychology	Sociology
Armstrong	X												X		
Bennett	X														
Collins	•	X	X	X	X										
Dalton	X															
Edwards	X															
Anthropology															
Business															
Political Science															
Psychology															
Sociology															
Harvard															
MIT															
Princeton															
Stanford															
Yale															

HOW TO PLAY TIME, MONEY, AND LOGIC
FORM D

You have:

- a logic puzzle,
- a play period of 20 minutes, and
- funding of $20,000.

At the end of each minute, we will collect $1,000 from you. Whenever you solve the puzzle correctly, you keep the remaining money. For example, if you solve the puzzle in 10 minutes, you keep the unspent $10,000.

The team with the most money at the end of the 20-minute play period (or whenever all teams have solved the puzzle) wins the game.

Notice that it is not that the fastest team wins the game, because you can also spend money to purchase additional information to help you solve the puzzle. For additional information, ask the facilitator a yes or no question similar to the ones on the A Dozen Questions and Answers handout. Your facilitator will give you the correct answer.

Additional information costs money. Here's how much the answer to each question will cost:

- First question: $ 1,000
- Second question: $2,000
- Third question: $3,000
- Fourth and all subsequent questions: $4,000

For example, if you ask a total of four questions, it will cost you $10,000. However, you may be able to solve the puzzle faster.

You may ask questions anytime during the play period, but only if you have the necessary funds. You have to pay in advance for the answer.

TEAM CONFERENCE: A LOGIC PUZZLE
FORM E

Solution Table for facilitator's use

Name	Department	University	Topic
Armstrong	Business	Stanford	Trust Building
Bennett	Anthropology	Harvard	Decision Making
Collins	Sociology	Princeton	Conflict Resolution
Dalton	Psychology	MIT	Goal Setting
Edwards	Political Science	Yale	Leveraging Diversity

33

INTERPRETING PERSONALITY DIFFERENCES

Karen Lawson

Overview This exercise is very effective in management development consultations to show the importance of recognizing and adjusting to various style differences.

Suggested Time 45 minutes

Materials Needed

✓ Form A (Personality Profile)

✓ 4 flip chart pages and 4 markers

Procedure

1. Distribute the personality assessment instrument (Form A) and ask participants to complete the assessment according to the written instructions. Walk around and check to make sure participants are completing the instrument correctly. Assist participants in scoring the instrument.

2. Next, group participants according to their styles: *Candid, Persuasive; Logical; Reflective.* Provide participants with these further descriptions of their styles:

   Candid: dominant, driving, direct

   Persuasive: amiable, influencing, expressive

   Logical: steady, systematic, thinking

   Reflective: conscientious, considerate, amiable

3. Give each group a flip chart page and marker and ask them to make a list of how they would like to learn how to drive a stick-shift car and the attributes they would most want in an instruc-

Contact Information: Lawson Consulting Group, 1365 Gwynedale Way, Lansdale, PA 19446, 215-368-9465, KLawson@LawsonCG.com, www.lawsoncg.com

tor. Further explain that if they already know how to drive stick-shift, they should not think about how they learned because how they were taught and how they would like to have been taught might not be the same.

4. Ask each group to post its list on the wall. Ask participants to compare the lists, noting the major differences as well as similarities.

5. Expect the following outcomes:

   ✓ *Candid*—List will be short and to the point; action-oriented

   ✓ *Persuasive*—List will be slightly longer than that of Candid; list will not be in any order and will emphasize importance of having a friendly instructor; will reflect social aspect of the experience

   ✓ *Logical*—List will reflect step-by-step procedure; need for structure and detail; may want to read manual and learn how everything works

   ✓ *Reflective*—List will be similar to that of *Logical* but will reflect a more cautious approach (and lots of opportunities to practice in a parking lot) as well as a need for a patient, caring instructor

6. Ask participants to give examples of how these style differences can be seen in the workplace or in their personal lives.

7. Conduct a discussion about the importance of communicating in the other person's style, not yours, in order to be more effective in both professional and personal relationships.

8. Point out the following strategies in communicating with each style:

   ✓ *Candid:* Get to the point quickly; emphasize big picture and bottom line; avoid details

   ✓ *Persuasive:* Emphasize the human element; express enthusiasm; socialize, establish relationship

   ✓ *Logical:* Provide details and approach the subject logically and systematically

   ✓ *Reflective:* Exercise caution and reservation; don't try to push for action; reflect and acknowledge emotions

9. Ask each participant to think about an individual with whom they have had difficulty communicating. Ask each person to speculate as to the other person's style. Then ask them to think about a typical scenario or interaction they might experience with this individual and write down how they might modify their approach to

communicate in that person's style. Invite a few participants to share their strategies with the entire group.

Variation Instead of using Form A, you may choose to use another assessment instrument. Be sure to use a personality or communication style assessment instrument that identifies four different personality profiles. Some suggested profiles:

I Speak Your Language (Drake Beam Morin)

Personality Profile System (Carlson Learning)

What's My Style? (HRDQ)

Behavior Profiles (Jossey-Bass/Pfeiffer)

PERSONALITY PROFILE*   FORM A

To get a flavor for style differences, read each of the following statements and circle the ending that is most like you.

1. When I am in a learning situation, I like to …
    a. be involved in doing something.
    b. work with people in groups.
    c. read about the information.
    d. watch and listen to what is going on.

2. When I am working in a group, I like to …
    a. direct the discussion and activity.
    b. find out what other people think and feel.
    c. remain somewhat detached from the rest of the group.
    d. go along with the majority.

3. When faced with a conflict situation, I prefer to …
    a. confront the situation head on and try to win.
    b. work with the other person to arrive at an amicable resolution.
    c. present my position by using logic and reason.
    d. not make waves.

4. In a conversation, I tend to …
    a. come straight to the point.
    b. draw others into the conversation.
    c. listen to what others have to say, then offer an objective opinion.
    d. agree with what others say.

5. When making a decision, I tend to …
    a. make a decision quickly and then move on.
    b. consider how the outcome will affect others.
    c. take time to gather facts and data.
    d. consider all possible outcomes and proceed with caution.

*Adapted from **The Art of Influencing.** Karen Lawson, Ph.D. Dubuque, IA: Kendall-Hunt Publishing Company, 1996.

6. I am seen by others as someone who ...
    a. gets results.
    b. is fun to be with.
    c. is logical and rational.
    d. is a calming influence.

7. In a work environment, I prefer ...
    a. to work alone.
    b. to work with others.
    c. structure and organization.
    d. a peaceful atmosphere.

Now count the number of times you circled each letter. The letter with the most circles indicates your preferred style:

a=Candid; b=Persuasive; c=Logical; d=Reflective.

34

LEARNING ABOUT CHANGE

Carol Harvey

Overview   This exercise is designed to teach participants that individuals react to change quite differently and that these differences need to be understood and acknowledged in the formulation and implementation of major organizational changes. It is designed for approximately 20 participants. If you have fewer or more participants, adjust the directions accordingly.

Suggested Time   30 to 45 minutes

Materials Needed
✓   Form A (Reaction to Change Sheet)
✓   Form B (Tan Team Instructions)
✓   Form C (Gray Team Instructions)
✓   Form D (Red and Green Team Instructions)

Procedure

1. Give every member of the group a copy of the Reaction to Change Sheet (Form A).

2. Tell the participants that they have 5 minutes to list as many words or phrases as they can that describe their individual feelings about change. (At first this seems easy, but as the time goes on they struggle with this.)

3. Call time at the end of 5 minutes.

4. Tell participants to rate each of their descriptions as positive, negative, or neutral and then to count the number in each category. List the totals at the bottom of the Reactions to Change Sheet (Form A).

5. Form four groups in the following manner:

Contact Information: Assumption College, 500 Salisbury Street, Worcester, MA 01615-0005, 508-767-7459, charvey@assumption.edu

- ✓ Divide the total number of participants by four. Use that number to assign quartiles to the participants' scores on Form A. For example, if there are 16 participants, 4 participants will be in each quartile. (The numbers in each quartile do not have to be exactly the same.)

- ✓ Designate the quartile with the *highest number of negative scores* the Red team and the quartile with the *highest number of positive scores* the Green team.

- ✓ Artbitrarily divide the participants in the two middle quartiles into two teams. Name one of these groups the Tan team, and name the other group the Gray team.

6. Conduct a brief discussion about why people think they had such different lists. Participants usually cite work experiences, perceptions, frames of reference, etc.

7. Give copies of Form B to the **Tan** team and Form C to the **Gray** team.

8. Give Form D to the **Red** (negative about change) team and to the **Green** (positive about change) team.

9. Allow at least 15 minutes for the teams to prepare their plans for the change.

10. Ask the Tan team to report their best plan for informing the positive people about the change. Follow this with a report from the actual high positive scorers, the **Green Team,** about how they wanted this change to be communicated and implemented. [Those who are positive about change often focus on the need for closure and ceremony such as a cake, etc.]

11. Repeat the procedure by having the Gray team report their plan for implementing the change for people who are more negative about change. Follow with the report from the actual high negative scorers, the **Red Team.** [Those who are more fearful about change often cite a need for more time to get used to the idea, want a say in how their peers are told, etc.]

12. In the discussion, all participants learn that there is *considerable* difference among managers' own attitudes about change, especially the way that it is communicated and implemented and the expectations of subordinates. While much of this is a product of personality and experience, it needs to be taken into account when announcing and implementing changes that employees will accept.

13. Participants learn that their development of change strategies is heavily influenced by their own attitudes toward change. This is particularly important when these are different from those of their subordinates. While changes may be inevitable in organizations, *how* managers implement change may be a determining factor in the more successful transformations. This exercise is a powerful way to experience change from another's perspective.

REACTIONS TO CHANGE   FORM A

In the space below, describe your feelings and reactions to the idea of change. Your answers should be limited to a word or a short phrase. In the time allotted, try to list as many reactions as possible.

	Rating		Rating
1. _____	_____	20. _____	_____
2. _____	_____	21. _____	_____
3. _____	_____	22. _____	_____
4. _____	_____	23. _____	_____
5. _____	_____	24. _____	_____
6. _____	_____	25. _____	_____
7. _____	_____	26. _____	_____
8. _____	_____	27. _____	_____
9. _____	_____	28. _____	_____
10. _____	_____	29. _____	_____
11. _____	_____	30. _____	_____
12. _____	_____	31. _____	_____
13. _____	_____	32. _____	_____
14. _____	_____	33. _____	_____
15. _____	_____	34. _____	_____
16. _____	_____	35. _____	_____
17. _____	_____	36. _____	_____
18. _____	_____	37. _____	_____
19. _____	_____	38. _____	_____

#P _____   #N _____   #Nu _____
(Positive)   (Negative)   (Neutral)

TAN TEAM INSTRUCTIONS   FORM B

As a group, devise a specific plan for explaining the following situation to an employee who has *positive* feelings about change.

Your employee's office is going to be relocated to another building at a nearby site. All that you know about this move is that the other members of his or her department will not be going along, the employee's job will essentially remain the same, he or she will still report to you, and you don't know why the employee has been asked to move.

Your plan should include, but is not limited to:

1. Details about how you tell the person (how, when, where, etc.).
2. Exactly what you would say.
3. Any other implementation actions you would like to include.

GRAY TEAM INSTRUCTIONS FORM C

As a group, devise a specific plan for explaining the situation to an employee who has *negative* feelings about change.

Your employee's office is going to be relocated to another building at a nearby site. All that you know about this move is that the other members of his or her department will not be going along, the employee's job will essentially remain the same, he or she will still report to you, and you don't know why the employee has been asked to move.

Your plan should include, but is not limited to:

1. Details about how you tell the person (how, when, where, etc.).
2. Exactly what you would say.
3. Any other implementation actions you would like to include.

RED AND GREEN GROUP
INSTRUCTIONS   FORM D

As a group, devise a specific plan for how you would like your supervisor to handle the following situation.

> *Your employee's office is going to be relocated to another building at a nearby site. All that you know about this move is that the other members of his or her department will not be going along, the employee's job will essentially remain the same, he or she will still report to you, and you don't know why the employee has been asked to move.*

Your plan should include, but is not limited to:

1. Details about how you are told (how, when, where, etc.).
2. Exactly what is said to you.
3. Any other implementation actions that you would like included that might make this change easier for you.

35
CREATING A TEAM-BUILDING OLYMPICS

Jeanne Baer

Overview
Often, one of the most important goals for a team-building retreat is to provide a way for participants to get to know each other better or to *bond*. An Olympic-style competition is an excellent way to achieve this goal. Like the true Olympics, your event can offer pageantry, color, excitement, and teamwork. However, yours departs from that world-renowned event in several ways: One need not be athletic to win, some of the events are silly, no injuries are anticipated, and cooperation replaces competition in your Olympics' final event.

Effective for groups of 15 to 300, your Olympics features fun events for people of all sizes, ages, and abilities. The events give people a chance to get to know each other in a nonwork setting and requires true teamwork to win.

Suggested Time
Open to several choices

Materials Needed
See details later

Procedure
Overall Design

1. The first thing to do is plan the individual events that will constitute your Olympics. Consider the following sample events:

   ✓ *Overachiever's First Aid:* This safety lesson will give four team members plenty of practice bandaging. The assumption is that one team member has three paper cuts—one on each hand and one on his or her forehead. Three teammates must wrap the cut fingers and head with about 20 feet of bandages, tucking the

Contact Information: Creative Training Solutions, 1649 South 21st Street, Lincoln, NE 68502, 402-475-1127, Jbaer@cts-online.net, www.cts-online.net

ends of the bandages in neatly. When a team finishes and its bandages are okayed by judges, the three bandagers remove the bandages, and a second team member is bandaged by the other three. Again the bandaging is okayed, after which the third and finally the fourth member are wrapped up. The first team to bandage all its members wins.

✓ *Collator's Nightmare:* The starter tosses a huge pile of various-colored, numbered sheets of paper into the air (40 for each team). The task facing each team of six athletes is to pick up the sheets in their assigned color and collate them in numerical order! The first team to finish wins.

✓ *Linking Up:* Athletes have 3 minutes to take large, colorful paper clips from a pile and link them into a chain. Since the three-member teams can only use one hand, teamwork is important! The longest chain wins.

✓ *Forms Management 101 (Wastebasket Basketball):* Working together in teams of five, the first player crumples a "form" into a ball, and it is thrown to the next player, and to the third, fourth, and finally to the fifth, who shoots it into a wastebasket. The team that scores the most baskets within 5 minutes wins.

✓ *Doughnut and Java Juggle:* Athletes must run with a cup of "coffee" (water) in both hands and a doughnut on a drinking straw, relay style. When they reach a teammate, they transfer the doughnut to the teammates' awaiting straw and transfer the coffee. The process is repeated to a third and a fourth teammate. First team to return (with doughnut intact) is the winner.

2. The last event of the Olympics should give participants a chance to work with each other instead of competing against each other and should involve all participants. Here's one possibility called *The Big Picture:*

✓ For this closing event, each athlete gets one or more giant jigsaw puzzle pieces, and must work with everyone to assemble the puzzle. The goal? To see the "big picture" as soon as possible!

✓ To produce The Big Picture, construct a giant jigsaw puzzle with an inspiring message on it. It might be the organization's mission or vision statement or a slogan such as, "We can't spell s ccess without U!" (*Note:* "Giant" really does mean very large. Four feet by eight feet is not too large to be considered a workable minimum.)

✓ Decide on the message and accompanying artwork. Transfer it to the material you have chosen for the puzzle. If you intend to use the puzzle repeatedly, consider constructing it out of 1/8-inch plywood. If not, corrugated cardboard is a good choice.

✓ Next, cut into interlocking pieces. You may cut it into the number of participants you are expecting, or you can cut it into many pieces and invite everyone to fit as many pieces as possible.

✓ If you want the event to go more quickly, you can number pieces sequentially and tell participants to find people with numbers close to theirs. Or you can label some pieces "top row," "bottom row," and so on.

✓ One option is to instruct participants that they must put the puzzle together without talking to each other. That way, you can later do a process observation about what behaviors did and did not work well, leading to some insights about teamwork and communication.

✓ Another option is to run the event twice; first without talking and then with talking. Time both tries so that participants can see how much faster they accomplish the goal when they are able to fully communicate.

✓ Regardless of how you conduct the event, be sure that everyone receives a prize for participating.

Planning Considerations

3. When you are brainstorming event possibilities, consider whether your Olympics will be indoors, outdoors with a hard surface, or outdoors on a grassy surface; some events may require a particular surface or setting. You will want to have diverse events calling on a variety of abilities and knowledge; while some events may call for speed or agility, not all should. Where possible, make success contingent on members working together as a team. Your final event should be one that brings the entire group together, competing not against each other, but against the clock.

4. The number of events that you organize depends on the total amount of time that you have available. Estimate the amount of time it will take to run any given event and then to award prizes for it. If you cannot set up for one event until you complete the previous one, you will also have to build in setup time.

5. You will also need to think about the number of athletes from each team that you want to participate in each event. This will depend on the amount of space you have, the amount of supplies and prizes that you want to provide, and the amount of time that you want to take for the event.

6. Be sure to have enough athletes competing in each event, and/or organize enough different events so that everyone can participate as much as possible. (While athletes are involved in an event, their remaining teammates should be nearby, cheering them on.)

7. Another factor in your selection or invention of games is the supplies required to run them. To keep the cost reasonable, use supplies you can borrow and return versus those you must buy and use up or have to store. Thrift stores can be an excellent source of some supplies. Create events that are especially appropriate to your industry. Often slight modifications of games you already know, accompanied by some creative descriptions, will customize them cleverly. You can also create a quiz bowl-style event, with silly and serious questions about the organization or any body of knowledge that you want to spotlight.

8. Decide whether you wish to do process observations on some, all, or none of the events. My personal preference is to debrief only the last event in this way. If too much process observing takes place, it slows the pace of the Olympics and can sap the energy of participants.

9. Some planning in each of the following areas is required. Just how much detail is needed will be determined by your own Olympics.

Creating Teams

10. The more teams you have, the more unwieldy the games become in terms of setup, supplies, and prizes. Three to six teams are easy, eight teams become a challenge, and any more than ten, a real headache. Each team should be made up of 5 to 20 members. In advance, decide who will be on what teams, making up teams of equal or nearly equal size. Assign each team a color, and instruct members to decide on a name to accompany their color (for example, the Green Giants, the Red Raiders, the Turquoise Tornadoes). This can be done before the Olympics in a promotional mailing or once the participants arrive for the retreat. At the site of the competition, create "camps" for each team by gathering chairs around team tables. If your budget permits, provide bandannas or T-shirts in team colors so that it will be easy to identify the members of each team.

Advance Promotion

11. Promote the games in advance to build anticipation and interest. If the purpose of the games is to organize a friendly competition

among already existing divisions, regions, or other groups, promotion is especially important. Also, if you make your Olympics sound too frivolous, some people will resist participating. Therefore, make your promotional mailing(s) fun, energetic, and creative, but also purposeful, promising a useful perspective on the skills that ensure successful teamwork.

Before the Games Begin

12. Before the Olympics officially starts, you will want to allow some time for team bonding. Coming up with their own team name, a team chant or song, and even a team flag are some possibilities.

13. The Olympics often take place after a meal. That way, athletes can begin to build esprit de corps while or right after they eat. Give each team a balloon bouquet in its team color and have participants decide on a team name. You may wish to supply felt-tip pens so that they can write the name on the balloons.

14. You may also invite them to come up with a slogan, chant, or very short song. That way, when their team wins an event, they can shout or sing it in unison, roughly equivalent to the playing of an Olympic winner's national anthem. To simplify song writing, assign each team a different, well-known tune, such as "Old McDonald." They only need to come up with a few lyrics to fit it.

15. Another option is to have each team make and fly its own flag. Provide each team with felt-tip pens in many colors, along with a large piece of white fabric or poster board. Also provide a stick that they can attach it to and a way to display the flags once the teams get them to the competition site.

Prizes

16. Award prizes to first-place teams. If you have many teams, sufficient funding, and the time to gather lots of prizes, award second and third prizes also. Silly prizes are often appreciated more than a serious prize would be. Specialty advertising companies can help you with imaginative prizes, and a company like Oriental Trading (800-228-2269) has thousands of inexpensive items. If your budget is more limited than your time, lead a shopping expedition to nearby thrift stores.

17. Try to select prizes that tie into each event. For instance, for "Overachiever's First Aid" you might award boxes of neon-colored "Band-aids," and for the "Big Picture" you might award magnifying glasses. Another option is to award Olympic-style medals for

each event. You can find gold, silver, and bronze medals hung on red, white, and blue ribbons at trophy shops.

Ambience

18. You can set an Olympics mood with some imaginative music and decor.

19. Erect large posters declaring, "Welcome World-Class Athletes!" or "Welcome to the _____-Lympics!" (combining the name of your organization with the word Olympics).

20. To further carry out the theme, spray-paint five hula hoops in the Olympics colors, wire them together in the Olympic rings configuration, and hang them prominently. Decorate with many brightly colored helium-filled balloons, preferably in colors not already assigned to teams.

21. Heroic-sounding, "epic"-style music should be played at the beginning and the end of the Olympics and may be played throughout.

Olympic Pageantry

22. You may wish to begin your Olympics with a parade of the athletes. They can march in with their flags or balloons, accompanied by Olympic-style music provided by a hired marching band or by tape. Music might include John Williams' "Olympic Fanfare" (recorded by the Cincinnati Pops on the Telark label) or Leo Armaud's "Olympic Fanfare" (part of "Bugler's Dream," recorded by The Concert Arts Symphonic Band, conducted by Felix Slatkin on the Angel LP "USA" label). Music from the film *Chariots of Fire* would be another good choice. For liability's sake, check with ASCAP or other licensing bodies and pay the required fees for using these pieces.

23. If teams have written a chant, slogan, or song, they can now perform them for the other teams. You or an Olympics "official" then welcomes the athletes, and then, "Let the games begin!"

24. If teams have created their own team chant, slogan, or song, you might invite the winning team to perform it when the prizes are given for each event. The entire team should be encouraged to perform, not just the athletes who competed in this event.

Logistics

25. To help your Olympics run smoothly, you will need to pay attention to various details. As you can imagine, the number of details

grows as the number of people grows. The following issues and questions are ones to consider:

Logo: Will you want a special logo designed to print on promotional materials, prizes, and uniforms? If so, start developing it *early*; allow adequate time for the approval process and for printing it on items.

Team uniforms: Will you identify team athletes with color-coded T-shirts or bandannas? Can you get them in the correct colors and sizes? Will they be printed?

Balloon bouquets: Can they be delivered by a balloon company, or must you rent a tank of helium and fill them at the site? After the Olympics are over, will the balloons be donated or will they be kept by participants?

Insurance: Are you covered for possible injuries?

Security: Is someone available to keep passers-by from joining in? While this is rarely a problem indoors, it can be if your Olympics are held in a public park.

Refreshments: Will you be providing light snacks and beverages? Will someone be needed to serve them or to be sure that the supply is continuous? If you don't provide them, are vending machines nearby?

Getting participants' attention: Do you have a public address system or bull horns with plenty of batteries available? Athletic-style whistles?

Restrooms: Are they nearby? If you are outdoors, consider renting portable toilets to be placed near your Olympics area.

Souvenir photos: Can you afford a videographer to tape the event? If not, can you arrange for people to take still photos? Will you copy tapes or photos for participants later? What will the cost be, if any?

Helpers: Do you have two or more helpers for setup, awarding prizes, and other tasks? If you have over 100 participants, consider having a special coach (facilitator) assigned to each team. These people will keep the teams organized, enthusiastic, and where they are supposed to be when they are supposed to be there.

Inclement weather: If you plan to hold your Olympics outdoors, do you have a contingency plan for bad weather? Do you have a backup, indoor site reserved? Do you have transportation waiting to move the whole group quickly? If you don't want to move the games inside, what will participants do if the games are canceled?

Cost

26. A team-building Olympics can be effective on almost any scale and budget. A small-scale example: an hour-long indoor Olympics for 50 participants on five teams, with supplies and prizes costing $85. A large-scale example: a 5-hour long corporate Olympics with 200 participants on 10 teams, requiring 6 months of preparation and six additional hired facilitators, with supplies and prizes alone costing about $8,000.

36

STIMULATING CREATIVE THINKING

Ernest Schuttenberg

Overview How widespread is creativity among your clients? Can creative thinking be learned? What are some of the skills associated with creative thinking? Is creativity an individual characteristic? A group characteristic? Both?

This activity will help your clients explore these questions and build seven creative thinking skills.

Suggested Time 2 hours
    Theory Session—15 minutes
    Warm-Up Creativity Exercises—20 minutes
    Creativity Simulation—70 minutes
    Debriefing Discussion—15 minutes

Materials Needed

✓ Form A (Some Ideas about Creativity)

✓ Form B (Warm-Up Creativity Exercises for Individuals and Small Groups)

✓ Form C (Team Creativity Simulation)

✓ One set of colorful plastic or wooden construction materials for each team, such as tinkertoys, Rig-a-Jig, or a comparable set, each containing at least 100 pieces of various shapes with connectors to link the pieces together.

Procedure

1. Distribute copies of Form A and provide a theory session on creativity using the ideas on Form A plus any additional information you may find helpful. (15 minutes)

2. Lead the participants (working in small groups of three or four) in the seven warm-up creativity exercises found on Form B. Use the

Contact Information: 6083 Park Ridge Drive, North Olmsted, OH 44070, 440-734-8249

Discussion Points following each exercise. After all the exercises have been completed, distribute copies of Form B to each person for reference. (20 minutes)

3. Ask the participants to remain in their groups. Distribute copies of Form C to the members of each group and review the instructions and time line for each phase of the simulation. Conduct the simulation.

4. After the simulation, lead a discussion on what the participants have learned about creativity and how they can apply what they learned in their work settings.

Variation Use actual work teams (regardless of their size) for the Team Creativity Simulation, Form C.

SOME IDEAS ABOUT CREATIVITY
FORM A

Characteristics of Creativity

Creativity means "bringing into being something that was not there before" (de Bono, 1992, p. 3). This "new thing" must have some value. The creative output should not be obvious or easy—it must be unique or rare. There is also an element of change in creativity, in the sense that the creative output changes the way people look at things. Rather than relying on Vertical Thinking, creativity relies on Lateral Thinking. De Bono explains the difference between these two thinking modes this way: "You cannot dig a hole in a different place by digging the same hole deeper" (pp. 52–53).

Seven Skills of Creativity

Creativity is not the province of only a few geniuses. There are a number of skills that promote creativity, and these skills can be learned and developed in individuals and teams. Listed below are some of the key skills of creativity and some questions to ask to promote creativity:

1. **Ideational Fluency:** the ability to generate many different ideas.
   Ask: What additional ways are there to...?

2. **Possibility Thinking:** the ability to see many ways of doing things.
   Ask: What are the possibilities...?

3. **Scenario Thinking:** the ability to conceive of a range of future possibilities.
   Ask: Can we look at it this way...and this way... and this way,...?

4. **Combinational Ability:** the ability to see relationships among seemingly unrelated objects or ideas.
   Ask: What are the similarities between...and...?

5. **Provocation Skill:** the ability and will to challenge traditional ways of thinking or doing things.
   Ask: Why does it have to be done this way?

6. **Disruptive Tendency:** the ability to disassemble familiar ways of doing things and to reassemble them in new ways.
   Ask: How about if we changed it from...to...?

7. **Paradigm Flexibility:** the ability to change one's frame of reference from prevailing ideas and beliefs.
   Ask: Maybe what we've been doing is no longer productive. How about...?

Reference: de Bono, Edward. (1992) *Serious Creativity: Using the Power of Lateral Thinking to Create New Ideas.* New York: HarperBusiness.

WARM-UP CREATIVITY EXERCISES FOR INDIVIDUALS AND SMALL GROUPS
FORM B

1. **Ideational Fluency:** Do each exercise as individuals, then share with team members:
   In one minute, write down as many uses as you can think of for:
   ✓ a brick.
   ✓ a baseball bat.

   Discussion Points:
   How many uses did you identify?
   How might you increase your ideational fluency?

2. **Possibility Thinking:** Do first as individuals, then share with your team:
   In one minute, how many possible ways can you think of to get from here to Beijing, China?

   Discussion Points
   How many of you listed geographic routes?
   How many listed methods of transportation?
   How many listed other possibilities?

3. **Scenario Thinking:** Discuss these in your team (3 minutes):
   Can you think of a set of circumstances in the future in which:
   ✓ Computers would be banned?
   ✓ Computers would be worshipped?
   ✓ Computers would be swallowed?

   Discussion Points
   Share some of the scenarios you came up with.
   To what extent was it helpful to discuss these items with others in developing your scenarios?

4. **Combinational Ability:** Discuss these in your team (2 minutes):
   If *up, in,* and *down* can be linked together by the word *shut,* what word links:
   ✓ *fish, cut,* and *cream*?   cold
   ✓ *apprentice, leader, and war*?   ship
   ✓ *baseball, fishing, and trousers*? fly

   Discussion Points
   How did you link each set of words?
   How helpful were your small group discussions in arriving at solutions?

5. **Provocation Skill:** Discuss this in your team (2 minutes):
For many centuries, there have been colleges and universities. How else might people become equally highly educated?

<u>Discussion Points</u>
What were your responses?
What assumptions did you make in arriving at your solutions?

6. **Disruptive Tendency:** Work on these individually, then share with team members. (Read one letter at a time for each cluster. Allow one minute after reading the last letter in each cluster):
Form known words by adding one letter at a time (in any order):
A—T—R—E—G—T   (AT, RAT, TEAR, GRATE, TARGET)
I—T—S—F—G—H—R   (I, IT, SIT, FITS, GIFTS, FIGHTS, FRIGHTS)

<u>Discussion Points</u>
What were the hardest and easiest parts of this exercise? Why?

7. **Paradigm Flexibility:** Work on individually (1 minute), then share with your team:
How could a person eat an iron bar? (Easily, if it was a candy bar, rich in iron.)

<u>Discussion Points</u>
What answers did you come up with?
What key skill was required here?

TEAM CREATIVITY SIMULATION
FORM C

Task: Using construction pieces provided, create, design, and build an object related in some way to "free enterprise." Or, if you wish, choose a concept that relates to your organization's mission, such as "customer satisfaction."

Criterion: The object must contain at least 50 pieces.

Materials: Each team will be given a set of construction materials.

Observers: Each team should select one or two observers who will not actively participate in Phases 1 and 2 of the simulation but will play a major role in Phase 3.

Phase 1: *Planning* (15 minutes): Each team should be given a Sample Kit, containing one of each kind of construction piece that will be provided.
✓ Plan what the object will be.
✓ Plan how it will be designed.
✓ Plan who will be involved in building the object.

Phase 2: *Construction* (25 minutes): During this phase, the Observers should take notes regarding the use of the seven skills of creativity identified on Form A. After Phase 2, the members of the teams should walk around and observe the objects built by each team.

Phase 3: *Presentation* (5 minutes each team): Each of the Observers should report briefly on the following:
✓ How the object relates to "free enterprise" or other concept chosen.
✓ How the seven creative skills were used by the team during planning.
✓ How team resources were used in constructing the object.

Phase 4: *Discussion* (about 15 minutes). General discussion about the experiences of the members of the teams during the simulation, about how to maximize team creativity, and about how participants can apply what they learned in their work settings.

37

GATHERING AND ANALYZING DATA

Cindy Bentson

Overview
This exercise is fun, high in energy, intense, noisy, and often a little frustrating. The point that teams will understand by the conclusion of the activity is that data gathering and analysis, solution generation and selection, solution implementation, evaluation, feedback, and adjustment are all critical elements of a logical and systematic problem-solving cycle.

Participants should be in teams of about 4 to 9. Standing or developing teams should be kept intact if at all possible to enhance the team development aspects of this activity. At least two teams are required to create opportunity for competition, excitement, and fun as well as opportunity for vicarious learning. The number of teams is unlimited except for physical space.

Suggested Time
45 to 90 minutes

Materials Needed

✓ A work table (approximately 3′ × 8′) for each team

✓ A gross (144) of multicolored, 7″ round balloons for each team (keep a few gross more on hand if needed)

✓ One sharp object to pop balloons for each team (e.g., poultry skewers)

✓ 3 to 4 clear (so that teams can easily see from a distance or close-up what's inside of them) lawn-size trash bags for each team

✓ Whistle or bell for the facilitator to use to call time

✓ Glue, tape, sticks, paper plates, ribbon/yarn (these are distracters, so you can get creative with what you provide the teams—just make sure each team gets the same materials)

Contact Information: Federal Aviation Administration, Air Traffic Division, Northwest Mountain Region, ANM-503, 1601 Lind Ave. SW, Renton, WA 98055, 425-227-1116, bentsonc@grieg.holmsjoen.com

✓ Flip chart, easel, tape, and marking pens for each team for data gathering and analysis

✓ One chair for each team for "Quality Specialist" to sit on, placed at least 20 feet away from team table

Procedure:

1. Before participants arrive, prepare each work table with the materials. Open the bag of balloons and dump it onto the table, and place the other (distracter) materials on the table. Place a flip chart and easel next to each work table.

2. Assign each team to a work table. Make sure there is space for participants to move around freely.

3. Have each team select a "Quality Specialist." Ask all of the "Quality Specialists" to go out of the room with one facilitator for "special training." Another facilitator should stay in the room with the teams to give them their instructions. (Note: If you only have a couple of small teams and you're the only facilitator, simply ask the nonspecialists to remain in the room relaxing while the specialists receive brief training.)

4. Out of earshot and view of the participants, explain to the quality specialists that their job is quality control. They will evaluate each balloon product as presented to them and either accept it as a quality product or reject it as a nonquality product. They may only accept or reject a balloon—they cannot in any way indicate why a balloon was accepted or rejected. If they accept the balloon, they place it in the large, clear garbage bag. If they reject it, they are to pop it with the sharp instrument. A quality product must be:

✓ fully inflated

✓ secured by a knot in the balloon

✓ presented to the Quality Specialist from the team member's left hand

✓ a different color from the previously presented balloon, regardless of whether it was accepted or rejected

✓ presented by a different team member each time, regardless of whether the balloon was accepted or rejected

The Quality Specialists need to know these rules cold so they don't make a mistake. Any mistakes will cause the teams to not be able to collect accurate data on what makes a quality product. Keeping track is a lot tougher than it sounds!

5. Bring the Quality Specialists back into the room and have them take their places in their chairs. Each chair should be a good 20 feet (or more) from the table, in a relatively straight line from it. You want the team members to have to travel a little bit during production times.

6. Explain that the teams are in a balloon factory and the product is an inflated balloon. The goal of each production unit (team) is to construct quality balloons using the raw materials at their work station. When a team believes it has a quality product, someone is to present the product to the Quality Specialist who will either accept or reject it. The Specialists are not allowed to talk or to indicate in any way why a balloon is accepted or rejected.

7. Indicate that they will have 5 minutes to plan their work . They are not allowed to inflate any of the balloons during planning time. They will then be given 3 minutes of production time. The beginning and the end of production will be indicated by a whistle.

8. After the first planning and production cycle, tell them that they'll have 10 minutes to plan for the next 3-minute production period. Again, use your whistle to indicate start and finish times.

   Answer any questions they might have without giving anything away or telling them how they should plan their production.

9. There will be several rounds of planning and production times. Each planning session should be about 10 minutes, during which time the team members are not allowed to produce (inflate) any balloon products. They may rearrange their raw materials if they'd like. Each production session should be about 3 minutes. [These times may be adjusted according to the needs of the teams—longer planning sessions are encouraged if they're using the time to collect, analyze, and evaluate the data. On the other hand, I've discovered that longer production times increase the likelihood that teams use trial and error methods and focus only on turning out quantity, rather than slowing down to plan and produce quality products. Emphasis should be placed on planning rather than on production, though this is almost guaranteed to cause frustration and impatience for team members.]

10. During the first 10-minute planning session (just after the first production period), gather the Quality Specialists together so they can review the rules and calibrate their judgments. They're likely to be a bit overwhelmed and unsure of their ability to remember all of the rules and judge the balloon products fairly. They're also

likely to be excited and wanting to talk about what has just happened, and maybe share their frustration at not being able to communicate with their own teams (or anyone else) during the production period. Make sure their discussions are out of earshot of the teams. Remind them that consistency is the key for successful data gathering and analysis by the teams.

11. Most of the time, the teams will start out in a pure trial and error mode, which is appropriate since they have no data yet. Unfortunately, a lot of teams don't keep track very well of what is accepted or rejected (they have no clues so they'll try all sorts of interesting things), and some pursue a trial-and-error course all the way through the activity instead of carefully gathering data and analyzing it. If your teams are not getting the point of collecting data (what is rejected, what is accepted) and analyzing it by the third or fourth round, start gently facilitating them to think about how to figure it out. Some teams might get very frustrated and claim that the Specialists are using random (and malicious) judgments. You'll have to challenge that thinking and get them to think about how they could figure out what the characteristics of a quality product really are. If they think of it, they can go and examine all of the accepted balloon products (and the rejected balloons as well—the pieces will be scattered, though).

12. A team has successfully solved the quality product riddle when it can present several balloons (use your own judgment on the number) in a row and get them all accepted. After they have completed this task, have them tell you (out of earshot of the other teams) what the characteristics are. This will help you determine that their work was not simply a fluke. After a team has successfully completed the task, they can either be cheerleaders for the other teams or coach them, without directly telling the other teams the solution.

13. After all teams have completed the task or you run out of raw materials (balloons) or time, it's time for a little stress reducer! Dump out all of the accepted balloons and invite everyone to pop them in any way they want. This will be incredibly noisy, but it does reduce the frustration that may have built up. Then everyone needs to help pick up the balloon cadavers.

Variation

Before each team selects its "Quality Specialist," have them brainstorm the characteristics of an effective quality specialist as a team resource. Then have them match those characteristics to someone on the team who is then the "Quality Specialist." This variation simply adds another dimension to the activity if it's appropriate.

Debriefing

The debriefing really depends on what the teams needed to get from this activity and how it applies to their work situations. It also depends on how sophisticated they were at collecting and analyzing data and how that skill shows up at work. You might also have a discussion around their ideas of cheating versus vicarious learning (some of my teams have thought that learning from the successes and failures of another team was cheating). Another fruitful area of discussion is that of competition. They had separate workstations, raw materials, and quality specialists, but there never was any rule against collaboration. Most teams will fall into the competitive mode instead of the collaborative mode. How does that relate to the work setting? Another area to discuss is the sharing of resources. Since they all work for the same company, did they share ideas, data, raw materials? Again, how does that show up at work? Another good area to debrief is their frustration around lack of communication from their Quality Specialists about a quality product. Let them discuss how poor communication, lack of clarity about goals, expectations, and so forth play a major part in frustration at work.

38
BALANCING CHANGE AND STABILITY

Mike Milstein

Overview   Organizational members often dislike and fear change because they may have to deal with many unknowns and they may have to let go of cherished practices. As a result, they often dig in their heels and resist change efforts.

Consultants need to recognize these typical responses to their initiatives and take them into account as they develop their strategies. This exercise is aimed at helping to create a balanced image of what will change and what will not change. The intent is to promote a realistic base of security while encouraging motivation for necessary changes by emphasizing what will not change as well as what will change.

Suggested Time   3 hours and 40 minutes

Materials Needed

✓ Newsprint, felt marking pens, and easel for each small group

✓ Facilitator's instructions on newsprint or as an overhead projection

✓ A room large enough for subgroups to work without disturbing each other; the space should also be flexible so the format can shift from small groups to large groups with ease

Procedure   1. Clarify the purpose of the exercise for the group: *The discussion will provide an opportunity for the group to explore whether it wants to keep or change important aspects of organizational life (structures, processes, products, behaviors, etc.).* As a result of the discussion, the group should be in a better position to decide what it will maintain and protect, what needs to be changed or eliminated, and what might need to be added. If the group is able to do

Contact Information: The Resiliency Group, Ltd., 4520 Compound Ct. NW, Albuquerque, NM 87107, 505-341-9450, Resiliencygroup@dellnet.com

these things, they should be ready to develop an action plan for change initiatives in the organization. (10 minutes)

2. Form small groups for discussion purposes (by work groups or across work groups). Ask the group to discuss this question: *What do we do that is excellent and should be maintained and protected*? A recorder should be appointed to list items the group agrees on. (30 minutes)

3. Ask recorders to post the agreements so all participants can see them. Each should read and expand upon the group's list. Ask the group to identify agreements that cut across small group lists that they feel strongly about maintaining and protecting, and post them on a sheet of newsprint. (30 minutes)

4. Ask members to return to their small group locations. Ask the groups to discuss the next question: *What do we do that is okay, but can be done better*? Agreements should be posted on newsprint by the recorders. (30 minutes)

5. As in step 3, have the total group discuss small group results and identify areas of agreement. (30 minutes)

6. Direct members to return to their small group locations for a final session. Ask the group to discuss the last question: *What are we not doing presently that we should consider doing*? Agreements should be posted on newsprint by the recorders. (30 minutes)

7. As in steps 3 and 5, invite the total group to discuss small group results and identify areas of agreement. (30 minutes)

8. Encourage the group to review the three lists:

   ✓ What should be maintained?

   ✓ What should be changed?

   ✓ What should be added?

   This is an opportunity to summarize agreements and to begin exploring appropriate action plans. (30 minutes)

Variations
1. Continue the group activity for the rest of the day, focusing on action plans. The added time can intensify the sense of ownership about agreements and add more depth and detail to the steps that should be taken to institutionalize them.

2. Separate the discussion into three segments and conduct it over a period of days or weeks:

   ✓ What to maintain?

✓ What to change?

✓ What to add?

Be sure to maintain the sequence as presented above. The longer time span can lead to fuller and more detailed discussions and, between discussions, time to reflect about what is identified and agreed upon.

39

BUILDING COACHING SUCCESS

Andrew Kimball

Andrew Kimball

Overview Conventional wisdom and most coaching experts recommend balancing positive and negative feedback in order to improve performance. Yet recipients of this "balanced feedback" often wind up feeling totally demotivated after a well-intended performance conversation. This activity provides a direct experience of a more successful approach to coaching. Using the tools presented in this simulation, coaches learn how to tell the most difficult truths in a way that leaves coachees looking forward to being coached again.

Suggested Time 90 minutes (See also Variations, Abbreviated.)

Activities	Minutes
Positioning	5
Round 1: Negative Feedback (with debriefing)	15
Round 2: Positive Feedback (with debriefing)	15
Round 3: Negative Ideas (with debriefing)	15
Round 4: Positive Ideas (with debriefing)	15
Round 5: Choose two of the above (with debriefing)	25
Total Time	**90**

Materials Needed For each two teams of 4 to 6 people:

✓ 3 unique, fun "bombs" to be hidden around the room (Note: To make the game more playful and to appeal to the kinesthetic and auditory modalities, use fun objects that make noise, such as a dinosaur that squeaks when squeezed or a bicycle horn.)

✓ 2 flip charts set up as score pads (see illustration at right).

✓ 1 flip chart set up to scribe notes

Contact Information: QBInternational, 824 E. Street, San Raphael, CA 94901, 415-457-1919, akimball@qube.com, www.qube.com

- ✓ 1 whistle or other device to signal the end of each round
- ✓ 4 blindfolds
- ✓ 1 stopwatch
- ✓ 4 sets of color-coordinated Direction Cards
- ✓ 1 pack of colored index cards
- ✓ Prizes for the winners (Be creative! How about a new BMW—a toy one, that is?)

Team A				
Task	Initial Time	Errors	Object Found	Total Score
Negative Feedback				
Positive Feedback				
Negative Ideas				
Positive Ideas				

Procedure

Note: You may play this game with as many as 30 teams. For every pair of teams, use a complete set of materials and designate a separate Bomb Zone.

Round 1: Negative Feedback

Setup

1. Divide participants into 2 teams. Explain that a terrorist organization has called in a bomb threat to your building. The bombs are due to go off in 5 minutes. Two rival bomb squads, Team A and Team B, have been called in. However, there is one problem. Today was the day when all the city's demolition experts went to the eye doctor to have their eyes dilated and examined. As a result, all the demolition experts are currently wearing blindfolds. They will be teamed up with expert guides who will act as their eyes. To make the situation even more explosive, the mayor is planning to cut the bomb squad's budget in half at the end of the month. Only the best team will survive the budget cuts.

2. Ask for a volunteer from each team to play the blindfolded demolition expert.

   Note: Some people have an aversion to being blindfolded. Once in awhile, an entire team refuses to be blindfolded. If no one on a team wishes to be blindfolded, ask for two volunteers from the opposite team. Trade one of the volunteers to the opposite team in exchange for one of their players. Announce that there has been an intersquad transfer.

3. Ask for a volunteer from each team to play the expert guide.

4. Explain that the rest of the team members will play the role of bomb squad efficiency experts.

5. Show the players the three bombs (noise-making objects). Explain that after the guides blindfold the demolition experts, you will place the three bombs around the room (or bomb zone).

6. Explain the role of the demolition experts:

   a. Designate two starting lines on opposite sides of the room. Try to ensure that both starting lines are equidistant from where you plan to hide the three bombs.

   b. Explain that the blindfolded demolition experts will have up to 5 minutes to find all three bombs and defuse them by ringing, squeaking, or holding them.

   c. Because each bomb may be found by more than one team, the demolition experts should be sure to return the bombs to where they found them once they have been defused. After the team has found and defused all three bombs, they must return to the starting line.

7. Explain the role of the guide:

   a. All demolition experts will have guides to help them move about the bomb zone. The guides and the demolition experts will act as teams.

   b. Guides may only provide information to the demolition experts in the form designated by their Direction Cards.

   c. Pass out the Negative Feedback Direction Cards (Form A) to everyone.

   d. Explain that in this first round, guides may not give any positive feedback or make any recommendations to the demolition experts. Guides may only give negative feedback about what the demolition experts have already done.

   e. Define negative feedback as negative judgments about past actions.

   f. Review the examples on the Negative Feedback Direction Cards (Form A).

   g. Elicit three or four other examples of negative feedback from the group.

8. Explain the role of the bomb squad efficiency experts:

   a. Team members who are not guides or demolition experts will be bomb squad efficiency experts.

   b. Each bomb squad efficiency expert should carry a pencil and an index card or pad of paper.

   c. Bomb squad efficiency experts are responsible for observing the opposing team's demolition expert and Guide and keeping track of their errors, including:

      • From the opposing guide: illegal directions.

      • From the opposing demolition experts: illegal bumps, brushes, or touches of objects other than the bomb.

   d. Each time they observe an error, the bomb squad efficiency experts should call, "Fault!" and briefly explain the error to the opposing team's guide. Then they should record the error on the index card or paper.

   e. Remind them that at the end of each round, the Game Director will add the bomb squad efficiency experts' fault points to the opposing team's score, so it is critical that bomb squad efficiency experts be accurate.

   f. Scoring:

      • The team with the *fewest points* at the end of the four rounds is the winner.

      • Teams will earn *1 point for each second it takes to find the three bombs* and return to the starting line.

Example:

If a demolition expert finds all three bombs and returns to the starting line in 2 minutes and 15 seconds, the team will score: 2 minutes x 60 seconds plus 15 seconds = 135 points.

   • If the 5-minute time limit runs out before the bombs are found, the team will receive 5 x 60 seconds = 300 points.

   • 50 penalty points will be added to a team's score every time the guide uses illegal directions.

Example:

In Round 1, if the guide slips up and says, "Turn left" (a recommendation) or says, "Good, keep going in that direction" (positive feedback), the team will be penalized 50 points for each occurrence.

- *10 penalty points* will be added to a team's score every time a demolition expert bumps into, brushes against, or in any way touches an object that is not a bomb.

Example:

If a demolition expert bumps into three chairs and brushes against one of the bomb squad efficiency experts, the team will have added to its final score 4 x 10 = 40 penalty points.

- *100 bonus points* will be subtracted from the team's score for defusing all three bombs.

Practice

1. Ask the guides to blindfold the demolition experts.

2. When demolition experts are blindfolded, ask a bomb squad efficiency expert from the opposing team to examine the blindfolds to ensure that the demolition experts cannot see anything.

3. Give the guides 1 minute to practice giving negative feedback commands, with bomb squad efficiency experts watching for faults.

4. Be sure to correct any mistakes that the bomb squad efficiency experts miss.

Play

1. Have the guides move the demolition experts to their respective starting lines.

2. Silently, and with great show, walk the bombs to their "hiding" spots, using hand motions to direct the attention of the guides to their locations.

3. Check one last time for questions.

4. Check to make sure everyone is ready.

5. Blow the whistle to begin play.

6. Keep track of time and call out each minute as it passes.

7. Count down the last 10 seconds.

8. When 5 minutes have passed, stop the clock and blow the whistle.

9. Ask the bomb squad efficiency experts to record the times, faults, and objects on the flip chart scorepads.

Debriefing Questions

How do you feel? *(to the demolition experts)*
What were you feeling during this round?

How do you feel? *(to the guides)*
What were you feeling during this round?

What happened? *(to the efficiency experts)*
What did you notice going on?
What happened next?
What happened after that?

What values were evident? *(to the group)*
If we start with the assumption that our values drive our behaviors, what values may have been driving the behavior of the demolition experts?
What values drove the other behaviors you observed?

What did you learn? *(to the group)*
As you reflect on what you observed and what the demolition experts have told us about their feelings and their choices, what general principles might you come up with to explain what you observed? (Elicit several responses.)
What else?

How does this relate to the real world? *(to the group)*
Assume for a moment that this game is a metaphor for something you experience every day in each of your jobs. What do you experience in your jobs that is governed by the same principles we discussed?

Round 2: Positive Feedback

Setup

1. Reset the clock for 5 minutes.

2. Explain that all roles will stay the same except the role of the guide.

3. Ask for a new guide from each team. Thank the old guides.

4. Explain the role of the guide:

   a. The new guides and the demolition experts will continue to act as teams.

   b. Pass out the Positive Feedback Direction Cards (Form B) to everyone.

   c. Explain that in the second round, guides may not give any negative feedback or make any recommendations to the demolition experts. Guides may only give positive feedback about what the demolition experts have already done.

d. Define positive feedback as positive judgments about past events.

e. Review the examples on the Positive Feedback Direction Cards (Form B).

f. Elicit three or four other examples of positive feedback from the group.

Practice

Practice as in the first round.

Play

Begin and manage play as in the first round.

Debriefing Questions

How do you feel? *(to the demolition experts)*
What were you feeling during this round?
What's changed since the last round?

How do you feel? *(to the guides)*
What were you feeling during this round?
What's changed since the last round?

What happened? *(to the efficiency experts)*
What did you notice going on?
What happened next?
What happened after that?

What values were evident? *(to the group)*
If we start with the assumption that our values drive our behaviors, what values may have been driving the behavior of the demolition experts?
What values drove the other behaviors you observed?

What did you learn? *(to the group)*
As you reflect on what you observed and what the demolition experts have told us about their feelings and their choices, what general principles might you come up with to explain what you observed? (Elicit several responses.)
What else?

How does this relate to the real world? *(to the group)*
Assume for a moment that this game is a metaphor for something you experience every day in each of your jobs. What do you

experience in your jobs that is governed by the same principles we discussed?

Round 3: Negative Ideas

Setup

1. Set up as before.

2. Explain that in the third round all rules stay exactly the same as before except the role of the guide.

3. Ask for new guides from each team. Thank the old guides.

4. Explain the role of the guides:

   a. The new guides and the demolition experts will continue to act as teams.

   b. Pass out the Negative Idea Direction Cards (Form C) to everyone.

   c. Explain that in the third round guides may not give any feedback or make any positive recommendations to the demolition experts. Guides may only offer negative ideas about what the demolition experts should do, beginning each statement with, "You should not...."

   d. Define negative ideas as recommendations about future actions not to try.

   e. Review the examples on the Negative Idea Direction Cards (Form C).

   f. Elicit three or four other examples of negative ideas from the group.

Practice

Practice as before.

Play

Begin and manage play as before.

Debriefing Questions

How do you feel? *(to the demolition experts)*
What were you feeling during this round?
What's changed since the last round?

How do you feel? *(to the guides)*
What were you feeling during this round?

What's changed since the last round?

What happened? *(to the efficiency experts)*
What did you notice going on?
What happened next?
What happened after that?

What values were evident? *(to the group)*
If we start with the assumption that our values drive our behaviors, what values may have been driving the behavior of the demolition experts?
What values drove the other behaviors you observed?

What did you learn? *(to the group)*
As you reflect on what you observed and what the demolition experts have told us about their feelings and their choices, what general principles might you come up with to explain what you observed? (Elicit several responses.)
What else?

How does this relate to the real world? *(to the group)*
Assume for a moment that this game is a metaphor for something you experience every day in each of your jobs. What do you experience in your jobs that is governed by the same principles we discussed?

Round 4: Positive Ideas

Setup

1. Set up as before.

2. Explain that in the fourth round, all rules stay exactly the same as before except the role of the guides.

3. Ask for new guides from each team. Thank the old guides.

4. Explain the role of the guides:

   a. The new guides and the demolition experts will continue to act as teams.

   b. Pass out the Positive Idea Direction Cards (Form D) to everyone.

   c. Explain that in the fourth round, guides may not give any feedback or make any negative recommendations to the demolition experts. Guides may only offer positive ideas about what the demolition experts should do.

   d. Define positive ideas as recommendations about future actions.

e. Review the examples on the Positive Idea Direction Cards (Form D).

f. Elicit three or four other examples of positive ideas from the group.

Practice
Practice as before.

Play
Begin and manage play as before.

Debriefing Questions

How do you feel? *(to the demolition experts)*
What were you feeling during this round?
What's changed since the last round?

How do you feel? *(to the guides)*
What were you feeling during this round?
What's changed since the last round?

What happened? *(to the efficiency experts)*
What did you notice going on?
What happened next?
What happened after that?

What values were evident? *(to the group)*
If we start with the assumption that our values drive our behaviors, what values may have been driving the behavior of the demolition experts?
What values drove the other behaviors you observed?

What did you learn? *(to the group)*
As you reflect on what you observed and what the demolition experts have told us about their feelings and their choices, what general principles might you come up with to explain what you observed? (Elicit several responses.)
What else?

How does this relate to the real world? *(to the group)*
Assume for a moment that this game is a metaphor for something you experience every day in each of your jobs. What do you experience in your jobs that is governed by the same principles we discussed?

Round 5: Choose 2

Setup

1. Set up as before.

2. Explain that in the fifth round all rules stay exactly the same as before except the role of the guides.

3. Ask for a new guide from each team. Thank the old guides.

4. Explain the role of the guides:

   a. In the fifth round the guides may use any two of the four coaching tools: Negative Feedback, Positive Feedback, Negative Ideas, or Positive Ideas.

   b. Remind the guides that this is the last chance they have to reduce the team's score. The BMWs are still up for grabs.

Play

1. Don't allow practice for this round.

2. Begin and manage play as before.

Final Scoring

1. When the round is over, total the scores from each of the rounds. The team with the lowest score is the winning team.

2. Award prizes: cash or the keys to the new BMW.

Final Debriefing Questions

How do you feel? *(to the demolition experts)*
   What were you feeling during this round?
   What's changed since the last round?

How do you feel? *(to the guides)*
   What were you feeling during this round?
   What's changed since the last round?

What happened? *(to the efficiency experts)*
   What did you notice going on?
   What happened next?
   What happened after that?

What values were evident? *(to the group)*
   If we start with the assumption that our values drive our behaviors, what values may have been driving the initial behavior of the demolition experts?
   What values drove the other behaviors you observed?

What did you learn? *(to the group)*

As you reflect on what you observed and what the demolition experts have told us about their feelings and their choices, what general principles might you come up with to explain what you observed? (Elicit several responses.)

What might we suggest as the optimal situation in which to use negative feedback alone?

What can we say about how to combine the different feedback tools?

What else?

How does this relate to the real world? *(to the group)*

Assume for a moment that this game is a metaphor for something you experience every day in each of your jobs. What do you experience in your jobs that is governed by the same principles as we discussed?

What if? *(to the demolition experts)*

What if we increased the number of bombs? How might that have changed your choices?

What if we decreased the time you had to defuse the bombs? How might that have changed your choices?

What if we increased the penalty for making mistakes? How might that have changed your choices?

What next? *(to the group)*

What might you do differently as a result of what you learned here?

How might you apply the principles you learned here to how you coach your people?

How might you apply the principles you learned here to how you receive coaching from your coaches?

Variations   1. Abbreviated: This activity can be compressed by eliminating less critical rounds. When pressed for time, you may eliminate Round 3 or Round 5 and develop those insights in the "what if" phase of the final debriefing. The richness of each round depends heavily on the time allocated for debriefing.

2. Houston Control: This game can be played with any exercise in which one person depends on another for information, advice, or instructions. In a recent variation, we used an electronic switch box to simulate a space adventure. One participant (the Astronaut) was required to throw 36 unmarked switches in a designated, patterned order. A second participant (Houston Control) called out instructions regarding which switches to throw in what

order. A buzzer sounded if the switches were thrown in the wrong order.

In Houston Control, we used the same series of Negative Feedback, Positive Feedback, Negative Ideas, Positive Ideas, and Choose 2 to communicate instructions, and we used the same debriefing questions to expand the learning.

NEGATIVE FEEDBACK DIRECTION CARD FORM A

Guides and demolition experts will act as teams. The demolition expert's goal is to defuse all of the bombs in the bomb zone and return to the starting line as quickly as possible. In this round, guides may not make recommendations or offer encouraging feedback. Guides may only offer demolition experts **negative judgments about past events** such as:

What Guides May Say	What Guides May Not Say
You shouldn't have turned left.	Turn right. Don't turn left.
You shouldn't have turned right.	Turn left. Don't turn right.
You shouldn't have walked past that spot.	Keep going in that direction.
You should not have raised [lowered] your hand.	Raise [lower] your hand.
	That's right, keep raising [lowering] your hand.
	Move your hand 30 degrees to the right.
You should not have leaned over so far.	Lean over farther.
You should not have sped up [slowed down].	Speed up [slow down].

POSITIVE FEEDBACK DIRECTION CARD FORM B

The demolition expert's goal again is to defuse all of the bombs placed around the room and return to the starting point as quickly as possible. Guides may not tell demolition experts to speed up, slow down, or turn. Guides may only offer demolition experts **positive data about past events** such as:

What Guides May Say	What Guides May Not Say
Turning left was a good idea.	Turn left. You shouldn't have turned right.
Turning right was a good idea.	Turn right. Don't turn left.
You were right to slow down.	Slow down. You shouldn't have been walking so fast.
You were right to have raised [lowered] your hand.	Raise [lower] your hand.
That's right, keep raising your hand.	Move your hand 30 degrees to the right.
You were right to have leaned over so far.	Lean over farther.
You were right to have sped up [slowed down].	Speed up [slow down].

NEGATIVE IDEA DIRECTION CARD FORM C

Guides and demolition experts will act as teams. The demolition expert's goal is to defuse all of the bombs in the bomb zone and return to the starting line as quickly as possible. In this round, guides may not make recommendations or offer encouraging feedback. Guides may only offer demolition experts **negative judgments about past events** such as:

What Guides May Say	What Guides May Not Say
You shouldn't turn left.	Turn right. You shouldn't have turned left.
You shouldn't turn right.	Turn left. You shouldn't have turned right.
You shouldn't keep going in that direction.	Keep going in that direction. You shouldn't have stopped.
You should not raise [lower] your hand.	Raise [lower] your hand.
	That's right, keep raising [lowering] your hand.
	Move your hand 30 degrees to the right.
You should not lean over so far.	Lean over farther.
You should not speed up [slow down].	Speed up [slow down].

POSITIVE IDEA DIRECTION
CARD   FORM D

The demolition expert's goal again is to defuse all the bombs placed around the room and return to the starting point as quickly as possible. This time, guides may tell demolition experts to speed up, slow down, or turn. Guides may only offer demolition experts **positive future-oriented ideas or suggestions about future actions** such as:

What Guides May Say	What Guides May Not Say
Turn left.	Don't turn right. You shouldn't have turned right.
Turn right.	Don't turn left. You shouldn't have turned left.
Keep going in that direction.	Don't keep going in that direction. You should have stopped.
Raise [lower] your hand.	Don't raise [lower] your hand.
	Don't move your hand 30 degrees to the right.
Lean over farther.	You were right to lean over farther.
Speed up [slow down].	Don't speed up [slow down]. You should not have slowed down [sped up].

40

MAKING MEETINGS BETTER

Susan Stites-Doe and Gary Briggs

Overview   This exercise seeks to raise awareness about the perils of poor meeting leadership and introduces simple ways in which one may improve the meeting experience and outcomes for participants. Participants will read a case that will serve as the basis for a group discussion. Groups will be charged with two objectives: to state the problems and to propose solutions.

Two successive rounds of meetings will be employed, one unaided and one aided (i.e., using the process for leadership we suggest). Debriefing will direct learning toward the benefits of employing the meeting leadership process we recommend, while at the same time acknowledging the difficulties of achieving shared voice and consensus among group members.

The case itself encourages participants to operate in teams and to consider fairness and the values of team-based performance in making decisions. It could be readily integrated into discussions of any of the following topical areas:

✓   Decision making

✓   Team-based organizational performance

✓   Team-based values

✓   Organizational justice, fairness

✓   Management development

✓   Organizational culture

Suggested Time   50 to 60 minutes

Materials Needed   ✓   Form A (An Introduction to Meetings)

Contact Information: Susan Stites-Doe and Gary Briggs, State University of New York College at Brockport, Department of Business Administration, 115A Hartwell Hall, Brockport, NY 14420, 716-395-5518 (Susan), 716-395-5526 (Gary), ssdoe@aol.com, gbriggs@brockport.edu

✓ Form B (The Case)

✓ Form C (The Problem-Solving Process Guide)

✓ Form D (Observer's Feedback Sheet)

✓ Form E (Participant's Feedback Sheet)

Procedure

1. *An Introduction to the Topic of Business Meetings:* This introduction provides a discussion of the types of meetings that are held in business contexts and how much time the average manager spends in meetings. (See Form A.)

2. *Subgroups Formed, Case Study Discussed:* Each group is given a simple case to read (Form B), and is asked to come to some preliminary conclusions regarding their proposed solution to perceived problems. Groups should work independently and unaided for approximately 10 minutes, and should then be prepared to give a 30-second synopsis of their solutions to the case.

3. *Problem-Solving Process Guide (Form C) is handed out.* Groups are instructed to use it to formulate new perspectives on the problem and to reach conclusions regarding best solutions.

4. *Feedback from Observers:* A single observer is appointed for each group. Observers are asked to fill out an Observer Feedback Sheet (Form D).

5. *Debriefing, Tips, and Tricks for Improving Problem-Solving Meeting Effectiveness:* At the close, participants fill out the Participant's Feedback Sheet (Form E) and discuss their reactions to the exercise in the teams. The instructor concludes, using a flip chart, board, etc. to record key points.

AN INTRODUCTION TO MEETINGS
FORM A

Managers and Meetings: The Bottomless Pit

One research study estimates that managers spend up to two-thirds of each business day in meetings. The same study reveals that among those meetings, half are regarded by attendees to be a total waste of time! Fact is, managers' jobs are getting tougher. Why? Primarily because there are fewer managers, and because they are responsible for more tasks.

Many of the tasks that managers were once responsible for are now handled directly by teams of subordinates. Groups such as self-managed work teams are now directly responsible for task accomplishment, and act independently from their managers. These groups need to understand how to assume the leadership roles once assigned to managers.

We should view the leadership of meetings as a topic whose time has come. The leadership of meetings makes a difference in the quality of meeting outcomes and in the extent to which members feel involved. Leadership of problem-solving meetings may be likened to an artful process that can be improved through training.

The History of Meetings: Structure and Parliamentary Procedure

Perhaps the most widely known meeting structure is commonly referred to as *parliamentary procedure* or simply *Robert's Rules.* These procedures call for fairly rigid adherence to a formal meeting process. For example, *motions* or suggestions for action, are made by attendees following a set of rules. These suggestions are then voted on by the meeting participants (a certain number, or *quorum,* must be present to vote), and the motion may or may not pass, depending on the outcome of the vote. Some motions are debatable and others are not. Other illustrations of formal rules of order are: One must be recognized by the meeting chair in order to contribute to the discussion, and proposed actions may be *tabled,* or pushed off to a future meeting.

Formal rules of order can be traced back as far as the sixteenth century, to the British Parliament. After ratification of the Constitution by the thirteen original colonies in the U.S., Thomas Jefferson, then president of the U.S. Senate, wrote the *Manual of Parliamentary Practice,* which was based on procedures used by the English House of Commons. In the late 1860s, Major Henry Robert wrote a set of rules that could be applied by society as a whole. This method combined parliamentary procedure with a single set of rules. Commonly known as Robert's Rules of Order, this hybrid set of rules is applied in board rooms and committee work across the world. These rules create a rigid structure that some critics say interferes with good decision making.

Types of Meetings

There are all kinds of meetings, and they have various purposes. Here are a few: training meetings, committee meetings, board meetings, summary, update, and review meetings, performance evaluation meetings, etc.

Edward Scannell ("We've Got to Stop Meeting Like This," *Training and Development,* January 1992, pp. 70–71) has sorted meetings into four categories:

Information meetings include training sessions.

Action meetings are brief, with two people addressing a problem to get closure and action.

Brainstorming meetings are called in order to generate a listing of creative solutions to problems.

Problem-solving meetings involve a group or team that gets together to attack a single problem.

Because it is our belief that much of a manager's job is spent in the process of solving problems, we focus here on the last category of meetings, the problem-solving meeting.

THE CASE FORM B

Instructions

1. Please read the following case.
2. After reading the case, work as a team to accomplish the following goals, and write them down as deliverables to present to the rest of the class:
   ✓ Decide what problem(s) exist in the case.
   ✓ Create a plan to solve the problem(s).
3. You have 10 to 15 minutes to work on this.

Introduction

Your company, Acme Pens, Inc., manufactures and markets fine writing implements, including high-end fountain pens and mechanical pencils. Acme's competition is mainly foreign, and you have a rich history and reputation for high-quality merchandise. Your work team, together for three years, is responsible for the development of technical documents and user support materials that accompany the fountain pens when they are packaged for delivery to customers. The unit is called the marketing support team. Its deliverables include the creation of "plain English" instruction sheets, replacement parts order forms, cross-selling order sheets for fine papers, ink cartridges, and wells, and the design of packaging materials that will keep damage to the pens in transit at a minimum. The marketing support unit is truly a self-managed work team. It makes hiring, firing, and salary adjustment decisions on behalf of the team. What's more, team members truly enjoy each other's company and have deep respect for each other's skill sets and talents. Several of you refer to this team experience as the best job you've ever had.

The Team

Each of the team members works a 40-hour week. Your team members have the following human capital characteristics.

Name	Job Tenure	Performance Rating*	Level of Education	Number of Dependents
Frances	18 years	4.9	Grad. Degree: English	Husband + 3 children
Wray	12 years	4.75	Grad. Degree: Liberal Arts	None
Drew	10 years	4.5	BS: Advertising	Wife
Alex	3 years	4.6	BS: Business	Wife +1 child
*Average, last 5 years; 5 = highest, 1 = lowest.				

The Challenge

Today you learned that the company is suffering from lowered third-quarter sales and profitability, and that the company is considering rapid cost reduction maneuvers to avoid further profit drains. The source of the problem appears to be in production costs, which are escalating due to milling and machining costs overruns. Your team has been charged with coming up with ways to reduce costs. Though you have not been explicitly directed to recommend layoffs, the team senses that downsizing may occur should costs not be contained. Mainly because of foreign competition, several of your competitors have recently announced their own intentions to downsize. Each of you works a full 40-hour work week.

Infrastructure and Product Line

The CEO and founder of Acme Pens, Mr. Thorton F. Inkwell, recently hired a human resource director to update the company's benefits package and to examine human resource costs across each of the functional areas. This addition relieved the burden of the office manager, who single-handedly managed both the office staff of 5 and a broad range of personnel issues for the entire plant of 146 employees. The new HR director, Susan Peoples, prepared a staffing report for Mr. Inkwell that suggested that the marketing support unit was top heavy, and that, in keeping with empowerment trends, *they* should be given the chance to respond to the challenge of quickly reducing costs. Like her competitors, and in response to Mr. Inkwell's directives, her initial thought was to recommend the trimming of Acme's labor force.

The Competition's Edge

Foreign competitors use highly-polished, colorful acrylics in manufacturing their pen casings, and their trendy, eye-catching designs, and low prices pack a powerful one-two punch in enticing buyers, particularly young buyers. Acmes' products are consistent, reliable, and functional, and tend to fall in the mid-priced range. Their pen casings are metal, and associated machining costs make annual price increases necessary. Fortunately, standardized casings—even acrylic ones—are now widely available in the industry, and these can be custom-milled for brand identity purposes (i.e., to permit the insertion of a trademark or logo) at little additional cost. Mr. Inkwell regards these cookie-cutter products as inferior to Acmes' and has not encouraged the newly formed new-product team to pursue these options. The new-product team, a cross-functional team made up of five members from throughout the company, including the marketing support team's Frances, disagrees with this hard line and sees this chance at introducing a line of low-cost pens as yet another opportunity slipping quietly away.

Hidden Costs, Secret Ambitions

Frances, the most tenured member of the marketing support team, sees the situation differently from Mr. Inkwell. She knows that her team's job is to work on supporting the product from the time it leaves the end of the production line to the time it arrives safely in the consumers' hands. A quick check with the sales department reveals that customer chargebacks were at an all-time high last quarter. "Has no one else seen this!" she wonders aloud upon reading the response to her E-mail query. It would appear that the packing materials that her unit recommended and inspected last quarter are no longer assuring safe passage of Acme's products. She vows to talk to the purchasing agent in the morning to try to understand more about what's behind this change. At the same time, Frances is tired. She would almost welcome a layoff, or the break a brief layoff would permit. Her daughter has just taken a job-sharing position, and she looks enviously at that arrangement! She considers what reduced hours might mean for several of her teammates...Would a layoff be good for them too?

The Bottom Line

The marketing support team has been asked to agree upon a possible method through which it can reduce costs for the work team. The team fears that management intends to lay off or even terminate employees, and it wants to protect the interests of all members.

THE PROBLEM-SOLVING PROCESS GUIDE FORM C

1. State your own *perceptions* of the problems that exist in the case. State problems as facts, limit their scope, be precise, clarify terms, and give whatever background statements are necessary to support your claim.

   _____

   _____

   _____

   _____

2. What are the possible *causes* of these problems? List as many causes as possible. If you get stuck, summarize what you *think* is going on, and then record it here.

   _____

   _____

   _____

   _____

3. How can we *solve* the above problems?

   _____

   _____

   _____

   _____

4. What are the *best solutions* to these problems?

   _____

   _____

   _____

   _____

OBSERVER'S FEEDBACK SHEET
FORM D

Your job is to observe **how** the team goes about the process of accomplishing its tasks. In the following spaces, please make notes about the process that the team used.

1. Arrive at a definition of the problem.

   _____

   _____

   _____

   _____

2. Generate possible solutions.

   _____

   _____

   _____

   _____

3. What are the problems in the case, as they define them?

   _____

   _____

   _____

   _____

4. What are their possible solutions?

   _____

   _____

   _____

   _____

5. How did they arrive at one *best* solution?

   _____

   _____

   _____

   _____

6. Did they carefully assess the solution that would best solve their problems?

_____

_____

_____

_____

7. Other comments:

_____

_____

_____

_____

PARTICIPANT'S FEEDBACK SHEET
FORM E

1. In the process of this meeting, I felt that my voice was heard. That is, I had an opportunity to voice my opinion, and was respected when I did so.

   _____ True   _____ False

   Comments:

   _____

   _____

   _____

   _____

2. I agreed with the solution(s) chosen.

   _____ True   _____ False

   Comments:

   _____

   _____

   _____

   _____

3. I think the process that we used to address this case was effective.

   _____ True   _____ False

   (If false, please provide your suggestions for improving effectiveness below.)

   _____

   _____

   _____

   _____

41

PRACTICING COACHING SKILLS

Doris Sims

Overview   We all know one of the best ways to develop management coaching skills is to practice, practice, practice. This activity provides a wide variety and a large quantity of scenarios that occur between employees and managers, so even with a large group, you will not run out of different situations to role play!

In addition to the 50 coaching scenarios, a feedback form is included with this activity for the observers in the group to provide written positive and constructive feedback for participants following their role play positions as coaches.

Suggested Time   15 minutes per role play

Materials Needed
✓ Form A (Coaching Skills Practice—Scenarios)
✓ Form B (Coaching Skills Practice—Feedback)

Procedure
1. Divide the class into trios and distribute Forms A and B. Designate several scenarios or allow trios to select one to use from Form A.

2. For each scenario, one person should take the role of *manager/coach* (all scenarios are written from the perspective of the coach), another person takes the role of the *employee,* and the remaining member of the group will become a *feedback giver* to the manager/coach using the Coaching Skills Practice—Feedback Sheet (Form B).

3. During and after each role play, the feedback giver will complete Form B and give it to the participant acting in the manager/coach role.

4. Rotate these roles for each scenario so that each person plays each role at least once.

Contact Information: FYI Incorporated, 3232 McKinney Ave. #900, Dallas, TX 75204, 214-953-7577, dorissims@fyii.com

Variations   1.   The scenarios can be chosen by the facilitator and read to the groups to create a more impromptu situation, or the group members can read and select the scenarios they would like to role play.

2.   The groups can contain more than one feedback giver.

COACHING SKILLS PRACTICE—
SCENARIOS   FORM A

1. Annette is responsible for obtaining monthly productivity statistics and creating the quarterly update report. The report is always accurate and Annette turns the report in on time, but those who use the report have complained to you that the format of the report makes it hard to read and understand. You decide to talk with Annette about the problem.

2. Brian is interested in becoming a supervisor. He has many leadership characteristics, and you agree he will make an excellent supervisor. The only issue you see is that others perceive him as somewhat arrogant because he frequently interrupts others to present his own ideas. He has no previous supervisory experience, and he has requested your help in achieving his goal.

3. Beverly and Mark are very effective, highly productive employees—unless they have to work together. They avoid communication with each other and often don't share information that is critical to the other, and their conflict is hurting the overall effectiveness of the team. They have recently been assigned to work together on a project to solicit vendors for an upcoming conference, and Mark has just entered your office to protest the joint project.

4. Bettina has been an employee with the company for 12 years, and she is a very productive, dependable employee who works well with everyone on your work team. However, now that the department has switched to personal computers rather than terminals to process work, she has been unhappy and her productivity is now much lower than the productivity of others in the department. Like others in the department, she has attended a computer training class and has been using the computer for a month, and she has now come to you asking to go back to using the terminal to process her work.

5. Crystal's wedding is one month away. Normally she is your most successful sales representative, but lately she has been busy with wedding preparations—during work hours. You have documented that she is spending an average of 80 minutes every day on the phone with her mother and various wedding preparation businesses. You have decided to talk with her about this issue.

6. Ben has been one of your employees for six months. He has a positive attitude, wants to learn new skills, and has a perfect attendance record. However, you have noted his error rate is 10 percent higher than other employees in your department over the last six months. You decide to discuss this with him at his standard weekly meeting today.

7. Casey has been with the company for two months. When she applied for the job, she indicated she had used spreadsheet software in her previous job to produce reports. As you have reviewed her work, you have found several calculation errors in her spreadsheets, and you are wondering if she knows how to use the spreadsheet formulas correctly. She seems quite happy in her job and she is an excellent team player in your group. You decide to meet with her to discuss the spreadsheet errors.

8. Chris is a data entry processor. The quality of his work has dropped significantly in the last two months. He has been a dependable employee with the company for three years, and this is the first time his performance has dropped below a satisfactory level. You've been documenting errors each week to see if improvement will take place without meeting with Chris, but the error rate is not improving, and you decide to meet with him.

9. Jack is an excellent employee with a positive attitude. However, he sometimes dresses inappropriately according to the company's dress code policy. He sometimes wears jeans when it is not casual Friday, and today he has on sandals, which violates a safety rule in the company. You ask him to meet with you to discuss this issue.

10. Dana's fingernails are so long they interfere with her typing on the computer. Her documents contain an average of five errors, and when you go into her cubicle to talk with her informally, you notice as she is typing that her fingernails hit different keys than her fingers are aiming for. She has an excellent knowledge of the company's industry, which is so critical to this position, and she knows the department procedures thoroughly, but the errors need to be addressed. You decide to discuss what you've observed at your next weekly meeting with her.

11. Hector has excellent technical knowledge; he is extremely helpful to the other employees in your department, fixing computer problems and answering software questions, and everyone, including you, appreciates his knowledge. The problem is that often he is so busy helping others with technical problems, he doesn't complete his work goals. In the last month, you've documented that he has only reached his daily call numbers 70 percent of the time. You decide to discuss this with Hector.

12. Normally, Robin has excellent attendance, and she has been with the company for six years. However, in the last three months, she has been absent ten days altogether. Because of this, your department did not meet a project completion deadline, which you have had to explain to your manager. Robin has just entered your office asking for three more vacation days next week.

13. Carol has been promoted to team leader in your group. She has natural leadership skills, but she does not know how to organize and lead a project through to completion, or how to create a project plan. You need her to lead a new procedure change for the group, and you call her into your office to explain the procedure change, and to discuss the project management skills she needs as a team leader.

14. David is a new on-the-job trainer in your department. He has created excellent training materials, and he has been meeting with new employees to go over department procedures. However, two of the most recent trainees have complained that he goes over the procedures too quickly and they don't have time to ask questions or to practice their new skills. You decide to meet with David to give him this feedback and to determine a plan of action together to address this issue.

15. Mark has been in your department for eight months. He seems eager to learn and to perform well, but he is in your office every 30 minutes asking for help prioritizing his work. Mark has just entered your office again asking for help.

16. Heather is a knowledgeable, competent employee, and she has been with the company for five years. However, when your group holds a department meeting, she never offers her ideas and opinions, which you know would be very valuable to the group because of her experience and insight. Today is your standard weekly meeting with Heather, and you decide to address this issue.

17. Jesse's job is to check the final documents for errors. Jesse has been with the company for three months. He is on time every day and appears to be working hard at his desk. The problem is that he is missing too many errors in his quality checks. In the random checks you conducted this week, you discovered six obvious errors that should have been caught during the quality check. Because Jesse is a new employee, you ask him to meet with you to determine if he is aware of his quality check goals, and to see if he has attended the training classes he was scheduled to attend.

18. You have just started as a new supervisor in the company, and you really enjoy your new job and your new work group. Hannah does the most accurate work in the department, and you really appreciate that. However, because of her perfectionist tendency, her speed is very slow. She is processing 13 customer research issues daily, while your other employees average 20 customer research issues daily. You decide to meet with her to discuss this issue.

19. Judith has expressed an interest in moving in her career path to a position as a trainer for the department. Judith is a natural people person, so you agree she would enjoy and succeed in this type of position. Her speaking skills are superior. The area she needs the most improvement in is her written communication skills, which will be important for the trainer position because new training materials need to be created and kept up to date. Judith has just entered your office to ask for your ideas about what training and skills she needs to reach her trainer career goal.

20. Wesley always puts in more than 50 hours a week, and his work is of high quality. However, you never know when he is going to arrive in the morning. While your department has a flex-time policy, Wesley didn't arrive this morning until 9:45 and you had no message he would be late. In fact, he has arrived after 9:30 four times in the last two weeks. He has been with the company for two years, and he is a very valuable employee, but this problem has been worsening recently. You decide to talk with him about it to see what has changed to cause this to happen.

21. Melanie has been with the company for four years, and she is one of your most knowledgeable employees. However, her desk organizational skills need work; for example, last week she found an investor's check in her drawer that everyone had been looking for all week. When she was absent earlier in the month, no one could find anything on her desk to complete two of her most urgent tasks. You ask her to meet with you this afternoon to talk about this problem.

22. Joseph is one of your supervisors. His employees seem to like working for him, and you feel the group looks up to him as a leader. You would like to see his time management skills improve. He forgot to attend two important meetings this week, and he doesn't prioritize his work well. Just last week he forgot an urgent project task item, and this has delayed a company project by two weeks. You decide to talk with him at his normal weekly meeting this afternoon about improving his time management skills.

23. Sarah is a whiz on the computer, she always has a smile on her face, and everyone enjoys working with her. Because of her strong system skills, she is often selected to work on project task teams. Her attendance at the meetings is consistent, but you've received three complaints in the last two months about her inability to follow through and complete specific project tasks assigned to her. This is causing some delays in major system conversion projects. You schedule a special meeting with her to discuss this.

24. Mike is one of your most effective supervisors. He has been with the company for five years, and he has just become a father for the first time. He has just entered your office to request a more flexible work schedule to allow him to come home earlier in the afternoon to spend time with his wife and new daughter.

25. Veronica is one of your supervisors. She has strong coaching skills and does an excellent job of ensuring departmental safety procedures are accurate and followed by employees. Her department safety record so far this year is 100 percent. However, one of her employees recently came to talk with you about problems that are occurring during meetings that Veronica leads. Veronica never seems to have a real agenda for her meetings, and when the meeting is over, no one seems to know what was decided or whether any tasks were assigned to the attendees to follow up on. You decide to talk with Veronica about this issue at her next weekly meeting.

26. Susan is going out on medical leave for six weeks. She has requested a meeting with you to go over the dates of her leave and the company medical leave procedures and policies. She does not know who to notify that her leave will start next week. She is also concerned about how her job responsibilities will be handled while she is out of the office. She has just entered your office to discuss these items.

27. Steven is an excellent customer service representative. His call productivity rate is high, and you've even received two complimentary letters from customers in the three months he has been here. The only problem is that the three employees sitting next to him have complained to you about the strong cologne he wears, and they've asked you to ask him to reduce the amount of cologne he puts on. Steven has just entered your office for his weekly meeting.

28. Andrew is a technical help desk employee who has been with the company for one year. His technical knowledge is excellent and he is able to help customers resolve problems easily, as long as the customer doesn't get upset or angry. He needs help learning to ease the anger of irate customers and then lead them into the information he needs to resolve the problem. Otherwise, you are afraid he is going to leave the company, because his stress level is very high and he is becoming increasingly frustrated in his job. He has asked to speak with you this afternoon about his frustration.

29. Maria would like to cut back on her hours and move into a part-time position. She is a steady, loyal employee who has been with the company for nine years. She has just entered your office to talk to you about her request.

30. Lonny always gets his work done and normally exceeds all his performance objectives. Customers and coworkers alike love Lonny's friendly attitude. The only problem is the monthly statistical report you need every month to present to the senior management committee; every month you have to ask him for the report because he has never given the report to you by the due date. The report is due today, so you decide to meet with him to ask for the report but also to discuss why this is happening.

31. Darlene has noticed a new position in the marketing department she is interested in. She has only been in her current position for four months, and the company policy states all employees must have at least one year of tenure in a position before transferring to another. She has just entered your office to ask you to complete the transfer paperwork.

32. Jenny is a new loan collector; she has only been with the company for one month. She is a very quick learner and she follows procedures precisely. However, she gets very emo-

tionally upset every day working with the customers and worries about their problems every night. You think she is an excellent employee for the company, but the loan collector position may not be the best fit for her. You ask her to meet with you to talk about this.

33. Kirk has taken on a new job responsibility within the department, and he is very excited about it. It requires him to meet with a variety of people in various other departments. He does not know any of the people he will be working with, and the other project team members don't know each other, but the success of the project depends upon the key people working together closely and effectively. He has come to you asking for advice on getting started with the new project.

34. Jade has been an employee of the company for four years, and she has just transferred into your department. She is learning your department procedures quickly, and she gets along well with everyone in your group except for John. You know that John is a little impatient and likes to get right to the bottom line quickly, and you have observed that Jade is very expressive and enjoys talking through details and many different ideas. You believe that might be the source of the communication problem. Jade has just stepped into your office, asking for your advice as to how to work more effectively with John.

35. George has ten years of experience working with system conversions; he has been in your department for eight months. He is so knowledgeable you know the department can really benefit from his experience and ideas. If only he would voice his ideas! Whenever you have a department or project meeting, he never says a word. But after meetings, he has come to you with new ideas that you wish he had presented in the meetings for discussion. This just happened again today, and he has just entered you office to talk about another idea that was discussed at the meeting.

36. Riley has been filling out his timesheet incorrectly. He has only been with the company for two months, so you believe he is not filling it out incorrectly on purpose, but that he just doesn't understand how to fill it out correctly. You ask him to come into your office to discuss the errors you've been finding on his timesheet.

37. Max sometimes has a problem using inappropriate language on the job. Yesterday, when you were walking by his cubicle with an excellent candidate for the open position in your department, you overhead him swearing on the phone, and so did the job candidate. Today, you asked him to meet with you to talk about this issue.

38. You have received complaints from customers about Marti, who has not been returning phone calls. This month, three customers specifically called to complain that Marti had not called them back in over a week. You decide to talk about this problem with Marti today during her weekly meeting.

39. In your department, it is important that employees arrive on time so the customer phone call queues are covered adequately. Aaron has been with the company for four years, and his customer service skills are excellent. But in just the last two months, you notice he has arrived late to work several times. Last week, you noted that he was more than 20 minutes late three times. You decide to talk with him to see what is causing the late arrivals.

40. Linda is a supervisor who reports to you. Her peers in the company respect her abilities and ideas, and she is a team member on several project task teams working to resolve issues. But you've had two employees who report to Linda complain that their perfor-

mance reviews and salary increases are several weeks overdue. They both say they've talked to Linda about it with no result. You call Linda and ask her to meet with you about this issue.

41. Nick is an account manager who reports to you. He handles several of the company's important accounts, and his clients respect him very much. In fact, you've had two other clients request him as their account manager. However, he seems to have a difficult time on many days prioritizing his work, and asks for your advice and help prioritizing his work and making judgment calls an average of three times daily. He always seems to have good ideas to solve his client's problems, but he just seems to lack the confidence to make the decisions on his own. Or, maybe he is not aware that you trust him and would like for him to make these decisions on his own. He has just walked into your office to ask how you would like him to handle the latest customer issue.

42. Sharon is upset about a company policy that has just changed, causing her to lose vacation time she thought she would gain when she reached her five-year anniversary with the company next month. She is very angry and has just come into your office to tell you she is going to go talk to the Human Resources director.

43. Walter is a special projects leader in your group. He will be presenting a new idea to the senior management team next week, and he is a little nervous. You know he has researched his idea thoroughly, and the idea is excellent. However, when he practiced the presentation for your work group earlier in the week, everyone had a difficult time hearing him, and he read the presentation directly from his notes word for word, even though you know he knows the presentation material inside and out. He has just entered your office to ask for your feedback on the practice presentation.

44. Melanie is working an average of three hours of overtime each day, but her productivity is the same as others in the department who are not working overtime. The quality of her work is excellent. But because Melanie earns time and a half pay for her overtime hours, and because you've been documenting in the last two weeks that she is taking excessive breaks, you've asked her to meet with you this afternoon.

45. Sean is new in your department; he transferred from the customer service area where he worked for two years. He has now been in your department for two months, and he seems to be working well with the other employees in your group. However, you were notified this morning that he did not attend the required safety course last Thursday, and he wasn't working at his desk that day either. You ask him to come into your office to determine what happened last Thursday.

46. Veronica is one of your most dependable and knowledgeable supervisors. Last Monday, during your weekly meeting with your supervisors, you told them about a new company product line that would be announced next week. You asked all of the supervisors to keep the information confidential until the announcement. However, after the meeting, the news spread through your division about the new product line, and Veronica's employees tell you they heard the news from Veronica. You decide to ask Veronica about the situation.

47. Craig is known for his sense of humor, and usually this fills a positive role in your work group, because he helps others lower their stress level and keeps everything in perspective. Unfortunately, today he went too far when he played a joke on another employee by giving her a dribble cup. The other employee was very upset about the stain on her cloth-

ing, and asked you to "do something" about Craig. You decide to ask Craig to meet with you about this specific incident.

48. To William, everything is a crisis. The good thing about this is that William is quick to handle all problem situations, but you find it difficult to tell when a situation really is a crisis and when it is not. Sometimes, William jumps to conclusions before researching the problem. William has just entered your office to apply for the open supervisor position in the group. You feel he is an excellent candidate, but he really needs to learn how to evaluate situations more carefully before reacting if he is going to be a supervisor.

49. Zoe is one of your most knowledgeable and dependable customer service representatives. She just transferred from another department in the company a few months ago, and she has been with the company for seven years. When you monitor her phone calls, you find that she always provides accurate information to the customer. However, her customer service skills need improvement; some customers have complained that she has been rude to them. On the phone conversation evaluation sheet you completed after monitoring her calls, you have noted she needs to remember to greet the customer and ask how she can help them, and thank customers for their business. You've asked her to meet with you this morning to talk about this.

50. Zane is your most creative manager. He always has good ideas for new products and he is a creative problem solver as well. Last year, the new product line he developed was the company's best seller. However, he is required to fill out specific paperwork for his employees and to track his budget each month, and he consistently "forgets" or is late turning the paperwork in. You decide to talk with him this afternoon to come up with a solution to this issue.

COACHING SKILLS PRACTICE— FEEDBACK FORM B

Directions: Please complete this feedback sheet for each person in the group who acts in the role of coach by circling the answer that corresponds with your observations. Provide comments as applicable to support the answer you choose.

The name of the coach I am observing is: _____

1. Did the coach provide both positive and constructive feedback during the coaching session?
   A. Yes, both positive and constructive feedback was provided.
   B. Only positive feedback was provided.
   C. Only constructive feedback was provided.

   Comments: _____

2. Did the coach provide factual information (what has been observed or heard, and the factual result(s) of the employee's actions) or subjective information (judgment statements based on feelings or personal perspective) about the problem?
   A. The coach stated the problem and the desired behavior using factual information.
   B. The coach stated the problem and the desired behavior in a subjective manner.
   C. The coach stated the problem both factually and subjectively.
   D. The coach stated the problem but not the desired behavior.
   E. The coach stated the desired behavior but not the problem.

   Comments: _____

3. Did the coach ask for and listen to the employee's perspective (their "side of the story") on the problem?
   A. The coach asked for the employee's perspective and listened attentively.
   B. The coach did not ask for the employee's perspective at all.
   C. The coach asked for the employee's perspective, but could have listened more attentively by _____.

   Comments: _____

4. Did the coach ask for and listen to the employee's ideas for solving the problem?
   A. The coach asked for the employee's ideas and listened attentively.
   B. The coach did not ask for the employee's ideas at all.
   C. The coach asked for the employee's ideas, but could have listened more attentively by _____.

   Comments: _____

5. Did the coach provide ideas for improvement or possible solutions?
   A. Yes, the coach provided at least one idea or possible solution.
   B. No, the coach did not provide any ideas or possible solutions.

   Comments: _____

6. At the end of the coaching session, did the coach schedule a follow-up meeting with the employee in the future to review the employee's improvement and the impact of the solutions or ideas implemented?
   A. Yes, the coach scheduled a follow-up meeting.
   B. No, the coach did not schedule a follow-up meeting.

   Comments: _____

   Overall Comments:_____

42

SETTING GROUND RULES FOR SUCCESSFUL TEAMWORK

Harriette Mishkin

Overview

New groups, as they form and organize to define their purpose and explore their team norms, need to address two critical issues up front: 1) how to create guidelines for attendance and timeliness, decision making, managing conflict, and confidentiality; and 2) how to engage in meaningful discussions and reach consensus on critical issues.

This activity provides a team with an experience in both issues by combining the need to engage in group decision making in order to reach consensus on a set of 12 normative behaviors that are essential in building successful teamwork relationships. It can be used in the first meeting of a newly formed group or team prior to dealing with task items on the agenda, or it can stand alone as the first task of an ongoing group or team.

The rank order chosen by the participants becomes their set of "Ground Rules." When the activity is completed, this document can be displayed (reorganized according to the chosen rank) for all to see and follow during ongoing teamwork processes.

Suggested Time

50-60 minutes

Materials Needed

✓ Form A (Building Ground Rules)

✓ Twelve 5 × 8-inch index cards, one containing each of the 12 items on Form A, prepared prior to this activity, typed using at least a 16-point font

✓ Masking tape or drafting dots or tack pins

Contact Information: Performance Concepts, 220 Locust Street, Suite 21 B/C, Philadelphia, PA 19106-3946, 215-923-6925, hmishkin@ssw.upenn.edu

Procedure

1. Tell participants that this activity will give them the opportunity to build their team ground rules, while simultaneously giving them practice in meaningful discussions and reaching consensus.

2. Hold a brief discussion on why it is important to establish team norms and guidelines for attendance, timeliness, decision making, managing conflict, and confidentiality; and on how teamwork outcomes improve when members engage in meaningful discussion and reach consensus.

3. Distribute Form A and explain that members have 10 minutes, working on their own, to rank order the 12 items, using the column "Your Ranking" to indicate which item is the most important to them (use #1 to indicate what is most important and #12 to indicate what is least important). There are no right or wrong answers.

4. Call time and tell participants that they have 25 minutes for team discussion. Review ways to make decisions: majority rule (voting), the leader decides (unilateral), powerful minority decides, everyone agrees (unanimity), and consensus (general accord/agreement; though it might not be your preference, you can live with it because it was arrived at fairly).

   Tell them to strive for consensus; try not to compete or compromise, or argue for their own choices. Avoid voting, bargaining, or coin flips. Involve all team members in discussing, deciding, and managing the time allotted.

5. As a group, they are to use the column "Team Ranking" to identify what is most important to them (use #1 to indicate what is most important and #12 to indicate what is least important). Original rankings in the first column should not be erased.

6. Call time and discuss the team ranking results. Using the prepared index cards each containing one of the 12 items, post them in view of the participants in the order of the newly agreed-to guidelines. Explain how to reference them during discussions and teamwork processes.

7. Debrief the teamwork process: How did they decide, involve all participants, manage differences, deal with obstructive behaviors, reach agreements, and manage their time? How close did individual rankings come to the team ranking? Ask participants to look at their top three and bottom three rankings and compare them to the team ranking. This will give you a sense of how well they worked together, the degree of synergy that was produced.

8. Ask team members to identify three lessons learned that they can use immediately. Capture them on flip chart paper and display for reference.

BUILDING GROUND RULES   FORM A   DOWNLOADABLE

Step 1: Each member of the team is to individually rank each of the 12 *"Ground Rules for Successful Teamwork."* (#1 is most important, #12 least). Place your responses in the first column under "Your Ranking." You will have 10 minutes to do so. Do not discuss the items until each member has finished the individual ranking.

Step 2: After everyone has finished the individual ranking, rank order the 12 items as a team. Use the second column—"Team Ranking"—to record your responses. Once discussion begins, do not change your individual rankings. You will have 25 minutes for the team discussion.

	Your Ranking	*Team Ranking*
1. If we must be late or absent, we will inform the team facilitator, liaison, or a team member at least a day in advance.		
2. We will always come to meetings prepared to work on the agenda that we will receive before the meeting. Our preparation and data collection will be complete, and we will be ready to discuss the issues on the agenda.		
3. We will always respect the opinions and feelings of all individuals. Each member has equal participation in our meetings. When discussing team business, members should expect to contribute to discussions and be listened to with respect.		
4. We will always avoid blaming people for the shortcomings of our team. If our team somehow fails to do its tasks properly, we will examine our team process and attempt to improve it. If individuals are having trouble meeting their commitments, the team will support them in every possible way.		
5. Members will support the decisions of the team after they are made. Undermining team decisions or second-guessing and bad-mouthing the team and its work outside the team setting to nonmembers is unacceptable behavior.		
6. Members will live up to their team commitments, recognizing that failure to do so affects the whole team's progress. When in jeopardy of not meeting their obligations, members will notify the team in time for other members to take supportive actions.		
7. When faced with a decision, we will first decide how to make the decision. Our general rule is to (1) state the problem, (2) discuss different ideas, (3) examine the benefits and risks associated with different approaches, and (4) select an approach we can all support.		
8. We will deal with conflict in a productive way. Our general rule for conflict is to understand the problem as best we can from each side's perspective. To do that, we will listen to all sides of the conflict, looking for facts and evidence. If there is still a conflict about facts, we will gather additional data. When the problem is understood, the team will help those in conflict create alternative approaches.		

	Your Ranking	Team Ranking
9. We recognize that working on a team usually results in high-quality ideas and decisions. If we find we are not experiencing these benefits of teamwork, we will pause to assess how we are working together until we better understand our team and our work.		
10. We will not engage in sidebar conversations, whether or not they relate to the topic under discussion or other issues. Relevant conversations will be shared with all team members.		
11. Because of the time boundaries of this project and our desire to engage all participants in discussions and decisions, external interruptions will be kept to a minimum.		
12. The discussions and decisions of this team will be kept confidential and not shared with anyone outside of this group, until agreed to by all participants.		

43

EXCHANGING EXPECTATIONS

Stephen Hobbs

Overview
In establishing a team, it is important to understand what team members bring to the team and what they require and request from the team situation. It is equally important for the organization to identify and state what it will supply to team members and what it expects and requests from the team situation. This activity achieves both objectives.

Suggested Time
1 to 2 hours

Materials Needed
✓ Overhead projector
✓ Flip chart and felt-tipped markers
✓ Form A (Team Accordion Form)
✓ Form B (Explanation of Terms)
✓ Form C (Folding Instructions)
✓ Form D (Two Stories)
✓ Form E (Overlay Suggestions)

Procedure
1. Distribute copies of Forms A and B to each person.
2. Define the task:

   You are asked to identify what you require of, request from, and bring to the team situation. Next, identify what you believe the organization expects of, requests from, and supplies to the team situation. You have ten minutes to complete these tasks.

3. If the group members have difficulty in brainstorming ideas, suggest two or three topics such as leadership, communication, vision

Contact Information: WELLTH Learning Network Inc., 2804 6th Ave. NW, Calgary, AB T2N 0Y3, 403-252-8188, stephen.hobbs@wellthlearning.com, www.welllearning.com

and mission, etc. Your suggestions are merely to help team members record some thoughts for the purpose of presenting later. Usually, no prompts are necessary.

4. On separate sheets of flip chart paper (six sheets minimum, set out like Form A on the wall or desk), record what each person has to say. Use your facilitation skills to determine in what order to collect data.

   ■ For the columns titled Person Requires and Requests, synthesis of the dialogue is possible. These two columns identify the assumptions, perceptions, beliefs, and values associated with establishing the team. The comments reflect the perceived reality for the team members as they begin to work together.

   ■ For the columns titled Organization Expects and Requests, synthesis of the dialogue is possible. These two columns identify what the team members assume are the organization's management principles associated with the team. The information can be compared with organizational practice. In the event the organization is new, the team is identifying the team norms.

   ■ For the Person Brings column, record what individuals say in their own words. This column records the knowledge and skill capabilities of each team member.

   ■ For the Organization Supplies column, team members identify what they believe are the helpful mechanisms and physical resources available to them. This information can be compared with organizational practice for confirmation.

5. After all comments are collected, ask the team members to fold Form A according to the folding instructions on Form C.

6. Next, ask the team members to fold Form A to correspond with the two types of stories described on Form D. Now you have provided two examples of stories possible from folding the paper.

7. Stop here and move to step 10, or continue.

8. Split the group into two or three teams and ask each team to create two stories for presentation. Possible combinations are found on Form D. During the 2-minute presentations, listen for additional ideas to be recorded on the flip chart paper.

9. Depending on the amount of information collected, you can lay an overhead slide of Form E over A and continue the dialogue.

10. The activity can be debriefed in terms of the metaphor of the team accordion. If the information recorded allows the team to work together in an effective and efficient manner, then the metaphor-

ic accordion music encourages the natural rhythm of the team. Conversely, if the information lacks clarity or is missing some vital pieces, then the accordion metaphorically becomes a rock crusher.

Ask these debriefing questions:

- Have we recorded everything that we know?
- What questions do we have of the organization?
- What questions do we have of ourselves as we move into a team?
- Who else has information useful to us?

Variations

1. If time is a concern, split the data collecting and recording by Person and Organization. Complete the task over two sessions.

2. Use this activity as a follow-up review process to ask team members how things are going at a time when the team is in its maintaining stage. The review will trace the progress of satisfaction and importance when the information gathered is compared to the information recorded during the baseline activity.

3. This exercise can be used with teams that are already established as a way to develop organizational norms for the team environment.

4. The category prompts outlined on Form E can be used to categorize the data drawn from the group dialogue.

TEAM ACCORDION FORM   FORM A   DOWNLOADABLE

Organization
Expects of
Requests from
Supplies to
T E A M
Brings to
Requests from
Requires of
Person

EXPLANATION OF TERMS   FORM B

The accordion diagram contains the following labeled segments (top to bottom):

Organization | ...the bottom-line needs that a person will not forgo to work on the team (e.g., quality of work life)

Expects | ...what the person asks of the organization, realizing that compromise is necessary to work on the team (e.g., work hour flexibility to meet family commitments)

Requests |

Supplies | ...what capabilities the person has such as knowledge, skills, and attitudes that contribute to team competencies (e.g., project management skills)

T E A M | ...the bottom-line needs that the organization will not forgo to have the team operate (e.g., job performance)

Brings | ...what the organization asks of the team members, realizing that compromise is necessary for a team to operate (e.g., work overtime hours)

Requests |

Requires | ...what the organization gives to the team members to do their jobs (e.g., office space and a computer)

Person | ...what the organization gives to be part of the team? the reciprocal question is, "What does the organiza-

Person requires from the team ...the bottom-line needs that a person will not forgo to work on the team (e.g., quality of work life)

Person requests from the team ...what the person asks of the organization, realizing that compromise is necessary to work on the team (e.g., work hour flexibility to meet family commitments)

Person brings to the team ...what capabilities the person has such as knowledge, skills, and attitudes that contribute to team competencies (e.g., project management skills)

Organization expects from the team ...the bottom-line needs that the organization will not forgo to have the team operate (e.g., job performance)

Organization requests from the team ...what the organization asks of the team members, realizing that compromise is necessary for a team to operate (e.g., work overtime hours)

Organization supplies to the team ...what the organization gives to the team members to do their jobs (e.g., office space and a computer)

Placement of Terms: The order of terms within the accordion is left to the discretion of the activity facilitator. It is important to maintain parallel placement of the terms as shown in the diagram above. If you start by asking "What do you (the person) *require* from the organization to be part of the team?" the reciprocal question is, "What does the organiza- tion *expect* of the team members who work in a team?"

FOLDING INSTRUCTIONS   FORM C

1. Fold along the lines marked with a number.

2. Mix and match the number lines to create different connections (playing the accordion).

1	2	3	4	5	6	7	8
Requires	Requests	Brings		Supplies	Requests	Expects	Organization

TEAM

Person

TWO STORIES   FORM D

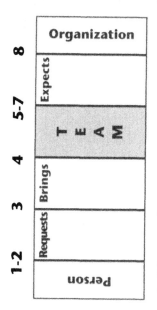

Person		Organization
1-2 Requests	**3** Brings	**4**	**5-7** T E A M	**8** Expects

In this story, the person states requests and indicates capabilities in light of organizational expectations surrounding the team.

Person		Organization
1 Requires Quality of life	**2-4**	**5-7** T E A M	**8** Expects Job perfor-mance

In this story, the person and the organization compare requirements and expectations of working through teams.

Possible Story Combinations (mix and match)

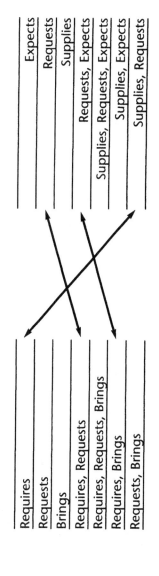

Requires
Requests
Brings
Requires, Requests
Requires, Requests, Brings
Requires, Brings
Requests, Brings

Expects
Requests
Supplies
Requests, Expects
Supplies, Requests, Expects
Supplies, Expects
Supplies, Requests

OVERLAY SUGGESTIONS   FORM E

Rewards and Recognition

Personal Safety

Technology

Communication

44

ENHANCING TEAM DIALOGUE

Malcolm Burson

Overview   The overwhelming success of *The Fifth Discipline Fieldbook* has highlighted the need for practical tools that consultants can use "on
Monday morning" to translate theory into practice. Given the increasing emphasis on teams and teamwork in organizations of all sorts,
Peter Senge's discipline of team learning is a natural model for helping
people develop more effective and productive ways to speak and work
with others. As the *Fieldbook* authors have pointed out, anyone
involved in team learning should be familiar with the key reflection-
and-inquiry skills of the mental models discipline. These skills include
balancing advocacy with inquiry, surfacing tacit assumptions, and
allowing others access to our beliefs and models of reality. The skills
become the shared property of the team for building understanding
and accomplishing tasks. This is especially true when these skills can
be practiced as part of the team's usual activity instead of in a laboratory or classroom setting.

Teams of all kinds, decision-making groups, or even the morning
coffee-break group, may find themselves at an impasse when the conversation engages deeply held beliefs, ideas, and convictions. The more
impassioned the discussion, the more individuals move into the stance
of advocacy. People are assumed to have an indisputable right to the
beliefs and values that inform their statements of truth or fact. As a
result, teams seldom take the time to inquire about the underlying
basis of a participant's assertions or to explore alternative models of
perception. The notion that everyone's entitled to her or his own opinion then creates a frustrating barrier to identifying the common
ground necessary for problem solving or conflict resolution.

Suspending assumptions is a skill generally associated with the
formal discipline of dialogue. It derives from physicist and dialogue
pioneer David Bohm's metaphor that we behave as if our assumptions

Contact Information: Malcolm C. Burson, 27 University Place, Orono, ME 04473,
207-866-0019, malcolm.c.burson@state.me.us

were hanging on a string just in front of our noses, where we and others can see and respond to them. Indeed, I've often put on an absurd headband, with glitter-covered styrofoam balls (assumptions) hanging from wires just above my eyes, as a lighthearted illustration of this approach. The concept is simple: In order to avoid misunderstandings of our beliefs and intentions when we're deeply engaged in conversation about something that matters to us...

- We take the time to surface our assumptions, by becoming aware of them ourselves.
- We then display our assumptions so others can see them.
- We invite inquiry so that others can be sure they understand where we're coming from.

We take the risk of making our thinking processes, and the structures and beliefs that inform them, more visible to others. At the same time, we become willing to explore the same aspects of others' thinking through respectful inquiry. The process allows new perspectives to inform the collective mind, creating knowledge and defusing avoidable conflict based on misunderstanding. The more skillful the team's discussions become, the more efficient its work and the greater the likelihood that decisions and their outcomes will be effective.

This exercise is intended to introduce a team to the value of exploring assumptions, using their real-world context as the learning environment. For a team already somewhat familiar with balancing advocacy and inquiry or with skillful discussion techniques, it can serve as a next step in deepening the quality of conversation and discussion. For a team just beginning this process, it can serve as an introduction. It's particularly helpful when a team is apparently stuck because of lack of "permission" to move beyond standard advocacy approaches based on assertion and confrontation. It can also be used as a classroom or laboratory learning tool.

Suggested Time   45 to 60 minutes

Materials Needed

✓   Blank paper, one piece per participant

✓   Lengths of string approximately 18" long, one per participant

✓   Assorted colored felt-tip markers (broad tip)

✓   Masking tape

✓   Flip chart

Procedure

1. Briefly present an overview of the reasons why learning to suspend assumptions can help the team work more effectively together. Point out that this is one among several ways of improving the quality of conversation and discussion in the team. If the team is not already familiar with the idea, briefly present the importance of balancing advocacy and inquiry. Stress that these skills are means to increase the team's pool of knowledge useful in accomplishing their task; that when we have a better sense of where people are coming from, we avoid unproductive conflict that may occur when we don't validate our assumptions about others' beliefs and ideas. Use Form A as an overhead projection, flip chart outline, or participant handout. You may want to add the point that suspending assumptions does not imply abandoning our convictions, but only allowing others to inquire about them.

   Use this as a closing hook: "Now I'm going to ask you to quite literally suspend one of your assumptions where others can see it."

2. Choose a particular issue or problem the group has struggled with recently, and write a summary of it on the flip chart in the form of a declarative statement. Example: "We need to cut costs while retaining high-quality service to our customers." Ask the team: "Is this an accurate statement of the issue? Is this something we're all concerned about?"

3. Invite all team members or participants to spend 3 to 4 minutes in individual silence to identify an assumption they currently hold about the topic. They should ask themselves if they're willing to suspend this assumption where others can see, inquire about, and reflect on it. Assure participants that they need not disclose any deeply held conviction or belief they're not comfortable sharing with others; but invite them to choose something about which they have strong feelings. Let the group know after 3 minutes that if they haven't chosen an assumption, they should try to do so in the next minute.

4. Ask each participant to write her or his assumption in bold print on a piece of paper, beginning with the words, "I assume ..."; attach a piece of string to it using the tape; and hang it around his or her neck so that others can read it. Explain that they will soon take turns asking questions about others' assumptions, but should refrain as much as possible from arguing or trying to convince others of their points of view.

5. Clear a space for the team to mingle. Have participants mingle in silence for 2 to 3 minutes, taking the time to read as many suspended assumptions as possible.

6. When you think the group is ready, invite them to choose partners whose assumptions they're interested in and inquire, "May I ask you about what you've written?" If the answer is "Yes" (assumed), then the inquirer asks a question intended to invite an alternative ("Have you thought about x instead of y?"); clarify what the person has written ("I'm not sure I understand what you mean by q; can you explain it?"); or work behind the assumption ("What evidence or experience leads you to that assumption?"). You may want to write sample inquiries such as these on the flip chart. The person being questioned responds briefly, without arguing. The point is to clarify, provide additional information, and so on. When the questioner is satisfied that he or she understands the assumption, the partners switch roles. When both have had a chance to inquire and respond, they separate, find other partners, and repeat the process.

7. When all have had at least two opportunities for exchange, invite participants to thank the persons they've spoken with for their willingness to surface and suspend their assumptions. Bring the group back together and debrief. Begin by inviting comments about the process: what it was like, how they experienced it, etc. Encourage feelings of skepticism as well as positives. Move on to invite people to name what they learned from the activity. Point out that while the questions may seem stilted or too much like recipes at the moment, we can all become more fluent with practice.

8. Continue by focusing on the team's actual task: determining the extent to which they have a changed sense of the issue; identifying new insights about causes; and evaluating the group's capacity to address new insights. Use divergent assumptions as an opportunity to seek new or creative approaches. Questions might include:

   - "Now that we have a clearer sense of some of the assumptions people used in forming their ideas, do we see the issue any differently?"

   - "Does the reality that we seem to hold very different assumptions about the issue(s) mean we should be sure of areas we agree on before we go further?"

   - "Do we need to explore any individual assumptions further before we move on?" (This might be particularly important if one or more surfaced assumptions revealed a previously unacknowledged generalization about a group in the organization; for example, "You seem to assume customer service representatives aren't capable of high-level problem solving." This then becomes an opportunity for the whole team or group to explore a suspended assumption together.)

9. Conclude by asking something like, "How do we want to apply what we've just learned to our continuing efforts?" Your goal is to gain a commitment to applying the new learning in future meetings of the group or team.

10. Thank members of the team or group for their willingness to take some risks and learn and practice new skills. Ask for feedback, particularly about whether this is the kind of thing they'd like to do in the future. Then adjourn or move back into the usual agenda, as appropriate.

SUSPENDING ASSUMPTIONS
FORM A

Suspending assumptions means...

- Standing back from advocating my position or imposing my views on others;

- Offering my thoughts, beliefs, and ideas instead of leaving them unspoken;

- Allowing others to consider and ask about my assumptions respectfully;

- Being willing to openly explore my assumptions so I and others can understand where they come from and how they affect my work in the team.

In order to suspend assumptions, we need to...

- Bring them to the surface by asking, "Just what is it that I'm assuming about _____?"

- Let others see them: "I assume that _____."

- Invite inquiry from others: "Can you help me see something I may be missing? What leads you to a different conclusion?"

45

ACHIEVING A POSITIVE CHANGE CLIMATE

Vicki Schneider

Overview   Charles Darwin theorized that the fate of a species was determined by how "fit" it was. Interpreting Darwin's statement, one might think that only the strongest or the fastest species would survive. Actually, it wasn't speed or strength that Darwin was referring to, but rather the adaptability of the species that would determine its fate. Just like our animal counterparts, only those businesses that are able to change quickly and effectively will survive in the tumultuous climate in which we find ourselves.

The following interactive exercise helps leaders and associates (i.e., nonmanagement employees) gain an appreciation of one another's challenges and needs as they Navigate the Sea of Change. By the end of the exercise, participants identify how they can help themselves and their organizations achieve a more positive change climate.

Suggested Time   60 to 90 minutes

Materials Needed
- ✓ Forms A and B (Leader's Worksheet)
- ✓ Forms C and D (Associate's Worksheet)
- ✓ Chart paper (one sheet per group)
- ✓ Colored markers, preferably scented (one set per group)
- ✓ Blindfolds (one for every two people)
- ✓ Masking tape, to create an outline of the Sea on the floor (You may use rope to create the border or draw lines in the ground, if the activity is done outdoors.)
- ✓ Toys (e.g., Koosh™ balls, plastic containers, plastic crates, lengths of rope)

Contact Information: Vantage Solutions, 4434 Waveland Court, Hamburg, NY 14075-2003, 716-627-3345, VantageSol@aol.com

Procedure

1. The Sea of Change is an obstacle course that blindfolded associates must cross safely. The leaders will give verbal instructions to their blindfolded partners to help them cross the course. The objective is to get the associates across the Sea without touching any of the "mines" (e.g., toys) that have been laid out. Once the crossing begins, the leaders are not permitted to touch their partners or enter the Sea of Change.

2. Before the session begins, lay out a rectangular minefield of the toys you've accumulated. The size of the field does not need to be exact. Following are suggested dimensions:

   Width = (Total number of participants ÷ 2) × 2.5 feet

   Length = Width × 2

   Take several trial walks through the Sea, modifying it to eliminate any particularly easy or difficult sections.

3. Divide the group in half. One half of the group will be the leaders and the other half will be the associates. If you have more than ten participants, select one person to act as a spotter for every additional eight people. The spotter will be responsible for ensuring the safe crossing of a maximum of four associates.

4. Before passing out blindfolds, ask if anyone objects to being blindfolded. (Assign anyone who objects to a leader's or spotter's role.)

5. Pass out blindfolds. (You may either distribute blindfolds to every other person, or distribute them to particular people based on the roles you want them to play.) If you have representatives from management and staff in your session, break them up evenly between the leader and associate groups.

6. Once blindfolds have been distributed, ask participants to pair up (one associate with one leader). If you have an uneven number of participants, use the extra person as a spotter or a historian (See Variations section.)

7. If possible, set up the Sea in an area that the participants can't see. Then have everyone walk to an area near the Sea, but still keeping the Sea out of sight. (The uncertainty of what lies ahead adds to the activity.) Have the associates put on their blindfolds and have the leaders guide them into the area where the Sea has been laid out.

8. Have the leaders line up the associates side by side, along the shortest edge of the rectangular Sea. The leaders are then to walk to the opposite end of the Sea and line up side by side.

9. Give the following instructions to the associates: *When you begin crossing the Sea, you might touch a mine. If you do, yell out, "I touched a mine, but I am fine!"* Have all the associates practice the yell on the count of three.

10. Give the following instructions to the leaders: *If your associate touches a mine, yell out, "You touched a mine, but you are fine!"* Have all the leaders practice the yell on the count of three.

11. Ask for quiet. Instruct the associates to turn 180° to their right, then 90° to their left, then 360° around. (It is expected that by this time, all of the associates will be facing a slightly different direction.)

12. Spotters should be positioned to watch the associates and make sure they don't lose their balance or trip on a mine. You and the other spotter(s) should enter the Sea to steady associates, as needed.

13. Tell the leaders they may start whenever they are ready. (All associates are to cross at the same time.)

14. When you see someone hit a mine, encourage the "yell" that they practiced earlier.

15. When associates step over the ending line (the end opposite where they started), they may take off their blindfolds and watch their peers.

16. After all of the associates finish their crossing, go back to the original meeting area. Create two or four breakout groups depending on size (one or two for the participants and one or two for the leaders). No group should be larger than eight people. Distribute Forms A and B to the leader group(s), and Forms C and D to the associate group(s).

17. Have participants individually complete questions 1 to 5 on their worksheets. Then have each group discuss their thoughts with the other members of their group. It is not necessary to reach a consensus on any question.

18. Advise the groups that when they come to the boxed section of the worksheet, they are to work together to formulate the message. They are then to create a poster that includes the words and associated drawings that convey their message. (Distribute a sheet of chart paper and a set of markers to each group.)

19. When all the groups have completed their posters, have each group select a spokesperson to share its message with all the participants. Have the associate group(s) report first. Encourage a

rousing round of applause following each presentation. Then ask if anyone has anything to add to the associates' messages. Repeat the procedure with the leaders' groups.

Variations

1. Select a historian and give that person a Polaroid™ camera to take pictures of the Sea of Change crossing. Create a poster that includes the pictures from the crossing and the messages from the associates and the leaders. Hang the poster in a prominent place at your work site.

2. If time permits, switch roles before you debrief the exercise and allow associates to become leaders and leaders to become associates. You may want to bring extra blindfolds for health reasons.

3. To increase awareness and empathy, place all management staff in the associate group(s) and all associates in the leader group(s).

4. Include additional debriefing questions. For example, "What did you yell when you hit a mine? How would you have felt if you had to yell, 'I touched a mine and I've failed'? What types of messages do we receive when we make a mistake at work? What messages do we give others when they make a mistake? How do those messages affect our behaviors?"

5. Have each group read its responses to the worksheet questions to the entire group.

6. Have each leader–associate pair meet privately to share their experiences during the crossing (e.g., what worked well for them, how they felt, what problems they encountered and how they overcame them, what they'd do differently if they had it to do over again.)

7. Conduct a "brain dump" at the end of the session. Ask participants to state the insights they gained from the session. You or a scribe should write the comments, without discussion, on a chart. Keep adding comments until all comments have been exhausted.

THE SEA OF CHANGE   FORM A

Leader's Worksheet (Page 1)

1. How did you feel during this exercise? How did your feelings change? What caused the change?

2. What did you need from your associate to ensure a safe and timely crossing?

3. What more could your associate have done to help himself or herself?

Leader's Worksheet (Page 2)

4. What did you do to help your associate cross the sea of change?

5. What other things could you have done?

> Write a message to the associate group, recommending ways they can help themselves "navigate the sea of change."

THE SEA OF CHANGE   FORM C

Associate's Worksheet (Page 1)

1. How did you feel during this exercise? How did your feelings change? What caused the change?

2. What did you need from your leader to ensure a safe and timely crossing?

3. What more could your leader have done to help you?

THE SEA OF CHANGE   FORM D

Associates Worksheet (Page 2)

4. What did you do to help yourself cross the sea of change?

5. What other things could you have done?

> Write a message to the leader group, recommending ways they can help associates "navigate the sea of change."

CPSIA information can be obtained
at www.ICGtesting.com
Printed in the USA
LVOW04s0001220217
525018LV00019B/162/P